Getting It Right

Getting It Right

Notre Dame on Leadership and
Judgment in Business

Viva Ona Bartkus
and Ed Conlon

JOSSEY-BASS
A Wiley Imprint
www.josseybass.com

Published by Jossey-Bass
A Wiley Imprint
989 Market Street, San Francisco, CA 94103-1741—www.josseybass.com

Readers should be aware that Internet Web sites offered as citations and/or sources for further information may have changed or disappeared between the time this was written and when it is read.

Limit of Liability/Disclaimer of Warranty: While the publisher and author have used their best efforts in preparing this book, they make no representations or warranties with respect to the accuracy or completeness of the contents of this book and specifically disclaim any implied warranties of merchantability or fitness for a particular purpose. No warranty may be created or extended by sales representatives or written sales materials. The advice and strategies contained herein may not be suitable for your situation. You should consult with a professional where appropriate. Neither the publisher nor author shall be liable for any loss of profit or any other commercial damages, including but not limited to special, incidental, consequential, or other damages.

Jossey-Bass books and products are available through most bookstores. To contact Jossey-Bass directly call our Customer Care Department within the U.S. at 800-956-7739, outside the U.S. at 317-572-3986, or fax 317-572-4002.

Jossey-Bass also publishes its books in a variety of electronic formats. Some content that appears in print may not be available in electronic books.

Library of Congress Cataloging-in-Publication Data

Bartkus, Viva Ona.
   Getting it right : Notre Dame on leadership and judgment in business / Viva Ona Bartkus and Edward J. Conlon.
     p. cm.
   Includes bibliographical references and index.
   ISBN 978-0-470-24588-0 (alk. paper)
    1. Problem solving. 2. Leadership. 3. Decision making. I. Conlon,
E. J. (Edward J.), 1951-II. Title.
HD30.29.B364 2008
658.4'092—dc22

2008015956

Printed in the United States of America
FIRST EDITION
HB Printing 10 9 8 7 6 5 4 3 2 1

Contents

Acknowledgments

No book dedicated to fostering collaborative problem solving as a critical leadership skill could be possible without broad assistance. Ours is no different. Dean Carolyn Woo, dean of the Mendoza College of Business at Notre Dame, and Mike Nevens, senior partner of McKinsey & Company, provided ongoing advice and guidance. Numerous classes of undergraduate and MBA students at Notre Dame challenged, tested, and through those challenges improved the problem-solving methods introduced in this book. For their contributions we thank, in particular, three students: John Waldron, Nicolas Picard, and Jason Wise. Our work benefited from the strong support of our publishers and the patient editing of Alan Venable, Sarah Smith, and Laura Gerber. Finally, we are grateful to the Bartkus and Conlon families. This book would not have been possible without their unwavering belief in our aspirations.

Getting It Right

Introduction

SOLVE THE PROBLEM

"He was my idol."

That is how the CFO of a major, global health care company described his former boss and CEO, Peter. Tall, energetic, and dynamic, Peter naturally gravitated to positions of ever greater authority, while colleagues gravitated toward him. He had put himself through college by working nights; then, in about twenty years, rose from lowly finance analyst to CEO. Passionate about serving the thousands of physicians and patients that used his company's medical products, Peter broadly communicated his vision for how the company would transform the world's health care systems. Having laid down performance objectives for each division, Peter promoted talented managers, provided the resources they needed, and then got out of their way. Many a senior manager benefited from his patient coaching and attention to their careers. Devoutly Christian, Peter lived his values every day. One of his first initiatives as CEO was a strict code of ethics for all employees.

If Peter sounds like a great guy to work for—he was. If he sounds like the visionary, authentic, selfless leader described in many a leadership book—he was. Bright, inquisitive, cordial to all, as CEO he focused on communication, decision making, execution—the behaviors of successful leaders.

Peter's successor as CEO, Paul, could not have been cut from a more different cloth. Ten years older, not exactly stern but certainly not as outgoing and charismatic as Peter, Paul was, to many, frustratingly cautious. Whether he was slowly trying to build as much consensus as possible or hunting for further evidence to prioritize investments, he routinely held up urgent decisions. Awkward in large groups and public debates, he did not even try to replicate Peter's inspirational style. However, he did travel widely to disparate divisions, building his own understanding of customers, competitors, and regulators, and the company's operations. Painstakingly systematic, Paul was nonetheless selfless as a leader in consistently putting company interests above his own and in going well beyond merely serving the interests of shareholders to serve patients, physicians, hospitals, employees, suppliers, and other stakeholders. It was just that those attributes stayed in the background as he directed the company and hand-picked senior managers who shared his careful approach.

Back from the Brink: A Cautionary Tale

So what happened at Peter and Paul's global health care company? On Peter's watch, the proud, seventy-year-old company performed ignominiously and destroyed shareholder value. Then, slowly, Paul nursed it back to health.

Close witnesses would agree that Peter possessed attributes and used behavioral styles that generally align followers, empower managers, and, at least initially, motivate employees. But there is no substitute for performance. Although attributes like Peter's can facilitate leadership, they do not ensure sound business decisions.

What Peter Lacked

Peter's faults involved problem solving and judgment. For years the company had been growing slowly, in line with its markets, or a bit faster, taking market share from smaller rivals. By contrast, Peter and his team believed that there was much more value in their R&D pipeline than shareholders saw, and that theirs was potentially a growth company. In the then-heyday of the biotech revolution—and given the company's extensive investments in science, engineering, and technology—perhaps this was possible. But other senior executives saw problems with Peter's direction at the time and tried to relay their concerns. Rather than triggering further analysis, these minority concerns were dismissed. Unable to influence the conversation, these managers departed.

Peter and his senior team significantly increased research spending, betting on new technologies that might transform the practice of medicine. They thought they comprehended the risks associated with such scientific investments, but in truth had little grasp of the associated technical hazards. Accelerating innovation is always complicated, especially for a company with thousands of employees spread across six continents. Anyone can underestimate how many new processes and capabilities are needed. Peter did. And after losing two key operating lieutenants within twelve months of each other—managers with critical ties to the marketplace—he and his team misread the signals coming from current and potential customers.

After three major research projects failed in clinical trials, two nearly disastrous acquisitions were made, and competitors began to gain market share in two of the company's three biggest markets, observers saw the writing on the wall. The company would fail to become the growth engine that Peter had promised to customers, employees, shareholders, and Wall Street analysts. It had not accelerated innovation as promised. No amount of sales and marketing of its traditional products could achieve the promised growth. Perhaps worse, no one within the company was examining the underlying problems.

What Paul Provided

Paul's approach contrasted sharply with Peter's. Peter had mainly rallied the troops around his ultimately flawed belief in rapid growth based on internal intellectual and scientific capital. Paul switched the company's focus to examining unmet customer needs, the company's market positions, and new capabilities that were needed to capture external opportunities. Many wanted him to move quickly, to divest poorly performing divisions in the portfolio, to cut expenses. Instead, he comprehensively evaluated options through the lens of unmet market needs, seeking all possible solutions for every one of the divisions. He traveled through the international organization collecting data and insight. Without hesitation, he examined in great detail Peter's previous mistaken assumptions. Only after he and his new team felt they had diagnosed the complex problems did they begin moves to bring the proud company back from the brink. This process took time, and impatient observers at first criticized Paul's methods as too slow.

Problem Solving—An Underrated Leadership Skill

Our cautionary tale reveals what most recent leadership books overlook. Many write about leaders' attributes and effective behavioral styles, how leaders came to have them, or how to produce a sense of shared purpose, empowerment, and persistent energy in an organization. They pay far less attention to solving both day-to-day and complex business problems. The trouble, then, is this: although certain attributes and styles do help leaders to energize the organization around a shared purpose, these same attributes and behaviors do not ensure that leaders can recognize and solve basic business problems.

In our experience, great business problem solvers are scarce; even less common are great leaders who are also great at solving problems. Why so rare? Normal business training emphasizes competence in individual functions, rather than how to integrate problem-related information from several disciplines. Not surprisingly, it is easy to find subject-matter experts in finance, accounting, purchasing, advertising, or human resources; harder to find are people who can think critically across business functions.

Hence, in solving complex problems, marketing managers may see challenges through marketing eyes; operations managers may seek solutions through modifying operational processes. But tough business problems are simply not that well behaved. They naturally defy such disciplinary boundaries. Problems may then be misconstrued to fit specialist capabilities, whose solutions in turn are at best incomplete and at worst, dare we say, just plain wrong.

We contend that rigorous problem solving is an underrated leadership skill. We further contend that the integral role of values in problem solving has been misunderstood. As a consequence, our book is not about leadership attributes such as authenticity or vision, nor about behaviors such as communication and execution. It is about how individual leaders and teams can simplify complex problems, develop pragmatic solutions, and make them workable throughout an organization. It is about how to become great at solving business problems.

The Misunderstood Role of Values in Problem Solving

Values underlie all leadership problem-solving efforts. Values influence the aims, division, and prioritization of analytical work, the choice of solutions, and their implementation throughout an organization. No problem-solving effort is value free, because one's values identify the problem. And because differences in values often cause conflicts during problem solving, one must examine one's own core values and develop ways to resolve the inevitable conflicts.

Today some adopt what we would argue is a misguided notion: that a "values neutral" stance is appropriate for business in a world of increasing globalization. Yet this situation leads to values being applied to business problems and their solutions without first being scrutinized, discussed, or debated. The foundation of effective problem solving lies in the firm embrace of meaningful, well-considered values.

To Be a Successful Executive, Make Values-Based Problem Solving a Habit of Mind

In our uncertain times, we assert, disciplined, values-focused, *problem-solving* leaders are needed more than ever before. Anxieties rightfully arise from the massive current changes driven by increased globalization, new technologies, demographic dislocations, and increasing cynicism toward governmental and corporate leaders. Our antidote is this: in times of great uncertainty, ever more rigorous habits of mind are required to solve problems. Further, we contend that people can learn how to systematically discover and enact solutions. Intuition, although essential, is not sufficient. With intuition, leaders may or may not find answers, but even if they do, they are still not equipped to answer credibly the question that employees and stakeholders anxiously ask: "What makes this decision the right one?"

Sound business decisions depend on disciplined, fact-based inquiry and systematic methods of problem solving. By developing the ability to ask probing questions, hypothesize solutions, examine assumptions, and collect necessary data and insight, leaders can dependably start the hard work of change. Our message is that one can work through even the most staggering challenge in a calm and confident way; that one can take comfort in, and draw faith from, the process. To truly lead, then, a general manager must develop values-based problem-solving habits of mind and action.

We define a problem as an intricate, unsettled question—one that causes distress, vexation, or frustration. A business problem is one that prevents an organization from achieving its goals, be they strategic, operational, or financial. In this book, we use the terms *problem* and *challenge* interchangeably. We focus on problems that span multiple issues and that challenge an organization's future sufficiently to require outstanding solutions and even better implementation.

Yet the iterative problem-solving framework introduced in this book can and should be applied not only to solve the most complicated problems but also to guide the daily discovery and ongoing thinking processes that constitute so much of business. A CEO can employ the described methods to determine a statement of annual priorities, for example, or the business unit manager could determine how to renegotiate suppliers' contracts or improve new product launches.

We define a habit of mind as a disciplined routine of inquiry and judgment into problems and solutions. Great problem solvers train their minds and their teams to ingrain certain habits of preparation, dissection of problems, and examination of assumptions. Certain routines of prioritization and implementation become second nature. For example, the habit of probing represents the ability to bring perspective to any problem. With this habit, one can quickly understand what one knows and how one knows it, not to mention what one does not know. Engaged in a line of questioning, one collects evidence specifically to prove or disprove working hypotheses of the solution. One constantly asks, "Why?" and "So what?"

Two mirror habits of mind are *analysis* and *creativity*. The first entails disaggregating a problem into its component issues and then logically reassembling those components into a solution. Pattern recognition frequently assists in prioritizing the most critical issues. Creativity means striving to rethink, from vastly different angles, all that has been learned about a problem thus far. Habits of action lead to effective communication, decision making, and execution. A problem solver must develop a predisposition to action—committing oneself to fighting the good fight once the analysis is done. There is no substitute for courage in overcoming the obstacles to change.

Strong habits of mind and action are part of expert problem solving. But crafting great solutions is more about recognizing and evaluating possibility than it is about depth of knowledge, intelligence, or keen analytical skills. In this book we hope to expand your perspective on the possibilities that problems contain. A problem solver must intuit that the problem can be solved, even in the absence of any obvious path toward a solution. One must also believe that the ultimate, broad benefits of the solution outweigh its costs of discovery and implementation.

How to Use This Book

To develop the basic ideas of this book, as authors we reached deep into the well of our own experiences. In particular, we leveraged Viva Bartkus's extensive experience helping major health care, retail, industrial, consumer goods, and high-tech companies to overcome their strategic, operational, and organizational challenges during her ten years at McKinsey & Company, the last four as a partner of the firm. Viva served as a consultant, but rest assured that the general manager of each client took responsibility not only for analyzing but also for actually solving the problem. We present her experiences as first-person narrative.

Ed Conlon's nearly thirty years as a leading academic and scholar on management issues came fully into play in drawing out the broader leadership implications of the challenges Viva undertook. Borrowing insights from consulting, management, and academia, we two together developed the parsimonious framework for mastering the art of solving real problems. Over the last three years we have collaborated on this book within the halls of the University of Notre Dame, and our approach has been deeply influenced by the values of that setting.

The Iterative Problem-Solving Framework

As we mentioned earlier, good business decisions rest on systematic, fact-based inquiry, particularly in times of great uncertainty. But what questions should be asked? Beyond asking what we might know, we need to probe more deeply into how we know it or why we *think* we know. Such deeper probing drives real insights. In a complex business challenge, these are basic, first-round questions:

- What are we asking and why? Is it the right question to ask?
- What is really going on here? What are we trying to achieve?
- How do we know what we think we know?
- How can we be certain that our ultimate recommendation will be right—or right enough?
- Can we actually change something?
- How should we get started?

Building on such questions, which move the problem solver beyond merely investigating symptoms, this book lays out its iterative problem-solving framework to identify and examine the root causes of business problems and then resolve them.

In our experience, problem solving does not rest on deep expertise in all facets of the problem. Rather, it requires first the ability to set a goal whose achievement *is* the solution. Second, it requires the ability to disaggregate or break down the problem sufficiently into pieces, or issues, and then prioritize them so that resolving them in sequence or in subsets ultimately reaches the overall goal. Third, solving complex problems requires being able to apply relevant frameworks to analyze and address the issues. Finally, it requires judging when to move on to action.

This book describes our framework in three parts, as shown in Figure I.1. Part One is about discovering solutions, Part Two about judging when to move from analysis to action, and Part Three about the process that drives a solution through the organization. For clarity, we will describe the three parts as occurring in a simple sequence; however, real life demands a constant iteration among the three.

Part One is mainly about systematically disaggregating and analyzing problems and from that, finding solutions.

Figure I.1. Iterative Problem-Solving Framework

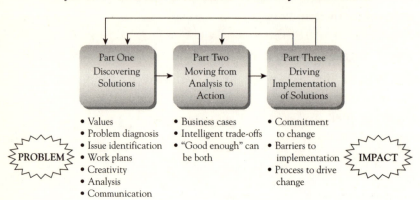

Chapter One begins by demonstrating how personal, organizational, and societal values underpin all problem-solving efforts. Chapters Two and Three describe methods to diagnose a problem from multiple symptoms, tools to break the problem down into component parts, and ways to prioritize issues based on estimates of possible impact. Because problem solving is art as well as science, Chapters Four and Five discuss creative and analytical approaches, respectively. Chapter Six is about how to communicate a solution.

The general manager constantly faces tension between demands for action and demands for certainty in decision making. Part Two focuses on making such difficult trade-off decisions. Chapter Seven starts with the use of business cases to test proposed solutions by rigorously examining their associated costs and benefits. Chapter Eight follows with a discussion of ways to make intelligent trade-offs between speed and accuracy, and among resources, investments, return, and risk.

Part Three takes on the thorny issue of implementing solutions. Sad to say, many an allegedly great solution sits gathering dust. Many business books focus on factors such as organizational culture and commitment to change. We contend that organizational and personal values should take center stage not only in determining solutions but also in the ways of executing them. Chapter Nine introduces tools to test leaders' commitment to the new solution. Chapter Ten describes additional barriers to executing new initiatives. Chapter Eleven proposes a high-level process to drive implementation through an organization. Once again, general managers must iterate between analyzing problems, judging when the solution is strong enough, and adjusting solutions for practical reasons. The book's conclusion reflects on situations to which our iterative problem-solving framework is well suited and what to do when it is not.

The Cases in This Book

Case learning can be especially useful to readers who have not already spent many years solving business problems. But even highly experienced managers may learn new material better by drawing their own lessons from real-life stories than by mainly reading basic principles.

Each chapter thus begins with and follows through on a real-world, difficult business problem that Viva, her consulting teams, and her general manager clients have faced and that speaks directly to the basic subject at hand. The cases allow you to practice asking questions, recognizing patterns, and applying useful frameworks. We believe the combination of principles and cases will speed your learning and strengthen your ability to apply what you have learned. Each chapter closes with a brief narrative from leaders at the University of Notre Dame, GE, Google, McKinsey, and other major organizations, providing insights into a problem the writer has encountered—whether solved or not.

A Debt to the University of Notre Dame

We gratefully acknowledge our intellectual debt to Notre Dame's scholarship and teaching emphasis on clarity of thought, tenacity in action, and uncompromising values. Notre Dame's perspective on leadership is, in a business context, what distinguished Paul's leadership from Peter's. Both Peter and Paul tenaciously promoted and protected their company. But Paul brought clarity of thought in examining and then marshalling sufficient information to solve his company's complex problems. In finding and implementing solutions, he overcame both internal and external constraints. And his process of discovery and decision making neither compromised the company's values—first and foremost to serve the needs of patients and physicians—nor dodged responsibility for improving economic performance and shareholder returns. Clarity in thought, tenacity in action, and uncompromising values became the foundation for our iterative problem-solving method.

Our Signs of Success

How will we know if this book has succeeded in helping to foster better problem solving? The toughest problems require not only systematic methods but also personal courage and daring. Although it is difficult to convey courage on a written page, we know that courage often flows, in part, from having the confidence to take on a challenge. By internalizing the ideas in this book, we hope you will gain confidence in your problem-solving ability and thus bolster your courage to take on some of the really difficult problems that businesses face today. Although courage may continue to be relatively scarce, we are quite certain that complex, multidisciplinary problems will never be in short supply.

We cannot promise that, having read this book and practiced on its cases, you will discover and develop the best solutions for every problem. But if the book prepares you to ask better questions as you take on current challenges or greater ones in the future, we shall consider it a success.

Part One

DISCOVERING SOLUTIONS

Chapter 1

STARTING FROM VALUES

A Tale of Values Conflicts

"No women. No minorities."

Within days of the start of the Mississippi Blood Services Organization (BSO) project, the general manager demanded that both I and my Chinese American teammate, Kevin, be replaced. He simply would not tolerate women and minorities on a team serving his organization.

It was the spring of 1993, and I had just moved from graduate school to the Upper East Side of Manhattan for my first real job, as an analyst with a major management consulting firm. Shortly after my arrival I had received a call. "You're going to Mississippi," Chris, the staffing coordinator, had told me.

My first reactions? "Mississippi—how do I get there from here?" "How hot is it down there?" "Will I understand their accents?"

"You'll be joining the team that is helping the Blood Services Organization of Mississippi get out of its financial problems," Bill, the partner and most senior leader on the project, had barked, also over the phone.

Our team's charter was to solve the financial problems facing the Mississippi BSO. For nearly half a century, the BSO had been collecting, processing, and delivering blood products to area hospitals. It was one of the pillars of the community, like the local university and major area hospitals. However, it was suffering from shrinking revenues, escalating costs, and mounting financial losses, not to mention low morale and departures of talent. In fact, it now sustained $22 million in annual expenses on only $20 million in revenues. It was hemorrhaging cash. Without a successful, substantial improvement in performance, the BSO would have to shut its doors.

Friends had warned me that the first few weeks, and especially the first few days, of a new job and a new project could be a bit unnerving. They were right. After quick phone conversations with teammate Glenn, the day-to-day project manager, and teammate Kevin, the business analyst, I tried to make sense of the facts (as I understood them) about the BSO. This Mississippi organization supplied blood products in-state by collecting voluntary blood donations and then testing, processing, and distributing these products to area hospitals. However, in the previous year or so the BSO's profits had swung into losses. The newly appointed chief executive of the national BSO was old friends with Bill, the partner in our firm. Both having come from the pharmaceutical industry, they had worked together on health care issues over the preceding ten years. The new BSO executive asked Bill to put a team together to assess and help turn around the deteriorating situation.

At least that is what I thought before I got to Mississippi. Once there, the challenge seemed to become that the general manager wanted neither women nor minorities on the team that would serve his BSO.

Growing up rather sheltered in Indiana, I had never encountered such outright prejudice. Shocked, I tried to determine how I might have caused the manager's reaction. Because it was only my first week on the job, I finally concluded that I had not had enough time to offend him. Then I was furious. How could the same person who had nearly bankrupted the BSO now think he could impose his beliefs—and prejudices—on the team dedicated to turning around his organization? From my perspective, he and his BSO were damn fortunate to get our talented, dedicated team.

After calming down, I quietly watched what happened. On the one hand, everything I had seen in our consulting firm—both on paper and in the way that everyone interacted—emphasized the importance of merit and serving clients well. On the other hand, Bill was a young partner under huge pressure, and the Mississippi BSO was our demonstration project for an entire network of potential future health care clients. Then, too, Mississippi was a long way from our home office in New York, and Glenn, Kevin, and I were very junior staff with little influence within our firm.

To his enormous credit, the following day Bill told the general manager that we were the best team to save his beloved BSO, and BSO could take it or leave it.

Although I did not fully appreciate Bill's courage until many years later, his stance earned him Kevin's loyalty and mine. My feelings for the general manager and his Mississippi BSO? Well, I felt a deep respect for the mission and good works of the BSO. And then there was my stubborn pride.

We stayed to prove our worth.

Values and Problem-Solving Efforts

A problem-solving effort begins and ends with values. Without some integrated system of values, one cannot say a proposed solution is optimal or even appropriate; one cannot even establish goals for a problem-solving effort. Values influence the division and prioritization of analytical work. In fact, without values, what is the reason to take the problem on?

By values, we mean the principles, standards, or qualities that you consider worthwhile or desirable. By norms we mean the principles of right action that guide and regulate proper and acceptable behavior within a society or organization. We argue that all problem-solving efforts encounter values conflicts. Consequently, you as the problem solver must examine your own values. But just knowing these is not sufficient. We argue that you must also stay true to them—first to your values, and then, if possible, to the norms of your organization.

We introduce practical approaches to resolving conflicts either among the values of different individuals or between individual values and organizational or societal norms. One can, and indeed must, harness values and norms toward developing pragmatic solutions to complex business challenges. Other scholars have written eloquently on business ethics and broader societal norms; where appropriate, we draw on their work and direct you to their contributions.

Values Conflicts in Setting Goals and Allocating Work

Bill's decision about the BSO team got me to closely observe the personal convictions of my teammates and the norms of our consulting firm.

Regarding goals and work allocation, right off we faced potential values conflicts even within our four-person team. Our day-to-day project manager, Glenn, wanted to complete the work as efficiently and quickly as possible. For efficiency's sake, he could have made Kevin responsible for building the financial model of BSO's operations by which we could test turnaround scenarios, analyze the profitability of products and customer accounts, and assess pricing and other opportunities. It would have been easy to do that, because Kevin, the more junior business analyst, had been staffed on the team as an expert in spreadsheet analysis and financial modeling from previous projects. But Kevin wanted to move beyond his current expertise. He wanted to interact more with clients, interview customers, broaden his experience.

Glenn did not take the easier, more efficient path, because our consulting firm also valued professional development. One could argue that it was one of our core organizational norms. As long as there was no negative impact on client service, partners encouraged teams to allocate project activities so as to build and broaden members' skills. Both Glenn and Bill, the partner, believed in and respected this norm. So Bill took Kevin to interviews and coached him on client interactions while Glenn and I sorted out the financials.

Values Conflicts in Prioritizing Options and Deciding on Potential Solutions

Bill, Glenn, Kevin, and I shared values (often implicitly) that helped us to prioritize options for BSO's financial turnaround. We stuck to the facts of the case, open to wherever our data and analysis might lead. We attempted to prioritize options in a straightforward, fact-based way. According to size and speed of potential impact, difficulty, and risk, we identified sufficient opportunities to return the BSO to financial solvency. Chapters Two and Three describe the problem-solving framework and process we followed. Specific solutions included cost reductions (in the nursing staff, laboratory procedures, and administrative functions) and revenue increases through improved blood product inventory management.

But from early on, there was a serious chance that the BSO general manager might reject our proposals because of the ongoing conflicts in values that went beyond the original ones over race and gender. Numerous BSO managers stubbornly opposed many rather straightforward ideas. After some reflection, I began to understand that the BSO managers were afraid that our team would make them look incompetent, harming their professional reputations and careers.

We eventually overcame this opposition by framing our recommendations in the context of the one fundamental value on which everyone agreed: the broad Mississippi community's benefits from a local blood supply. In retrospect, the confluence seems obvious: the community valued a local blood supply, especially in times of disaster and need. Mississippi BSO's mission actually rested on this goal, and at some level every employee's and consultant's personal convictions supported it.

Having discovered this overarching common good, we set out to turn the BSO around as humanely as possible, trying to avoid major layoffs. Fortunately, most of the savings could come from eliminating overtime expenses for nurses during blood drives, so BSO could avoid laying off its three hundred dedicated nurses.

Values Conflicts and Bottom-Line Trade-Offs

The preceding discussion raises the question of what leaders should do when adherence to personal values might compromise the bottom-line objectives of the firm—as was Peter's experience as CEO of the global health care company in the introductory tale.

As another example, take a publicly traded, major retailer that consistently provides value for customers while—unlike its competitors—also granting employees such generous health care and other benefits that applications for positions far exceed hiring needs. Despite growth and profitability that also far exceed the competitors', Wall Street analysts consistently criticize the CEO for higher-than-necessary expenses. To date, the CEO has weathered criticism and garnered praise for affirming his company's norm of fairly treating employees. But the bottom-line fact remains: the CEO's tenure depends on the company's delivery of excellent economic value to its shareholders. Were performance to deteriorate, all improvement options would certainly be on the table, including benefit reduction. At that point, the CEO might be forced to compromise the fair treatment principle to the extent required to lift shareholder returns.

Articulating Your Own Bedrock Values

The bedrock of leadership and problem solving lies in the values that each of us holds dear. Yet sometimes it is difficult to know just what those values are. This section may aid your examination of your own values and surrounding norms. We begin by discussing four cardinal virtues that influence business decisions, then take on the tough topic of motivation, before continuing with a few ways to deepen your understanding and commitment to values.

Personal Values and the Four Cardinal Virtues

Values are principles that individuals may hold worthwhile; virtues are those values that a society deems right. Aristotle, Aquinas, and many other philosophers in the Western tradition have argued moral character rests on four main ("cardinal") virtues: prudence, justice, temperance, and courage. Basically, prudence is a strong, steady disposition to choose appropriate means toward good ends. Justice is the continuing commitment to render unto each his or her due. Temperance is the rational disciplining of desires. And courage enables one to do the right thing despite the threat of personal injury or loss. We maintain that these four cardinal virtues are essential to sound business judgment.

I still greatly respect the tough nursing manager at Mississippi BSO for how she handled my difficult messages regarding the high costs of her nursing department. A major portion of the BSO turnaround depended on modifying scheduling procedures for blood drives to eliminate most overtime nursing costs—which was deeply unpalatable to nurses wanting overtime pay. The nursing manager displayed all four cardinal virtues in handling the decision. Prudently, she did no more and no less than was necessary, but she did eliminate all overtime pay. She was eminently just in the way she accomplished this, not looking at seniority or performance or even her favorites in the nursing staff, but applying the policy equally to all. She displayed temperance in patiently explaining why her decision was correct and appropriate, given BSO's overall challenges. Finally, she showed tremendous courage in abolishing overtime pay despite loud resistance from the nursing union.

Aristotle, Hobbes, and Human Motivation

My often comical experiences in the world of investment banking illuminate two opposing perspectives on human motivation
and on related contrasts in organizational norms. Aristotle and
Thomas Hobbes defined the basic distinction: whether people's
motives lean more toward cooperation or competition. The ori-
entation can be attributed to an individual's nature or to the
social context.

About 2,400 years ago, Aristotle made the case for cooperation as the basic human motivation, arguing, "Man is by nature a
political [social] creature," designed to live in the *polis* or society.[1]
The state, he said, is a creation of nature whose purpose is to teach
its citizens how to live a virtuous life.

Contrarily, about two millennia after Aristotle, Thomas
Hobbes argued that humans are basically more competitive
than collaborative. Without a strong power to keep all forces in
check, a situation of " . . . war of everyone against everyone"
naturally ensues. Government, Hobbes maintained, is based on
the need for security, not—as Aristotle contended—on fostering the good life. Absent some central authority to keep man's
natural aggression in check, said Hobbes, " . . . the life of man
[is] solitary, poor, nasty, brutish, and short."[2]

Understanding your own natural disposition and the motivation of colleagues is a way to determine the degree of harmony
or conflict in your work environment. As for me, I was an
Aristotelian in my mind, living in a Hobbesian world. That, in a
nutshell, was my challenge when serving a large New York City
bank in 1995.

My Indiana, Catholic, and immigrant upbringing emphasized helping neighbors, friends, colleagues, and those in need.
Naively, I assumed the same in others. I quickly learned these
expectations were completely inappropriate on the trading floor
and among international banking executives whose success
depended on fostering raw competition and conflict.

Of course, no industry or organization is entirely cooperative or competitive. Contrast the ruthless vendor management of American car manufacturers with the more Aristotelian cooperation across the automotive supply chain of their Japanese counterparts—with vastly different long-term results. In many industries and companies, the sales force's performance incentives are specifically designed to encourage competition. By contrast, however, in rapidly evolving industries in which intellectual capital and creativity are a competitive advantage, companies specifically foster cooperation to ensure the combination and exchange of knowledge.

In the absence of values, there is nothing inherently right or wrong with either an Aristotelian or Hobbesian organizational mindset. Still, we would not be two Notre Dame professors if we did not argue for rather more Aristotelian approaches.

Neoclassical economists took a page directly from Hobbes in developing their assumptions: that humans are selfish, rational, and atomistic. Yet Hobbesian rationality and competition cannot provide the full foundation for all economic activity. For example, no matter how detailed, contracts cannot foresee every possible future contingency, and are thus incomplete. Under conditions of cooperation and basic trust, transaction costs among individuals and firms will be lower, because every contingency need not be written into a contract. As one of our colleagues pointed out, even economists cooperate.

Cooperation within an organization or society can further lead directly to more positive payoffs for its members. Within a community, dense horizontal relationships reinforced by commonly held norms yield the benefits of freely flowing information, surveillance of and sanctions against deviant behavior, and overall encouragement toward collective action. Within a firm, the payoff of increased cooperation can be a competitive advantage. Think about recent investments that many professional firms, research and development organizations, and high-tech companies have made in the knowledge economy. In our rapidly changing world, their investments aim to increase their competitive advantage by fostering cooperative networks that create and manage knowledge.

In short, it is worth your while to spend some time reflecting on your own and your organization's cooperative and competitive views.

Broadening One's Experiences and Perspectives on Values

Further broadening your perspectives regarding values can prove indispensable. To this end, an overseas posting presents at least one unique benefit: it can help managers not only learn about the norms deemed important by a foreign society but also come to recognize more clearly their own values back home.

Because of the shift in cultural context, overseas assignments also frequently give rise to business conflicts. In 1998, I was assigned to a large team assisting a Southern California biotech firm in integrating an acquired Austrian health care company. For six months, our team shuttled constantly between Los Angeles and Vienna. But it was not the travel and long hours worked that caused the most tension. The tensions stemmed primarily from conflicts between American and Austrian business and societal norms.

They started with seemingly trivial matters. On the first day, the two sides disagreed about appropriate formality and salutations. In Austria, meeting attire was "business casual." Austrians understood that to be conservative dress—dark suits—whereas Americans understood it as any casual clothing except jeans. The Austrians expected much more formality in conversation. For example, Austrian business colleagues would greet each other as "Herr Doctor" and "Herr Professor" even after twenty years of working together.

These tensions escalated, complicating and massively slowing integration. In the political context, Austrian society valued gradual broad-based consensus, so major business decisions required consulting with unions, city officials, health ministers, and other stakeholders. Major Austrian corporations played vital roles in social services and beyond, so business decisions in Austria sometimes ran counter to the American tendencies to first and foremost maximize shareholder returns. And culturally, Austrians were not the "rugged individuals" that the Americans considered themselves to be. Indeed, an Austrian's place in the community is incredibly important to his self-perception.

Given the extensive need for consensus across disparate Austrian and American stakeholders during the course of the study, I longed to find just one person who might have the sign that President Truman had on his desk, "The buck stops here." It would never be that easy to make decisions in Vienna.

The six-month assignment in Vienna helped me better understand not only Austrian norms but American ones as well—and also just how American I was.[3] With increased globalization, effective leaders must expand their horizons to deal with different values systems, even within the United States. As the Austrian example strongly suggests, business executives disregard societal norms at their own peril—even here at home.

Organizational Commitment to Norms

Organizations vary in how they adopt, modify, and disseminate their own norms and support certain personal values. They vary also in how their norms compare with the norms of the broader society.

Company Ethics and Societal Norms

Historically, many American economists and business leaders defined company norms narrowly: first, efficient use of resources; second, fair competition. Indeed, in 1970 the *New York Times*

Magazine quoted the Nobel economist Milton Friedman: "The doctrine of social responsibility . . . is fundamentally subversive . . . There is one and only one social responsibility of business—to use its resources and engage in activities designed to increase profits so long as it engages in open and free competition without deception and fraud."[4]

Current vibrant academic and public policy debates sound quite different. Not surprisingly, two separate considerations drive this recent transformation: responsibility and money. Citing the four cardinal virtues, longtime business scholar Keith Davis proposed, "If business has the power, then a just relationship demands that business also bear responsibility for its action . . . The Iron Law of Responsibility is that . . . in the long term, those who do not use power in the manner which society considers responsible will tend to lose it."[5] Business leaders ignore changing societal values to their own detriment. Although most probably agreed with Friedman in 1970, by 2000 a *Business Week*/Harris poll revealed that only 5 percent did so. Well over 90 percent of Americans surveyed believed that business had some obligations toward its employees and communities.[6] Other polls have shown similar changes.

Scholars besides Davis have argued that more ethical and socially responsible firms tend to be more successful financially.[7] Widely differing reasons drive this commitment. Perhaps most frequently, companies adopt ethics policies to manage risk—avoiding legal or financial problems arising from wrongdoing by employees. Companies may also do so to align personal values with organizational norms, thus improving performance and encouraging employee commitment and trust. And companies may adopt ethics policies to enhance market position and build better relationships with customers. There may be some additional benefit in being perceived as a good global citizen.

Disseminating Company Norms by Credo or Osmosis

Observing my colleagues' actions on the BSO project helped me understand both their personal values and our firm's norms.

Some organizations disseminate their values through formal positions like the Johnson & Johnson Credo. The Credo asserts simply that J&J has four responsibilities. The first and foremost is to provide its customers with high-quality products at fair prices. The second is to treat its employees with dignity and respect and to pay them fairly. The third responsibility is to the communities in which J&J operates, to be good corporate citizens, and to protect the environment. The fourth and last is to provide its shareholders with a fair return. In 2002, Ralph Larson, the Chairman and CEO of J&J, outlined his thoughts about the Credo, saying, "In the final analysis, the Credo is built on the notion that if you do a good job in fulfilling the first three responsibilities, then the shareholder will come out all right."[8] The principles underlying the Credo go back to J&J's founding.

Others let values permeate their organization through a more informal, osmotic process. Our consulting firm definitely transmitted values through osmosis. How does the osmotic process work? How (and how well) did it work for me personally? Consider, for example, two norms frequently affecting work assignments: excellence in client work and ongoing professional training. At first, my commitment to my firm's norms arose from the end-of-study performance evaluations, which explicitly asked partners to evaluate whether each associate and project manager created professional training opportunities for their teammates. Later, my inspiration to help others develop professional skills came from a strong desire for external recognition within my office. Every year our office publicly honored the best mentors, and I vowed that I would make that list. By the time I was elected a partner, I constantly thought of development opportunities for my colleagues—even when no one would ever see or know about my efforts. The institution's norms had become my own values.

Scholarship suggests my experience is in keeping with a common pattern. Daniel Katz and Robert Kahn delineate three sources of commitment: rule enforcement, external rewards, and internal motivation.[9] Initially one obeys rules out of respect for authority and avoidance of penalties for wrongdoing. Secondarily, one responds to financial and recognition rewards for prescribed behavior. Finally, one internalizes organizational norms into one's personal values.

Resolving Inevitable Conflicts

Regrettably, there is no magic formula for resolving values conflicts in problem-solving efforts. After much reflection, however, we offer these thoughts:

- Make explicit the hierarchy of values and norms.
- Search for "the oasis in the storm," or common ground.
- Stick to "the safety of the data."
- Stay aware of the bottom-line requirements.

Hierarchies of Values and Norms

Although at times controversial and certainly never transparent, a hierarchy of values and norms always exists in some form. Recognizing this hierarchy enables making the difficult trade-offs that solutions to tough problems require.

The BSO achieved its turnaround without laying off its nurses. Let us, however, examine a hypothetical solution that required BSO to lay off a quarter of its nursing staff. How should BSO managers react? The implicit hierarchy of values would be as follows: first and foremost, the societal norm of maintaining a local blood supply; second, the needs of individual nurses. If all other avenues of cost reduction had been exhausted, and there were no other alternatives, then the Mississippi BSO would have to execute the layoffs despite the hardships imposed on individual nurses. One should characterize the implications of different solutions for the organization, society, and individual managers. In this case, societal and organizational needs outweighed personal ones.

One can test the hierarchy of values by talking through its implications for solutions. At the BSO, I had to explain to the nursing manager how her stubborn protection of the nurses' compensation threatened the BSO's entire existence. Once she understood that, she changed her decisions toward doing everything possible to save the BSO.

Another test of often implicit values is to delve into the criteria by which potential solutions would be judged. Between the judgment criteria and the proposed solution's implications, one can unearth the values hierarchies that different managers hold dear. For the good of the problem-solving effort, these hierarchies need to be as transparent as possible.

Oasis in the Storm

Frequently, values come into conflict because various parties' objectives are not aligned. The problem solver should try to find the common ground, which we call the "oasis in the storm." The mission or objectives of the organization are always a good place to start. In the Mississippi BSO case, the common ground was the unquestioned benefit to the community of a local blood supply, especially in times of disaster. As long as our team focused on that objective, managers would be more willing to commit to our recommendations.

If your current perspective yields no common ground, then keep expanding your perspective until you discover it.

Let the Data Speak for Themselves

When managers argue about, say, BSO's market share in Mississippi, the argument should be short. One can define the market, estimate the sales of BSO and its competitors, and then calculate the appropriate market share. The lesson? The safety of data—their relatively less controversial nature—can significantly reduce conflicts in problem-solving efforts. In tricky circumstances, let the data speak. People may see different implications in it, but presenting the data without commentary sometimes can be the most effective way of beginning the problem-solving process. The more difficult discussions arise from what to *do*, based on the information.

Stay Aware of Bottom-Line Requirements

Organizational norms tend to address the means by which results should be achieved. For example, the J&J Credo addresses the treatment of customers, employees, and communities before talking about creating economic value for shareholders. But stay aware that they are *means* to providing that value. J&J's attentiveness to customers establishes its reputation, customer trust, and, consequently, repeat business. Good treatment of employees builds a culture of loyalty and, among other things, minimizes the disruption of turnover. By respecting its communities, J&J builds good will. The three norms form the basis for effective top- and bottom-line financial growth and performance.

Bill's Decision and Lessons for the General Manager

Many years after the Mississippi BSO project, I ran into Bill at Chicago's O'Hare airport. Those first days with BSO had made such a lasting impression, I had to ask him how he had decided on his response to the general manager's demand to replace me and Kevin.

Having been elected a partner by that time, I could imagine the pressures on Bill as a young partner trying to prove himself. Bill observed that, sadly, we do not always know our own personal values, nor can we predict what we would do when confronted with specific challenges. Most of the time, we are lucky simply to get things right. We laughed and agreed.

However, Bill then described staying up all night thinking about how changing out the team would make him feel. "Lousy," was the answer. Thinking about how to tell the client that his demand was wrong and would not be accommodated also made Bill sick. From there, he meditated on how he would advise a colleague facing the same decision, then on how he might be remembered for his choice. Still no help. Finally, he thought about how he might explain this to his recently deceased mother. In that light, the decision became crystal clear.

When I asked where he had learned such a sensible approach to making difficult decisions, surprisingly Bill cited Saint Ignatius of Loyola and the "discernment rules" that Loyola developed to address his own challenging times—the 1500s.[10] How relevant could a sixteenth-century Spanish priest's thinking be to modern-day business? Loyola understood the challenges of moral uncertainty, empathized, and gave good pragmatic advice: Involve the whole person—feelings, intellect, and will. Ask oneself imaginative questions, such as Bill had asked: "How would I counsel a colleague facing a similar problem?" "How would I feel at my own deathbed looking back on the choice?" Human reason comes up with the useful questions. One's heart and will finally make the choice.

Integrity in Problem Solving

Success in solving problems depends on integrity. Absent values, solutions tend to be based on weak standards or unguided by established principles. To general managers facing complex business challenges, we suggest examining one's own personal values often and making them as explicit as possible to colleagues. Diligently and frequently explore one's organization's and community's norms. The foundation of the effective discovery of solutions, and their implementation, is a thorough consideration and embrace of meaningful values.

Values are a pervasive, complicated, conflict-engendering part of problem solving. Resolving these conflicts by finding common ground strengthens efforts to determine solutions. The following essay by Father Theodore Hesburgh, CSC, President Emeritus of the University of Notre Dame, speaks more to the challenge of discovering common values. The next chapter moves into diagnosing a problem's root causes from the usual mess of symptoms.

My Toughest Problem:
The U.S. Commission on Civil Rights

Father Theodore Hesburgh, CSC
President Emeritus, University of Notre Dame

> *We discovered that we didn't have three Southerners and three Northerners on the U.S. Civil Rights Commission—as everyone thought—but rather six fishermen.*

Serving on the Civil Rights Commission was certainly an honor that no one seeks, yet its work and impact on American society is one of the proudest achievements of my life. In 1957, President Eisenhower appointed and the U.S. Senate confirmed the six members of the commission: John Battle, former governor of Virginia; Doyle Carlton, former governor of Florida; Robert Storey, dean of the Southern Methodist Law School; John Hanna, president of Michigan State University and former assistant secretary of defense; J. Ernest Wilkins, undersecretary of labor and the only black member of the commission; and myself.

Whichever way we turned, we faced immediate and major challenges, even to the extent of finding places to conduct our work. Many of my students at Notre Dame now cannot even fathom how segregation and discrimination had scarred our society fifty years ago. Our only power was to subpoena testimony to document the dismal state of civil rights in the country in general, and voter disenfranchisement in particular. Because no hotel or restaurant in the South would serve both the white and black members of our commission together, President Eisenhower had to intervene personally to clear the way for us to stay at military bases and conduct our hearings in federal buildings. It was no wonder that Commissioner Hanna called ours "a God-awful job."

After two years of work and before making our recommendations to the president and Congress, we were to conduct one more set of hearings in Shreveport, Louisiana. Under the scorching heat and humidity, and the noise of military aircraft landing at all hours at the SAC airbase accommodating the commission, tempers frayed as fatigue set in. Then a federal marshal announced that a federal judge had enjoined us from holding our hearings, on the grounds that the U.S. Civil Rights Commission was unconstitutional. Well, I knew then and there I had to get my fellow commissioners out of Louisiana. We would never reach agreement as to our recommendations under these trying circumstances.

We went from what felt like Hell to as close to Heaven as possible. With the generous donation of a Notre Dame benefactor's private plane, we flew from Shreveport to the university's retreat in Land O' Lakes, Wisconsin. Calling ahead, I made sure that we would have steaks, corn on the cob, baked potatoes, and cold martinis waiting for us when we landed. Then, as my fellow commissioners collapsed from exhaustion and slept on the flight, I went to the back of the plane to confer with our excellent staff. During the five-and-a-half-hour flight, the staff and I worked out the resolutions that the commission should recommend.

All I can say is that the Spirit was with us. During dinner at Land O' Lakes we discovered that all six of us were avid fisherman. I quickly called our guides and got our boats ready for an evening of fishing for bass and walleye at twilight.

Afterward, we settled in our screened-in porch to discuss the commission's recommendations. John Hanna handed the role of chairman to me for the evening, because, as he pointed out, I had spent time with the staff developing the resolutions. I think the whole environment—cool air, pine trees, good food—provided the magic we needed to discover the common ground that I fervently believed we shared. We passed eleven of the twelve resolutions unanimously, covering issues as wide-ranging as voting, employment, administration of justice, housing, and education. The twelfth—on school integration—passed 5 to 1, with former governor Battle voting against.

While holding Mass the following morning, I overheard the three Southerners discussing what had happened the previous night. They agreed that the atmosphere was so pleasant, they had not wanted to fight about the recommendations. True Southern gentlemen, they kept their word. And all twelve resolutions became the law of the land in 1964 with the passage of President Johnson's Omnibus Civil Rights Act.

Tough problems require bold and brave actions, and the occasional inspiration as well. My fellow commissioners were dedicated leaders who, on hearing the repeated stories of racial injustice across America, felt a call to action. A peaceful evening of fishing and the subsequent black, starry night in northern Wisconsin supplied the inspiration to enable those actions.

Chapter 2

WHAT REALLY IS THE PROBLEM HERE?

After our intense, emotional first day with the Blood Services Organization in Mississippi and our partner Bill's principled stand not to change the makeup of our team, we turned with relief to the relative peace of data gathering, analysis, and interviews in the service of solving BSO's strategic, operational, and organizational problems. As a team, our day-to-day project manager Glenn, business analyst Kevin, and I began to try to figure out the real problem at the BSO.

A business problem is whatever prevents an organization from achieving its strategic, operational, or financial goals. The Introduction outlined the three parts of the overall iterative problem-solving framework: discovering solutions, deciding when to move from analysis to action, and implementing the solution throughout the organization. The framework must be understood as iterative, because in the course of any problem-solving journey one may need to implement parts of the solution, then alter other parts in light of ongoing reexamination. Although the BSO problem is one that outside consultants helped to solve, the approach we describe can and should also be used by business leaders by themselves.

This chapter focuses on determining problems, identifying issues, and planning the work. The process starts with a rapid diagnosis of the symptoms that leads into the underlying problem—a perspective that we will gradually refine, disaggregating the overall problem into issues to be addressed by the longer-term work plan. At the BSO, everything described in this chapter was accomplished or at least substantially begun by the end of our first week.

Starting to Diagnose the Problem

The challenge was enormous; our team quickly realized we would need to draw on all our resources, combining logical problem structuring and analyses with creativity and intuition about the people, the problem, and a vision of the organization's potential. We would need to leverage our finance, operations, marketing, and strategy expertise to properly diagnose the causes of the BSO's financial problems. Although common sense and resourcefulness were essential, empathy with the BSO's challenges and aspirations was shaping up as perhaps the most important element in helping its managers overcome problems.

We got started with eyes toward a rapid initial assessment of the problems.

Early, Quick Determination of Problems

We quickly determined what exactly the BSO did: it supplied blood products to Mississippi by collecting voluntary blood donations and then testing, processing, and distributing these products to area hospitals. At the time, federal regulations prohibited air shipment of blood products; limited blood product viability required ground transportation to local hospital customers. As a consequence, most blood centers had near monopolies of blood products in their immediate areas.

Next, we looked into the symptoms of BSO's problems.

Problem solving, and even proper diagnosis, is complicated by the fact that most business problems manifest first as symptoms. Interpreting symptoms requires a basic facility in all business functions. Hence the problem-solving framework proposed here requires integration across business disciplines. At BSO, our team combined accounting skills, operations process flows, marketing evaluations on market share declines, and financial assessments—to name but a few analyses—to identify the BSO's core problems.

A cursory glance at the BSO's annual income statement showed that revenues had shrunk by 2 to 3 percent per year for several years, and nursing and laboratory costs were much higher as a percentage of sales than at other, comparable regional blood centers. As a result, the Mississippi BSO was bleeding cash, losing a staggering $2 million per year on only $20 million in revenues. Cash flow constraints meant we had only three months to turn it around.

On the afternoon of our first day in Mississippi, Bill, Glenn, Kevin, and I entered the conference room for our kickoff meeting with BSO managers. Seventeen employees were waiting for us: the directors of nursing, lab, distribution, marketing and donor relations, hospital accounts, finance, and human resources, and their deputies. Nearly three hundred collective years of BSO experience in the room was wondering whether our team had any new insights.

They sat in stony silence as we four limped through the introductions and kickoff. You could taste the cynicism; clearly, these BSO veterans had seen outside "consultants" before. After the meeting, we began to interview department directors individually about the current situation.

Financial statements showed the symptoms of BSO's poor performance; we hoped that the interviews with staff would move us toward underlying problems. We needed to build trust with BSO managers quickly, to harness their experience to our problem-solving methods. We tried to convey our caring for the BSO managers as people, add energy and optimism, and provide a quiet leadership that would help them find courage to change the ways they conducted business.

Partnering with Glenn throughout these general interviews, I observed how he conveyed these messages. He repeated the project's purpose, then asked detailed questions on how the BSO actually worked, followed by more open-ended questions about what department directors thought had gone wrong and what might turn things around. All the while, he tried to help them see that we were here to help, and so gain their trust. He hoped to gain a few useful insights, while avoiding passive aggressiveness or outright confrontation.

Moving Toward a "Week One Answer"

From the first day of the project, our team was prepared to offer a working solution based on our knowledge and evidence at that time. We call it a *hypothesis statement*. It was part of a more extended plan to reach a firmer preliminary recommendation by the end of the first week. Our steps are outlined later in this section. Beyond the first week, we would focus on gathering more data and conducting analyses to either prove or disprove aspects of the Week One Answer. This process of recording an answer after the first day, refining it after the first week, and continuously revising it thereafter forced us to make our assumptions explicit. In the following days, we systematically released each of the constraints and assumptions to see how that might affect the working solution.

Getting started early and quickly—and, as we shall see next, deductively—is critical to the process. Formulating answers after the first day of working on a problem and then revising those answers by the end of the first week may feel uncomfortable at first, but it will enable you to target your work much more effectively. Solutions formed at the outset are often not the correct ones and will need to be revised often, but they enable faster learning as subsequent data are gathered.

The process of discovering solutions follows six basic steps. Like the entire problem-solving process, it is part science, part art:

1. Define the problem and its context, and generate a hypothesis of the solution (based on available information).

2. Disaggregate the problem into issues, discard minor issues, and begin to prioritize the remaining issues.

3. Develop a detailed work plan.

4. Employ creativity and conduct critical analyses to solve the problem.

5. Build the argument from the findings into a storyline.

6. Repeat the process, as needed.

The rest of this chapter outlines Steps 1, 2, and 3, which we essentially completed during the first week at the BSO. It describes tools that enabled us to diagnose the problem quickly and posit a broad solution. The next chapter introduces techniques for prioritizing issues and options. Chapters Four and Five address ways to bring creativity and analytical rigor into the problem-solving process. Chapter Six discusses methods to communicate ultimate recommendations. Before describing Step 1, however, we want to give you more insight into the strengths (and weaknesses) of the hypothesis-driven approach.

Our Iterative, Hypothesis-Driven Approach

Coming up with early answers means relying on deduction, which is essential to rapid problem diagnosis. In an *inductive* process, you would not try to identify the answer, or even the exact nature of the problem, until you had collected all of the data. By *deductive* process, we mean a hypothesis- or "answer"-driven approach in which your search for data or information is guided by your early guess about the causes and potential solution to the problem, and is targeted to those areas that will either support or refute the hypothesis. We will use the terms *hypothesis*, *working solution*, and *Week One Answer* interchangeably, to refer to your best guess with respect to the problem, its causes, and potential solutions.

Our iterative approach combines the best of deductive and inductive reasoning. It depends on deductive logic in its early stages, to develop a hypothesis of the solution which becomes essential to organizing further activities. With a hypothesis in

hand, the problem solver adopts inductive logic, thereby deriving conclusions from the results of collecting and investigating
more data. Deductive logic is how one formulates the hypothesis
or Week One Answer, whereas inductive logic is how one tests,
proves, disproves, and revises that hypothesis. The problem-
solving approach is fundamentally iterative, with the problem
solver moving back and forth between these two reasoning
methods on the path toward discovering the solution.

Although we are aware of no body of formal research that
establishes the superiority of a hypothesis-driven methodology
over other problem-solving approaches in terms of efficiency
and effectiveness, we do have logic for using it on complex
business problems. In our experience, this approach affords a
quicker workable understanding of a problem and offers several
related benefits:

- It focuses and guides the search for additional information,
  first by limiting the initial questions asked to the most
  pertinent ones and then by providing quick feedback about
  whether the team is on the right track.

- It enables early sharing of thoughts, facilitating timely reactions and help.

- It provides the problem solver with a history of thinking and
  analyses that can be used to examine other solutions, should
  they be needed.

Focusing and Guiding the Search

Let us look at how a hypothesis-driven approach helped focus
team efforts at Mississippi BSO. We brainstormed two reasonable
early hypotheses for what was driving the BSO's financial problems: one involved revenues—more specifically, ineffective pricing and marketing of blood products; the other involved costs,
particularly inefficiencies in managing the blood supply chain.

If we chose to pursue the pricing and marketing hypothesis, we would head down a path that included comparing the prices charged by Mississippi BSO for blood products with those of other such organizations across the country. Analyses might focus on market price elasticities of demand or medical reimbursement regulations. If we pursued the cost-reduction hypothesis, we would need to study BSO's entire supply chain. We would look at labor costs, inventory costs, and blood product waste. Note that the two hypotheses require very different information, sending us in very different directions.

Enabling the Sharing of Thoughts and Reactions

The hypothesis-focused method enhances communication and facilitates debate. By sharing our hypotheses with others, we can get their reactions to what we are considering. Suppose we shared with the BSO management a hypothesis that pricing might be a root cause of its problems. Their reaction could accelerate the problem-solving process. For example, they might respond that they had already considered that problem, and could provide us with research on the BSO's and others' prices for each blood product as well as reimbursement rates paid by major insurers and government agencies. Or they might say that their policy was to offer the lowest available price in their market for every product. Or they might indicate that they had focused almost exclusively on costs. Each would suggest a different path for our team to pursue.

Enabling Problem Solvers to Examine Other Potential Solutions

Hypotheses help us build a useful history of our thought processes. Complex business problems crossing multiple disciplines are seldom solved in one day or even one week. As a result, the solutions we consider, and the hypotheses we advance, are seldom completely correct on the first, second, or even third try. Having an explicit trail of the hypotheses the team has considered and refuted can prevent nonproductive backtracking and retesting of ideas that have already been eliminated.

Risks of the Hypothesis-Driven Method

This approach is not without its risks. First, for complex problems elusive of structure, it is important to begin the deductive process with a set of assumptions that act as constraints. The assumptions need not hold for the final solution, but they enable the team to get started. The team must be disciplined, however, to release those assumptions periodically to investigate how that might change the hypothesis.

Problem solvers must never "love their hypotheses" so much that they are unwilling to give them up in the face of new, and perhaps conflicting, evidence. Indeed, the problem-solving mindset requires an aggressive search for possibly contradictory data in order to quickly prove or disprove the current working solution. Solving problems also requires a thick skin and a short memory of criticisms that others may have of the hypotheses and problem-solving process.

We understand that developing a Week One Answer is difficult if one has never done it before. Further, some organizations' norms may make it all the more difficult, if there is a premium on not being wrong or never changing one's mind. Throughout this chapter and the ones that follow, we describe real case histories—symptoms and all—to provide you with opportunities to attempt to determine potential hypotheses of the problems and their solutions. We also discuss examples of Week One Answers and how subsequent data and analysis proved them wrong and forced their revision on the path to the ultimate solutions. There is no substitute for practice in developing this important skill of generating constructive hypotheses early in the problem-solving process.

Problem-Solving Step 1: Defining the Problem and Generating a Hypothesis of the Solution

Earlier in this chapter we described the first-week efforts at BSO to pose a solution to a problem not yet certainly defined. In those phases, we were already working on a hypothesis, which would change but increasingly clarify the problems that had spawned the mess of symptoms. That work continued in later weeks. In the first week, hypothesis statement in hand, we also defined the situation further by context and background.

The Hypothesis Statement

A good hypothesis statement is a guess of the solution—not a fact—and the more thought-provoking, the better. It must also be specific to the situation, debatable, actionable, and relevant to future decision making. Without a good hypothesis statement, problem-solving efforts will be unfocused, even ineffective. Here are some *poor* examples:

"The Mississippi BSO is losing money despite its regional near-monopoly in the supply of blood products." (Statement of fact.)

"Should the Mississippi BSO turn around its worsening operations?" (Not debatable.)

"Can the Mississippi BSO be managed differently to increase profits?" (Too general.)

Here is a good one:

"How should the BSO become the low-cost, broad-based, local blood supplier by restructuring its operations and reassessing its blood product line to improve profitability by $2+ million per year?" (Specific to the situation, debatable potential solution, actionable, and relevant to future decision making.)

Arriving at a Hypothesis Statement for BSO. Actually, we took our first cut at a BSO hypothesis statement before we went to Mississippi, and we refined it over the first few days. These were our two candidate statements:

> "What opportunities exist for the Mississippi BSO to turn around its financial performance by eliminating unprofitable products and customers in order to become a significantly scaled-back player that focuses only on its core products and customers?"

versus

> "How should the BSO become the low-cost, broad-based, local blood supplier by restructuring its operations and reassessing its blood product line to improve profitability by $2+ million per year?"

Both worked in that they took a debatable position on a future direction that might return the BSO to profitability. Both placed the crux of the problem in the BSO's operations, not its strategy. We believed that the BSO faced a choice in how to improve its operations: either continue to be a full-service, broad-based player, or divest peripheral customers and products, shrinking back to a smaller, presumably still profitable business. Both statements made assumptions about what mattered to decision makers, what the organization considered to be success, and what aspects of the organization could be examined and changed. Our subsequent analyses would test whether either of these hypotheses was on the right track.

Expanding on Problem Context and Background

As we noted earlier, in conjunction with developing a hypothesis statement, the team must define the full problem context and background. It must be explicit about scope, decision makers and their success criteria, timeframe, the accuracy or precision of solution that decision makers will need in order to move ahead, and any other constraints on the problem-solving effort.

Define the Scope. Without a clear scope of the problem, the team risks recommending solutions that go beyond an organization's willingness and ability to change. Teams must consider the business's current capacity to absorb change, and they must avoid approaches beyond its reach in time, attention, or resources. But teams should not define the problem so narrowly that their proposals risk not solving the entire problem. Frequently, recurring discussions are required among critical stakeholders to refine the problem's scope as new data and potential solutions appear.

Identify the Key Decision Makers and Their Success Criteria. The team must ascertain the values, interests, and any *professional and personal* criteria that decision makers will apply to solutions. Without meeting their expectations, a recommendation is unlikely to succeed. The ultimate solution needs to meet both organizational criteria and the personal criteria of its most powerful leaders.

Define the Timeframe. Deadlines drive the process. The shorter the timeframe, the more likely it is that a team must aim for temporary, incomplete, but immediate results. Stabilizing the situation provides time for future iterations to develop ultimate recommendations.

Determine the Accuracy of the Solutions Needed to Move Forward. When is a solution good enough? When does it need additional work? The timeframe and decision-making criteria often drive that determination. Those conducting analysis must find the point of diminishing returns, weighing the additional time and effort required to move from, say, a reasonable solution to a more ideal one. When more team time is spent distilling the solution, the improvement is not usually proportional to the increased expense of time, energy, and resources. Most of the time will be spent refining the final 20 percent of the solution, which may not even be needed to make a sound business decision. There will be times when an 80-percent solution is good enough, enabling the team to move on to other problems. In highly uncertain and risky conditions, however, business leaders may need greater accuracy. Rarely, though, should teams seek the perfect 100 percent.

Determine the Constraints. Constraints determine the solution space. Which aspects of the organization are open to change? Which are not? Would a profitable BSO not serving indigent populations be considered a success? The BSO served every Mississippi county. Was it open to serving only selected counties? Or was coverage of the entire state sacrosanct? Regarding organizational norms and values as constraints, for example, the solution space for the BSO turnaround was bounded by its long-standing mission of serving the general public of the entire state. Thus it was unacceptable to make the BSO profitable by, say, eliminating service to less-profitable hospital customers.

Or consider a company with a customer service problem. Normally, operations would own and solve that problem. But IT innovations can frequently fix customer service problems. If the operations group assumes that the current IT approach cannot change, then operations has effectively constrained the problem-solving effort. The good news is that labeling IT as a constraint simplifies the field of options. The bad news is that we lose those additional options.

Table 2.1 shows a diagnostic tool—the hypothesis statement and general problem context worksheet—describing the Mississippi BSO problem. The initial round of interviews with

Table 2.1. Hypothesis Statement and Problem Background for Mississippi BSO

Hypothesis Statement

How should the BSO become the low-cost, broad-based, local blood supplier through restructuring its operations and reassessing its blood product line to improve profitability by $2+ million per year?

Decision makers	Criteria for successful effort
CEO of national Blood Services Organization General manager of Mississippi BSO Director of nursing	Financial turnaround for BSO
	Clear set of actions and accountabilities to execute turnaround
	Senior management of BSO committed to overall program
	Measures of success
	Quick improvement in cash flow
	Modest profitability in next year's income statement

Key concerns/constraints acting on decision makers		Timeframe/accuracy for solution
CEO	Quick solution would enhance credibility in new position	Plan needs to be in place within three months
	Insufficient local skills or resources to implement recommendations	Financial turnaround must be achieved in twelve to eighteen months
	Limited investment possible	80/20; directional answers sufficient, detailed accuracy not needed
GM	Political, community pressure for local blood supply	
	Owns current budget and plan	
	Employee mindset	
Director of nursing	Upcoming union contract negotiations	

senior BSO managers that Glenn, Kevin, and I conducted allowed us to fill it in, confirm our initial assumptions, generate a hypothesis statement, and generally better understand the challenges.

Problem-Solving Step 2: Disaggregating the Problem into Issues

The Mississippi BSO case may seem complicated, with multiple issues from multiple disciplines; however, it is typical of many business problems. The best way to handle such problems is to disaggregate them into issues that are as unconnected as possible. An issue is one aspect of the problem that is generally independent of all other aspects of the problem. To disaggregate, we use an "issue tree."

Develop the Issue Tree

An issue tree is a tool for breaking down a problem easily and quickly. Ideally, it is made up of a set of independent issues that include all possibilities within the problem—in other words, with no overlaps and no gaps. It may sometimes be helpful to develop several issue trees that lend different insights into the problem. The team will need to judge which tree seems most useful in setting up subsequent paths of inquiry.

Why spend time on an issue tree? It focuses work on the most pertinent issues. Moreover, a good issue tree maintains the integrity of the problem solving. In driving for comprehensiveness, it ensures that solving the component issues will actually solve the entire problem—in aggregate. It also simplifies the work planning. And in brainstorming the issue tree, teams can tap their collective creativity and experience. Consider the hypothesis statement provided earlier:

"How should the BSO become the low-cost, broad-based, local blood supplier by restructuring its operations and reassessing its blood product line to improve profitability by $2+ million per year?"

As Bill, Glenn, Kevin, and I tried to create our first issue tree, we stood around the white board listing issues from our multiple interviews, bringing each other up to speed and clarifying our own intuitions. Our list of potential issues was not short: revenues shrinking; significant blood product waste, loss, and expiration; high nursing costs; union demands; ever-increasing lab costs; morale issues; and departmental antagonisms.

We then tried to impose some structure or hierarchy. We needed to make the subissues of the issue tree as exhaustive as possible. Obviously some subissues deserved more attention because of their potential impact, difficulty, or urgency. Figure 2.1 shows an issue tree for the Mississippi BSO.

Our issue tree identified three types of issues: cost reductions, revenue and other performance improvements, and possible trends in the marketplace. This was not the only possible set of issues nor the only way to describe them. We could have written:

- Are temporary market fluctuations affecting profitability?
- Can product waste be reduced by changing inventory management processes?
- Are labor costs unnecessarily high?

And so forth. In Figure 2.1, each issue is a possible *independent* contributor to the overall problem. This schematic plan for tackling each issue formed the basis of the detailed work plan we discuss later in the chapter.

If the team is having trouble starting from the "trunk," it can try building backward from the "twigs" of the issue tree. For example, our team might have brainstormed the actions for the right side of Figure 2.1, such as "restructure administrative functions," "streamline lab processing," "drive efficiencies in

Figure 2.1. Issue Tree for the Mississippi BSO

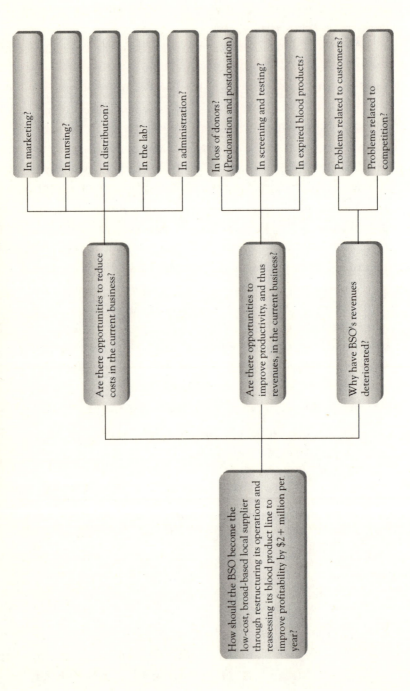

distribution," and then combined them leftward as "opportunities to reduce cost."

Because the early objective is a Week One Answer, the team should not spend too much time on developing the issue tree. It will probably change as the team learns more. Teams must always be ready to question assumptions and prune off branches. They must ask themselves "How wrong could we be?" and "How does that change the answer?" Other helpful questions are the plain "So what?" and "Why?"

Further Disaggregation at the BSO

We gained further insights into the BSO's problems by a few simple analyses of internal data—we had not yet interviewed the BSO's customers, the hospitals. Among the essential facts was this one: one pint of blood yields different amounts of several products—red blood cells, platelets, plasma—with greatly different prices and shelf lives. Implication? Because the BSO's economic performance was based on maximizing the number of unexpired blood products per unit of donated blood that it delivered to hospitals, optimizing revenue became a complicated equation.

Further interviews with local BSO blood drive employees revealed striking inefficiencies in donor recruitment and blood collection. Simple operational benchmarking against comparably sized blood centers revealed poorer BSO performance, including much higher nursing costs and a much higher loss of products through waste.

These analyses helped us prioritize further investigations to focus on blood collection, nurse staffing, and product waste in lab processing. We always kept in mind the turnaround goal of $2+ million in annual improvements—the required amount to return the BSO to sound financial health.

Even though we had brought structure to the problem, we still did not know whether the combination of all our ideas for improvement would generate enough improvement to turn the BSO around. If not, we would have a different set of problems on our hands. We made a quick, back-of-the-envelope sensitivity calculation of what a 10-percent improvement related to each idea would mean to the BSO's bottom line. We also estimated the potential difficulty and timing of the improvements. By the end of our first week in Mississippi, we had assessed all our known potential areas of improvement.

Our quick Week One Answer showed that if the BSO's managers could capture half of the improvement opportunity in the timeframe required, the BSO could do more than break even financially. In other words, a 50-percent solution would be good enough to eliminate the crisis and give the BSO some desperately needed time to solidify turnaround efforts.

Problem-Solving Step 3: A Detailed Work Plan

Once the main issues are prioritized in the first week, disciplined work planning can significantly accelerate efforts. Thoughtful work plans outline how the team will analyze, assess, and, ultimately, address issues. (Our actual work plan was derived from the issue tree in Figure 2.1.) The plan includes the analyses required to prove or disprove the hypotheses, the likely data sources, whose responsibility it is to conduct each analysis, and the timing and level of accuracy needed for each end product. The work plan should be as specific as possible about analyses and their data sources, with many near-term milestones and check-in points. It should not extend further than two to four weeks because the project priorities often change rapidly in the early stages. Table 2.2 shows what is contained in a good work plan.

The team should not wait on data to create the work plan, but should revisit and revise the plan in light of subsequent data. In most cases, senior colleagues guide the project manager's drafting of the plan.

Table 2.2. Example of a Work Plan

Issue	Hypothesis	Analysis	Data Source	End Products	Responsibility	Timing
Starts with issues from issue tree	A statement of the likely resolution of the issue	Work to be done to prove or disprove hypothesis and therefore resolve issue	Likely location of data (such as company financials, market data, interviews)	Output of analysis	Teammate	Date Degree of accuracy required

The work planning process for the BSO was fast and efficient. Glenn, our project manager, drafted the work plan after our team brainstorming session very early in the project. We then (still within the first week of the project) divided up the data gathering and analytic tasks.

Dividing up the work among team members requires thought and discussion. To maximize coherence and efficiency, analytical work should be divided by the questions or issues addressed—which frequently arise from the issue tree—rather than by specific analytical tasks such as analysis of financial statements, operational flow charts, or customer interviews. These specialized tasks are merely useful means in solving a particular issue. In keeping with this advice, in the case of the Mississippi BSO, each of us took on a significant issue such as reducing expenses in nursing or maximizing revenues. Then we used all the data, analysis, and creativity we could muster to try to address our particular issue. That meant that both Kevin, the business analyst, and I would analyze the BSO's financial statements and conduct interviews toward answering our own specific questions.

Table 2.3 displays the first-cut work plan for the BSO project. This work plan balanced complicated, and at times conflicting, priorities among the BSO executives and our team. The BSO's general manager, for example, was very concerned about external publicity, particularly pressure from civic and political leaders to maintain a broad-based, local blood supply.

Table 2.3. Work Plan – Mississippi BSO Example

Issue	Hypothesis	Analysis	Data Source	End Products	Responsibility	Timing
Turnaround sales decline	Changing competitive landscape— has a new competitor entered the BSO market?	Hospital purchasing patterns	Interview 3 to 5 largest customers Interview marketing directors in BSO corporate headquarters	Description of hospital purchasing decisions Estimate of size of opportunity by optimizing sales to customers	Kevin	One week
Improve nursing costs and efficiency	Reduce nursing costs through improved staffing of blood drives	Benchmark staff levels and cost per staff on blood drives versus other blood centers Analyze staffing process including union contract	Other blood centers Interview staffing director Interview union representatives	Estimate of size of improvement opportunity in nursing First cut at ideas on how to capture opportunity	Me	One week (first week)
	Improve efficiency of nursing time at blood drives through reduction in loss of donors	Benchmark loss of donors Develop ideas to improve donor retention	Other BSOs' data Observe blood drive Interview marketing person who schedules blood drives	Estimate of donor recruitment improvement opportunity	Me	One week (second week)

	Hypothesis	Analysis	Interview	Purpose	Who	When
Improve lab costs and efficiency	Production scheduling involves too much down time	Production flow analysis FDA requirements Analysis of labor and material costs	Interview BSO lab director Map process to test, spin, process blood into products BSO financials	Identify process improvements in production flow	BSO colleague	One week (first week)
	Reduce blood product loss through improved testing	Benchmark losses vs. other BSOs FDA requirements	Other BSOs	Perspective on degrees of freedom to change testing	BSO colleague	Later
Blood product expiration	Drivers of product expiration mainly internal (vs. external drivers)	Describe internal process for last week prior to blood product expiry Benchmark expiry rates vs. other blood centers Track expiry over time and by product line	Interview BSO lab director Interview other BSOs on their internal processes	Identify bottlenecks in the process to get products to hospitals Expiry by product line vs. other BSOs	Kevin	One week (second week)

The director of the nursing department expressed concerns about the upcoming contract negotiations with the nursing union. Within our own team, Kevin's career development needs were considered. Me, I just wanted to sink my teeth into a hard problem and solve it from beginning to end.

After much discussion, we decided that Glenn and Kevin would partner in tackling the urgent need to raise declining revenues, interacting with hospital customers to assess evolving competition. Ultimately, they needed to understand customer accounts, various product sales and expirations, pricing policies, and the distribution network. A BSO colleague would address potential performance improvements in the lab. I would focus on the front end of the blood drive process, including potentially reducing nursing costs. And so Bill, Glenn, Kevin, and I were off and running, trying to fill a $2+ million annual financial gap.

For Problem Solvers Working Solo

Throughout Part One, we are discussing problem solving by teams rather than by lone individuals. The team brings together diverse skills, experiences, and perspectives that strengthen the debate and, ultimately, the proposed solutions. But what if you are on your own? Managers frequently do face daunting problems without a supporting cast.

In fact, the problem-solving approaches outlined here also apply to the solo practitioner—with a bit of additional advice. Foremost, find "thought partners"—one or more individuals with whom to share the details of the situation as both collaborator and sounding board. Thought partners need not be in the same function or even the same industry—just intelligent, experienced, trustworthy, and responsive. When you find yourself alone facing a difficult problem, think of a person or persons who, despite their busy schedule, will still return your phone call.

Then engage with them as frequently as possible, especially early on while diagnosing the problem from its symptoms. Focus your discussions on critical junctures such as hypothesis generation and the Week One Answer. You will need to provide enough information and context for the partner to contribute perceptive questions and feedback.

The single problem solver cannot hope to complete analyses, data gathering, and interviews as quickly as a team. The time-frame has to be longer. But if, by working alone, he or she gains more time than a team to think through possible solutions, that may actually be an advantage. Longer timeframes mean more time for mulling things over, which can improve the ultimate solution.

In Short, More Erasers Than Pencils

Problem solving is a dynamic process, and good problem solvers generally wear out many erasers. Applied diligently and aggressively, the framework proposed here can enable problem solvers to answer, in a preliminary fashion, a difficult problem within a week. The process is fundamentally iterative. By diagnosing the problem from its symptoms early on and then quickly generating hypotheses about the working solution, the team can focus only on data and analyses that test the weakest parts of hypothesized solutions. Weeks subsequent to the first are dedicated to refining the working solution through further data gathering and analysis. Along the way, several tools may be helpful: the problem context, hypothesis statement, issue trees, and work plans.

In the next chapter we describe how we prioritized both potential avenues of inquiry and then potential solutions on the Mississippi BSO project. No organization has infinite time and resources. Smart priorities are integral to problem solving.

Diagnosing the Problem

Shona Brown
SVP, Business Operations, Google

When tackling business problems, unearthing the real issues may take patience and perseverance. In my experience, senior executives often start debates by making assertions such as "We are suffering margin erosion" or "We need to have a presence in China." The typical reaction to such observations is often either to poke a hole in their logic or to simply make a counter assertion.

It's often more fruitful to probe the original statement first. Asking, "Can you explain your rationale?" or "What do you mean by that?" can prompt colleagues to elaborate on their thoughts. Try not to immediately judge whether the assertion is true, but rather take the time to clarify and understand its basis.

Your first goal should be to get a deeper understanding of the nature of the assertion. This not only gives you clarity on the matter, but may also, through the process of explaining it to you, clarify your colleague's thinking.

The second goal is to further clarify the assertion by breaking it into logical chunks, perhaps even reshaping it, given your better knowledge of the context, before starting to problem solve. For example, if you say, "My margins are falling," further questioning could yield these insights:

- The volume of products sold is decreasing on a high fixed-cost business.
- Raw material costs or labor expenses are increasing.
- Prices are falling.
- Volume is shifting away from high-margin toward low-margin products.
- The low-margin part of the business is growing much more quickly.

You could then put forward a hypothesis of the working solution: "If I understand you correctly, you believe we have product mix issues that are driving the erosion of our margins." Only to the extent that you have deeper knowledge, through collaborating with your colleague to clarify the actual issues, can you offer insight. Together the two of you will be much better prepared for gathering the evidence necessary to address each question. The collaborative environment is essential.

Collaborative problem solving is not unlike assembling a large jigsaw puzzle without the picture on the box. Usually, the simplest path forward is to start with the border or some uniquely distinguishable piece. After connecting the first few pieces, you add more based on their fit with the first few. Discovering the solution means you build a common understanding of the picture—the problem you're trying to solve.

Chapter 3

PRIORITIES

Without first prioritizing, the problem solver can become lost and overwhelmed by the sheer amount of data and options. Every set of priorities, in turn, rests on a set of values. This chapter introduces practical tools for prioritizing the work.

Recall that the Mississippi Blood Services Organization (BSO) collected blood, tested and processed the donations into separate blood products, and distributed the products to Mississippi hospitals. But the BSO's revenues were decreasing, and the BSO was losing over $2 million annually.

Bill, Glenn, Kevin, and I were charged with turning the BSO around financially within three months. By the end of Chapter Two, our hypothesis statement was, "How should the BSO become the low-cost, broad-based local blood supplier by restructuring its operations and reassessing its blood product line to improve profitability by $2+ million per year?" The statement reflects our suspicion that the BSO's problems were more operational than strategic. Now we were gathering data, meeting with BSO executives, interviewing hospital customers, and conducting various analyses in a race to prove or disprove our hypothesis. There were quite a few operational inefficiencies and, thus, improvement options, so we needed to prioritize our time, effort, and, later, the options themselves.

Prioritization in Action

After a week of gathering information, our team of consultants congregated in our small, windowless team room, excited by what we had learned. We felt we understood enough about the BSO's operations and external environment to make some inroads into its problems.

At that point our senior leader, Bill, asked Kevin, the business analyst, to run a simple analysis of the profit impact associated with a 10-percent improvement from each idea. For example, if administrative costs were reduced by 10 percent, what would be the financial impact? If blood product waste were reduced by 10 percent, how much would revenue improve? This analysis was purely financial, with no assessment of how hard it might be to achieve each option. When we examined Kevin's spreadsheet, three high-potential-impact options stood out: reducing nursing costs, reducing lab costs, and reducing blood product expiry and waste. The "Potential Impact" column in the issue tree in Figure 3.1 shows how much the three stand out. On the issue tree, the top eight "twigs" were operational, the bottom two strategic. The bottom two served to remind our team that once we had improved BSO's financial performance operationally, we needed to explore its strategic positioning. We added the strategic questions to our work plan to be investigated later on.

Potential impact was only one of the criteria we needed to apply in order to prioritize options. Impact aside, which of the eight operational options could the BSO achieve most easily and quickly? To chart these factors, Glenn drew a simple graph on the white board, with the vertical and horizontal axes representing time and difficulty. We would plot the eight operational ideas on that matrix, also recording their potential impacts.

By timing, we meant whether the BSO could capture one option faster than another. With our current knowledge, we could hardly estimate the absolute time required to implement an option (that could take weeks or months), but we could judge the *relative* length of time for each.

We assessed the difficulty and risk of each option according to how much control the BSO would have. In general, the less BSO control, the more difficult the option. But how

Figure 3.1. Potential Priorities for the Mississippi BSO

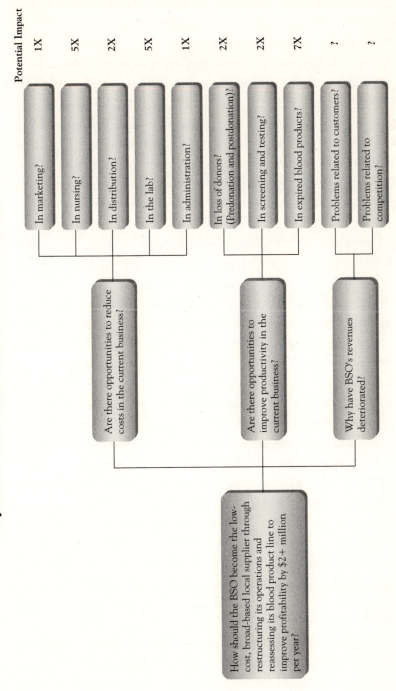

Potential Impact

How should the BSO become the low-cost, broad-based local supplier through restructuring its operations and reassessing its blood product line to improve profitability by $2+ million per year?

Are there opportunities to reduce costs in the current business?

- In marketing? — 1X
- In nursing? — 5X
- In distribution? — 2X
- In the lab? — 5X
- In administration? — 1X

Are there opportunities to improve productivity in the current business?

- In loss of donors? (Predonation and postdonation)? — 2X
- In screening and testing? — 2X
- In expired blood products? — 7X

Why have BSO's revenues deteriorated?

- Problems related to customers? — ?
- Problems related to competition? — ?

to determine the degree of control? For several high-impact options, we surmised that external parties would dictate both the timeline and difficulty of the option.

In our estimation, three of the eight options offered relatively high potential impact but, unfortunately, relatively low BSO control: reducing lab costs, improving screening and testing, and improving donor retention. The U.S. Food and Drug Administration (FDA) would scrutinize each change. Reducing lab costs would certainly involve changing internal processes and procedures (which included staffing and shift schedules), and we did not know how long the FDA would take to approve them; consequently, we rated "reduce lab costs" as big-impact, relatively easy, but of an uncertain (therefore longer) timeframe. We relied on Bill's and Glenn's extensive health care experience to judge how the FDA review process could be managed.

Potentially, the FDA might scrutinize process changes in blood screening and testing even *more* than lab procedures; federal regulations might give the BSO little room to maneuver. Therefore, we rated blood screening and testing changes as even slower and more difficult. We rated donor retention improvements also as more difficult and time-consuming than lab staffing, because education targeted to local audiences would take time to create and perform.

Figure 3.2 graphs all eight options, including those over which the BSO had more control, such as reducing blood product waste or nursing costs. Lab personnel would need to learn new warning procedures to address when the blood products would expire. The BSO might need to sell products at short notice or ship them farther afield. These were complex steps but, we argued, not too arduous or time-consuming.

By contrast, any nurse staffing or compensation changes required union approval. Overtime pay, which made up a significant portion of the expenses, was not directly covered by the contract. Negotiations were starting in earnest on the union contract, which would expire later that year. Consequently, our

Figure 3.2. Potential Matrix for the Mississippi BSO Turnaround

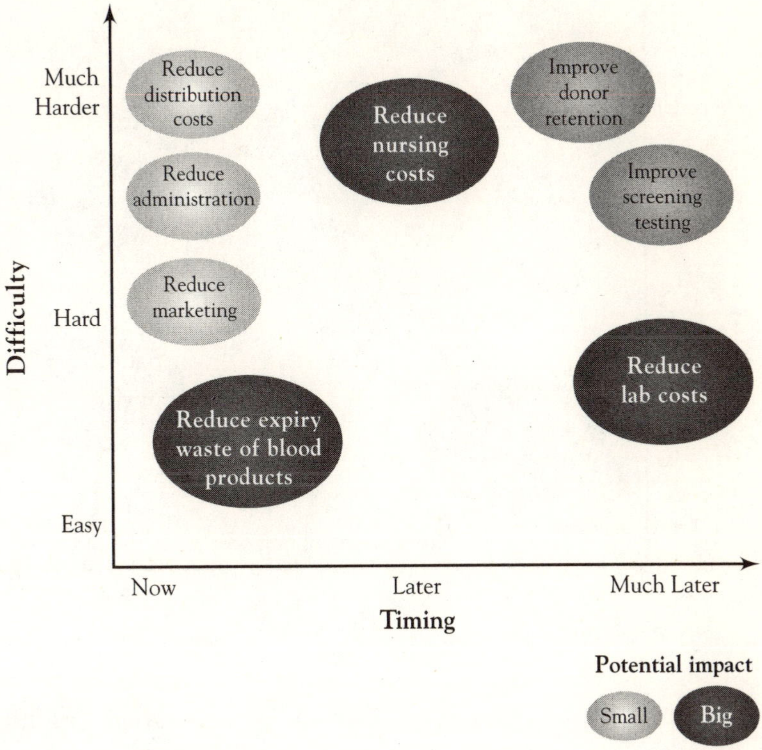

team decided that blood product expiry reduction would probably be a faster, easier option than substantially reducing nursing costs. We thought logistics changes could reduce distribution costs quickly, albeit with some effort. The BSO had no contractual obligations about when and how it delivered its blood product to the hospitals. However, it would have to notify over one hundred hospitals and get their approval of changes—which would take some time.

Finally, we asked, how about those opportunities that might have a relatively smaller impact, yet could be accomplished more quickly? For example, reducing administrative costs and marketing initiatives could be done quickly and without

Figure 3.3. Potential Priorities for the Mississippi BSO Turnaround

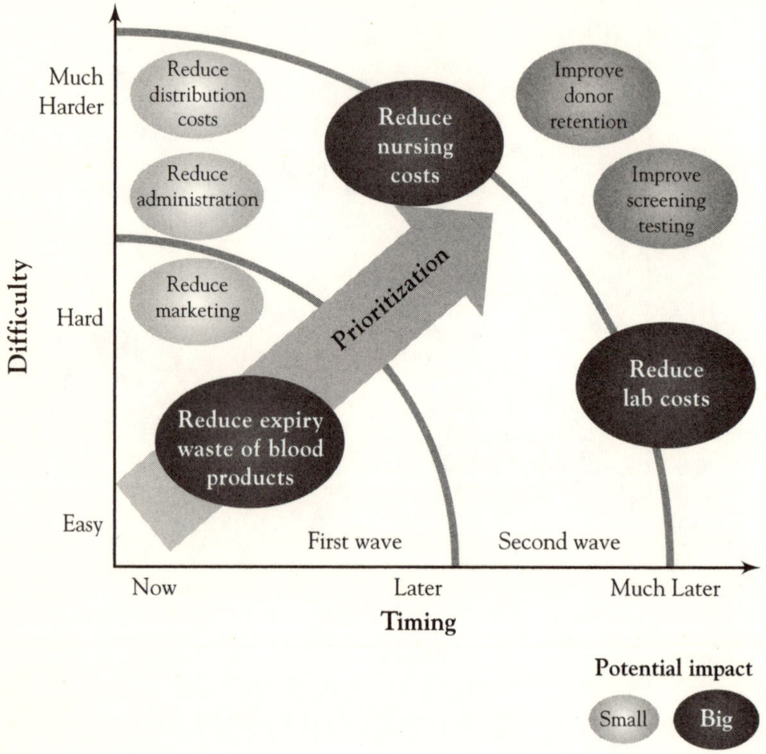

external approval. Although these ideas would not substantially increase profits, they could help stabilize the BSO's financial position.

We then started to prioritize options, beginning with those in the lower left quadrant of the graph (easy and quick) for our first wave of work. We would look at other quadrants later. Figure 3.3 shows our first three options: reducing blood product expiry (large, relatively easy and fast); the two others—reducing marketing and administrative costs. However, we were constantly assessing whether the options would prove sufficient to solve the problem—whether the combined profit impact of these options would close the $2 million financial gap. We thus moved immediately to other options, including reducing nursing and distribution costs. The combined impact needed to be enough to save BSO from bankruptcy before moving on to execution.

Despite the summer heat, the frequent misunderstandings with local restaurants about crawdads, grits, and okra, and the long flights from New York City, for three months we diligently helped senior management identify turnaround opportunities and capture them, too. Collaborating intensely, our joint BSO-consultant team returned the BSO to financial health, and the people of Mississippi retained their local blood supply.

Complex problems frequently lend themselves to multiple, independent solutions. Prioritizing helps problem solvers identify which possible solutions to pursue. We have shown how priorities were set for one problem. The next two sections generalize more, with further examples.

Setting Aspirations

Each problem-solving effort needs to aim toward appropriate aspirations. Consider how medical personnel might treat a trauma victim. When paramedics first arrive at the accident, their priority is to save the patient. They must stabilize the patient's condition, to preserve the opportunity for further treatment at the hospital. In a similar manner, our goal was not to build a thriving BSO organization, but to save it from bankruptcy. (Down the road, after the BSO escaped bankruptcy, its senior executives labored to return it to its former glory.) Strong problem solvers assess the current state of the enterprise and set aspirations accordingly.

Looming over questions of aspirations and prioritization is the issue of diminishing returns: When has enough analysis been done to decide on a proposed solution? Perhaps more important, when is the improvement "good enough"? Ultimately, the decision to move from survival to having a good or even a great future depends on the mix of aspirations, organizational capabilities, and next-step options and their associated risks. Chapter Eight takes on the question, "How much is good enough?"

Criteria for Prioritization

In the BSO case, our team simultaneously considered three aspects of each possible option:

- Potential impact
- Ease of execution and degree of risk
- Speed of execution and accrual of benefits

Business problems rarely allow for straightforward prioritization, but these three considerations can help prioritize almost any set of options.

Because a single option rarely scores well on impact, ease, *and* speed, teams frequently give priority to options with the greatest impact and to those "low-hanging fruit" that can be plucked quickly and relatively easily. Such rapid assessments are not detailed; they depend heavily on the team's good judgment.

Potential Impact

Assessing the potential impact requires answering an "if—then" question such as, "If the solution were achieved, then how much would the organization benefit?" In the BSO case, two "if—then" questions were "If we could reduce blood product waste by 10 percent, then what would be the effect on revenues?" and "If we could reduce nursing overtime by 10 percent, then what would be the effect on expenses?" We framed questions in terms of 10-percent reductions, but we could have easily framed them in smaller changes, such as 1 percent. Such analysis clarifies the incremental impact of small improvements.

The team should analyze the impact of potential solutions independently of difficulty and timing. At this point, we simply want to understand whether or not an option can produce sufficient benefit to warrant further consideration.

Ease of Execution and Degree of Risk

Some solutions are inherently more or less difficult to execute, and therefore more or less risky. At the BSO, our team was sensitive to the difficulty of each option—meaning its probability of success or failure in implementation. The primary source of uncertainty was the inability of the BSO to control particular aspects of execution; for example, FDA scrutiny of changes in lab procedures and union approval regarding changes in nurses' compensation. In both cases, the BSO would have to rely on external parties to help it implement changes.

Risk assessments require technical expertise and knowledge of the situation. By benchmarking the BSO's lab procedures against those at comparable labs, we were able to gauge improvement potential at the BSO. We also informally gauged laboratory personnel's current room for improvement. For example, if the laboratory process had been revised within the previous eighteen months and was now considered state-of-the-art, we would have doubted the likelihood of another 10-percent increase in efficiency.

Speed of Execution and Accrual of Benefits

Teams should estimate the *relative* time required to achieve a desired percentage improvement in performance. At the BSO, if 10-percent reductions in blood product waste could be achieved relatively quickly, those benefits would accrue earlier than those of nursing or lab improvements. In most cases, the timing of benefits is critical to meeting the business imperative, as a unit of benefit that is realized sooner is more valuable than one realized later. Although timing correlates to execution risk in many cases, a relationship is not automatic. In an iterative problem-solving approach, further improvements may depend on the earlier, successful implementation of faster solutions.

Teams need to keep the goals always in clear sight, consistently evaluating whether the combined options will be enough to solve the problem. In most cases, the tough work of execution should not start until the options are clearly sufficient.

A Disciplined Managerial Habit

After diagnosing a problem from its symptoms, the prioritizing of options lays the foundation for all remaining problem-solving efforts. Good prioritizing depends heavily on informed, careful judgment and a set of (often implicit) values. General managers will never have the time or resources to uncover perfect solutions, but a disciplined habit of considering each option's potential impact, timing, and ease of execution can assist in prioritizing them and their related activities.

Once the priorities have been established, a team can focus its creative and analytical abilities on areas of highest potential return. Chapter Four discusses how to stimulate creativity when discovering solutions. Chapter Five describes how creativity and analysis together can turn the science of problem diagnosis into the art of discovering solutions.

Problem Solving as Leadership, Culture, and Process

Keith Sherin
Vice Chairman and CFO, General Electric

"Your recommendations are intellectually unstimulating and emotionally unpalatable."

With these words of crushing feedback, the CFO of one of GE's divisions condemned to oblivion the carefully developed recommendations of my audit team. Sure, the general manager had a reputation for being a tough guy, but he also had a reputation for embracing good ideas. I had to figure out what had led to this debacle.

This was one of my early opportunities to lead a team of auditors. We had about twelve people working on two projects at once—identifying ways that independent customer contracting and IT support operations could work more effectively and save costs. The auditors worked long hours over a three-month period to understand the issues and develop recommendations. Our solution consisted of consolidating the separate organizations into centers of excellence that could provide timely and superior customer service while also reducing costs. We thought we had a winner here—so what happened?

It wasn't that hard to dissect what had gone wrong. I had made the same mistakes that new general managers frequently make: they try to do too much with too few resources, and consequently their teams struggle to achieve the objectives laid out before them. For my own audit team, the story was similar. We had spread our resources too thinly and thus did not get to the depth of analysis—of both the issues and the implications of our center-of-excellence idea—that the CFO felt he needed in order to support consolidation. Hence he found our recommendations "intellectually unstimulating."

Furthermore, as leader of the initiative I had not developed a fluid communication process with him and his team as our findings had emerged. Without this level of communication, my team had not understood the constraints under which we were problem solving. The solution was "emotionally unpalatable" because the division was not ready to undergo significant layoffs.

Despite my feeling bruised from the feedback, this was a very important learning experience for me. It helped shape how I operated with future teams and gave me a valuable teaching experience that I have used often.

We have a wealth of tremendously talented leaders at GE, and I think most of them would think of themselves as proficient problem solvers. Furthermore, over many years at GE we have put in place a framework involving leadership development, common culture, and process rigor, that helps enforce the leaders' already good problem-solving instincts.

As an example of GE's approach to solving tough problems, consider the decision-making process on investments and acquisitions of the GE Capital Board. First, we ensure that the right people are in the room—ten to fifteen leaders bringing together both the necessary knowledge on the part of the business leaders—about the specific market opportunity, technology, and competitors—and the required functional expertise in finance, legal, and risk, as well as Jeff Immelt, GE's chairman and CEO, and myself.

Second, we ensure the right culture—which in our case is collaborative and data-driven, with an obligation to argue for one's point of view. We expect every person in the room to objectively weigh the business case presented and then attempt to convince the other participants of his or her perspective. Everyone has a voice, and we value and respect that broad input. But once the group has reached a decision, we also expect any dissenters to be committed to the attitudes and actions needed to make that decision successful. In the end, our investment decisions are usually consensus-driven.

Third, we wrap the GE Capital Board's monthly deliberations with a disciplined process to harness the organization's extensive intellectual capital. Indeed, much of the early foundation for a new investment is laid during GE's strategic planning process, which annually updates a three- to five-year "Growth Playbook" for each division. Every business has five to eight growth priorities, some of which may take major investment. Investment decisions that come to the Capital Board are driven by the strategic priorities laid out in the growth playbook. For a specific investment, the responsible business team develops and circulates their detailed business case, including the results of due diligence, the pro forma financial results, and the risks and opportunities associated with the transaction. Independently and simultaneously, GE's chief risk officer writes and circulates a memo assessing the investment opportunity. We also evaluate the opportunity against our available investment resources using a "checkbook" process, which tracks our investment capacity. If the decision is made to go forward with an investment, we use processes to support acquisition integration using the lessons we have learned from previous transactions so we can optimize the results of the current investment.

Solving problems for GE really is a matter of unflinching leadership, a collaborative yet outspoken culture, and extraordinarily disciplined processes. For myself, having come a long way from my initial disaster, problem solving represents a daily opportunity to get the best inputs available, to allocate appropriate resources, and to wrap the decisions in thoughtful communication to do the best job possible.

Chapter 4

ONE PERCENT INSPIRATION

> Genius is 1 percent inspiration . . .
>
> —*Thomas Edison*

Inspiration—creativity—can make the difference between a good solution and a great one. This chapter is about harnessing creativity to business problem solving. Chapter Five discusses the other 99 percent.

The Electric Town Case and Creativity

"A newbie?! You mean you are assigning a rookie to this really important effort to develop a client project proposal? You have got to be kidding."

That was my reaction.

Our staffing coordinator answered me placidly, "His name is Gerald."

Developing project proposals can wrack any consultant's (or manager's) nerves. Time is way too short, the stack of information to process too high, the pressure to impress one's boss or potential client too intense. Normally, seasoned veterans develop proposals. And who did I get on my team? Gerald, a brand new recruit—his third day on the job. So I was expected to train him, inside this pressure cooker? Fortunately, at least three other very experienced colleagues also staffed the team. Little did I know then that later I would be thanking the heavens for—Gerald.

Straightforward Processes, Sensible Policies—But Dismal Results

Electric Town (ET), a national discount retailer of appliances and electronics and a long-standing client of our firm, was keenly interested in whether we could improve the effectiveness of its marketing programs—particularly the disappointing results of its Sunday newspaper advertising supplement. In less than a week, we would need to present ET's senior marketing executives our best preliminary ideas. But ET had also decided to solicit proposals from two other major consulting firms.

This was my first competitive negotiation as a project manager, and I vowed that we would not lose—not on *my* watch. To get started, my team employed the same problem-solving method that was integral to the Mississippi BSO project. In the few days before the presentation to ET executives, we needed to understand ET's business, specifically its advertising problems; we also needed a working hypothesis about how to raise ET's poor returns on its supplement promotion dollars. Through early interviews with marketing managers, we began to grasp the symptoms. Once we had a good hypothesis statement and the problem context in hand, we moved on to brainstorm an issue tree of potential improvement options. Meanwhile, as project manager I quickly developed a work plan to organize everyone's activities.

At least initially, the problem appeared fairly straightforward. For the last three years, Electric Town had placed a ten-page supplement in the Sunday edition of every major paper in ET's local marketing areas. To judge ET's performance, we benchmarked its results against those of other retailers. The news was disheartening: ET spent 90 percent of its print advertising budget on the supplement, but sales were 15 percent below expectations for retail supplements of its type and a whopping 30 percent below those generated by one of ET's major competitors. These results were particularly surprising because ET's supplement was the most read among male customers ages eighteen to fifty. ET's other major marketing channel—sponsoring nationally broadcast television shows and sporting events—yielded returns slightly above the overall retail industry average and about average for appliances and electronics.

So how could ET better allocate its marketing budgets? How could ET promote and advertise more effectively? Needing more information before we could hypothesize possible solutions, we turned to studying ET's marketing organization and processes in creating the supplement. Maybe something there was broken.

An ET marketing manager kindly explained that within the overall marketing department there were marketing managers (worriers about ET's overall message to consumers), category managers (in charge of the marketing initiatives for specific product lines), and advertising specialists (responsible for coordinating with television, newspapers, and other media). If ET's marketing organization seemed a bit convoluted, by contrast its internal decision-making processes about the Sunday supplement content seemed fairly straightforward. Every week, senior marketing managers allocated page space in the circular to each of the product category marketing managers. For example, the category managers for computers might get two pages, category managers for televisions and video equipment two pages, DVD managers one page, and so forth. The marketing department would then determine the overall advertising copy that would appear in each space. The most senior marketing director reserved the front and back pages for special promotional items. Category managers submitted copy by 8:00 A.M. on the Tuesday prior to the weekend the supplement would appear. The supplement was sent to press on Thursday and by Saturday morning was printed and ready to be inserted into the newspapers of over two hundred publishers around the country.

Our further marketing interviews with the advertising specialists revealed fairly sensible-sounding policies: each product category group decided which items to include in its section, generally based on margins, current sales trends, manufacturer's discounts and special promotions, and how long it had been since the last time a certain brand had been featured.

Fairly straightforward marketing processes, fairly sensible advertising policies, yet dismal results. How could that be? Something did not add up. And this was a problem that ET's hardworking, smart marketing managers had struggled with for years.

After several days of quick but rigorous analyses before the presentation deadline, my team and I still lacked a good working hypothesis. Where was the insight that would unlock the solution? Somehow, we needed to turn the problem on its head. I had publicly vowed not to lose this engagement. I now felt a bit apprehensive. Oh, who am I kidding? I was scared.

Systematically Hunting for Solutions

Back to the issue tree and work plan—back to work the process. We continued gathering data, interviewing, analyzing. We evaluated internal performance through advertising yields, profiled what competitors were doing, even rapidly investigated how customers made purchase decisions. In our team meeting, members diligently presented analyses—except Gerald, of course, whom I had told to tag along with a more experienced teammate, conducting interviews with marketing and advertising managers. "Just listen and learn," I'd said.

From the reports, we learned more about ET's process of creating the supplement and about readers' responses to it. The supplement varied less in the amount of page space allocated to different product categories, compared with more effective competing supplements. Also, male and female customers treated the supplement very differently, which the current use of space neither reflected nor optimized. Male consumers between eighteen and fifty tended to look at the first and last pages to identify the week's discounted items, then skip to inside pages dealing with products that interested them most—mainly large-screen televisions and car audio systems. By contrast, females between eighteen and fifty were less interested in the front and back pages unless the pages promoted products like DVDs of popular movies, top-artist CDs, and small kitchen appliances.

Amid these discussions, we discovered additional con-straints. ET's assistant advertising director had complained that within the overall marketing department, the advertising, mar-keting, and category managers were supposed to be of the same status within the organization, but in fact, the category managers tended to be very powerful, highly regarded people, and tremen-dously autonomous. Although the advertising group could dic-tate the total page space allocated to each category management group, it had little say about how that space was used. From this we were able to conclude that, whatever solution we came up with, we would need to make a compelling case to the advertis-ing department—and especially to the category managers.

What's more, Electric Town's category managers differed significantly amongst themselves in how they decided what to put in the supplement. The large appliances (white goods) category group generally featured at least two refrigerators, two washer-dryer combinations, and two dishwashers in each issue, and they featured every major brand name at least once a month. The CD music group allocated two-thirds of its space to the week's *Billboard* magazine chart toppers, and the remain-ing third to "special interest" categories like classical artists or show tunes. The computers and peripherals group dispensed advertising space to subgroups of products (desktops, laptops, printers, and so on), then focused on the best-sellers within the subgroups.

Our conclusion: any positive results from ET's current pro-cesses were purely accidental! Through painstaking interviews and analysis, we had discovered a massive disconnect between what we took for the supplement's goals—to drive revenue and brand awareness—and its process of creation. Apparently, these goals were unknown or simply disregarded. Upon reflection, our team thought it a bit odd that no one at ET had yet even *mentioned* the supplement's goals.

Immediately we hypothesized some potential solutions: improve the communication of the supplement's objectives to all category managers and develop incentives for them to follow the objectives. Also, stop allocating a fixed amount of space to each product category. Also, get the various product groups to agree on standard policies for deciding what to include, how to advertise them, and certainly which to prioritize. Following the hypothesis generation, we turned quickly to how to revise ET's internal policies so that revenue and brand awareness objectives would drive the space allocations.

Creative Surprise: A Great Analogy

Gerald had been very quiet up until now, as he was still in his first week on the job. Now he piped up—about his former career in commercial real estate and the similarities he saw between a valuable piece of land and the page space in a Sunday supplement. A major land developer never builds shacks on expensive property. Similarly, a category manager should not waste valuable advertising opportunities on low-valued items.

Sometimes creative ideas go unappreciated. Those who lack a deep understanding of the problem context may not recognize a creative insight. But because our team had invested so heavily in a comprehensive knowledge of ET's unique marketing challenges, we could immediately see the power of Gerald's analogy. It was a phenomenal insight.

The room filled with excitement as everyone began to contribute to Gerald's metaphor. We considered the characteristics of an expensive piece of property, its use, the means by which land tended to be subdivided and allocated, and the factors that gave some lots higher value than others. We noted that all property, regardless of location, needs to be both accessible and unobtrusively served by utilities. Then we considered the Sunday supplement. Our team enthusiastically generated new ideas about the mechanisms that could be used to allocate page space for maximum impact on revenue. These ideas included internal pricing approaches that would force category managers to make important trade-offs.

Not only did Gerald's analogy uncork new ideas, but it also actually transformed our basic hypothesis statement. No longer would we merely change communication and incentives to prioritize the category and advertising managers' goals for the supplement; we would propose that ET create an *internal market* for supplement space.

And the analogy held other potential power: if we could convince the category managers to think of the supplement as we did now—as valuable real estate—we might change their behavior. We tried to anticipate all the questions they and other ET managers might raise about pricing, potential category rivalry, internal incentives, and so forth. From that we developed a presentation that did, indeed, engage the influential category managers.

ET's managers loved our recommendations. Its CEO remarked, "I do not think that, even in a hundred years, we would have come up with such a solution ourselves."

Why Creativity Is Hard

Creativity is a problem within a problem. For example, the fundamental problem at Electric Town was improving the sales yield of the Sunday supplement. A secondary problem was finding a way to think differently enough to come up with the best solution. In this case, Gerald's creativity transformed our team's good solution—change communication and incentives to prioritize management's goals in the supplement—into the far better one—create an internal market for supplement space so that ads would generate the highest revenue.

As we all know, flashes of inspiration when they are most needed are fleeting, unpredictable, and never guaranteed. Why? We see at least five factors impeding creative insight:

- The brain's efficient wiring
- Conventional wisdom
- Investment required to recognize good creative ideas
- Organizational routines
- Personal risk

The Brain's Efficient Wiring

Evolution has organized our normal cognitive processes in a reasonably energy-efficient way. Hence, the way we think about a problem is usually similar to the way we have tried to solve similar problems in the past. These neurological patterns limit our ability to see things in new and different ways.

Conventional Wisdom

Frequently, conventional wisdom artificially limits the development of solutions. In the Pulitzer Prize–winning book *The Soul of a New Machine,* Tracy Kidder documented how engineers at Data General designed and brought to market an entirely new mini-computer in less than one year. Most experienced computer engineers would have predicted that the feat was impossible. The project manager in this situation overcame this assumed constraint by recognizing that it arose more from human nature than from technology development. By populating the team with very bright, very hungry, and very inexperienced engineering graduates from top universities, who did not know that the proposed timeline was ridiculous, Data General reached the goal.

Investment Required to Recognize Good Creative Ideas

To appreciate a creative insight, you must already deeply understand the problem and its context. Creative solutions must be rooted in the same analytics and reality of the original problem, as these provide the baseline against which any future solution must be judged. There is no substitute for comprehensively analyzing a problem. By identifying the best practices of other producers of Sunday supplements and then applying these to Electric Town, our team already had developed some good working solutions, which could produce immediate improvements. Gerald's creativity built on that.

Organizational Routines

Most organizations support routine, repeated activities. They tend to channel information to individuals based on its presumed relevance or past usage. The operations manager is not as likely to receive information about changes in tax law as is the comptroller. The comptroller is not as likely to receive the latest market survey data as is the sales manager. Thus people are shielded from the broader perspectives on which novel thinking depends.

Personal Risk

Creativity sometimes means acting outside one's role in an organization—at the risk of losing a future promotion, or of failure to do one's immediate job, or of suffering in reputation. People are often rewarded for performing in a well-defined area. For innovation and creativity outside that area, they may get no reward. Making creative, risky suggestions outside one's area generally offers little upside. A sales manager who takes the time to study competitive products and imagine ways to improve on them may not receive a proper hearing and, even if given a hearing, may receive only a "thank you" for reward.

Creativity from Conscious Planning

Creativity in problem solving rarely occurs without some degree of conscious planning and effort. How can problem solvers build it in? First, cover all the obvious bases: identify the problem, disaggregate it, create a constructive hypothesis statement, analyze it, and generate possible options in a straightforward manner. Then consider the following tools and techniques (and others) that foster creativity.

Lateral Thinking Slows Normal Convergent Thinking

Faced with a problem, the mind seeks a satisfactory solution as quickly and simply as it can. When faced with familiar problems, or even new problems that seem similar to familiar problems, we tend to recall (converge on) the same sorts of facts and details that we have used in the past to solve them. Although this tactic saves routine time and energy, it rarely leads to distinctive ideas.

To counter convergent tendencies, creativity theorists such as Edward DeBono have offered contrasting "lateral thinking." Lateral thinking means deliberately slowing convergence, forcing individuals to consider a wide range of definitions, lines of reasoning, and potential solutions. For example, you have coffee, sugar, cream, and no silverware at your cabin in the woods. How to stir your coffee? The usual solutions could include visiting a neighbor to borrow a spoon or driving into town three miles away to buy one. But both alternatives would mean cold coffee. You could stir your coffee with your pencil, but ugh, which end? Or you could redefine the problem. You do not have to *stir* your coffee to blend it. How about shaking it up? In an empty jar?

Lateral thinking is all a matter of perspective. The fact that the alternatives we develop through lateral thinking may seem silly merely reveals the value that our minds may mistakenly place on efficiency and the use of familiar concepts.

Questions to Stimulate Inspiration

To offset the mind's efficient wiring, sometimes you must consciously ask yourself perspective-changing questions. Amid the hectic energy of the problem-solving process, pause to ask funny questions—and pointedly disregard your judgmental reactions to the answers.

Perhaps the original question should be reversed: "What would it take for ET to *prevent* category managers from allocating supplement space in an economically productive way?" Or take a historical or futuristic approach: "How might merchants have solved this problem five hundred years ago? Five hundred years in the future?" Or a "donut" solution: "How could ET cut its disappointing Sunday supplement problem out of its current situation?" You could even try to solve the problem like a favorite character or superhero: "How might Winnie the Pooh do it? Or Spiderman?" Or explore the edges of the constraints: "What would ET never be willing to do to fix its supplement problem?" Or write the problem out and quietly stare at each word to ask what could happen. *The problem itself will always contain a seed of its solution.*

Forced Analogies

This is what Gerald brought to our team. Forcing analogies encourages creativity by exploring comparisons between the current problem and other seemingly unrelated activities. We benefited from Gerald's comparison of the spread of newsprint with a spread of expensive open land. The forced analogies approach involves four steps:

1. Define the target problem.
2. Identify productive analogies.
3. Make a comparison table.
4. Formulate creative solutions.

Define the Target Problem. At Electric Town, the general problem was increasing the effectiveness of the Sunday supplement. We honed that down to "How can Electric Town best allocate content to page space in its Sunday supplement?"

Identify Productive Analogies. A productive analogy can be hard to catch, as it needs to seem immediately valid and yet be a "stretch." Immediate validity means that the analogy does appear somehow related to the problem, usually because the two share some basic similarities. Commercial real estate and ET's supplement both involve segmenting valuable physical space and allocating something to the segments.

By *stretch* we mean how well the analogy invites thinking beyond surface similarities. In the real estate analogy, effective allocation of land creates economic value. But the means of allocations could not have been more different between newspaper supplement and land. A bureaucratic, inconsistent process allocated ET's supplement space, whereas most often a competitive market system based on price allocates property.

By analogy, our team uncovered potential ways to use a market-based pricing mechanism for the supplement. Rather than administratively dictating allocations for users, could users buy and sell space according to its anticipated value in generating revenue? A good analogy suggests ideas that go beyond the obvious. We garnered some immediately fascinating ideas from Gerald's metaphor. We got even more value by comparing in more detail.

Make a Comparison Table. After deciding on the target problem and problem analogy, one should place them in a comparison table, as shown in Table 4.1. Begin on the left, identifying aspects of the analogy. For example, in real estate a developer would subdivide the property into lots, assign prospective prices to the lots, allow for rights of way, and so forth. Try to build a comprehensive list of ideas first, disregarding the original target problem.

Once the left, analogy column is complete, one can complete the right, target problem column. Individual teammates should look at the items on the left and, on the right, add whatever ideas surface. "Subdivide the plot into lots with different prices" might trigger "Segment each page into logical components having different presumed values." For example, typical reader behaviors make the top third of the page more valuable than the bottom third and the right side more valuable than the left side. "Allow for rights of way" might trigger "Add tables of contents, front and back, for what is on the inside pages."

Table 4.1. A Forced Analogies Table

Comparison: Developing a Piece of Land	Target: Designing a Sunday Advertising Supplement
How should the lots be divided? Should all lots be the same size? Which lots are more valuable?	Not all pages are of the same value; the most valuable should carry more ads.
How do we price the lots?	The most profitable items should get the prime ad space.
How do we make sure all lots are accessible?	We need a policy, perhaps internal pricing, to allocate space across product groups optimally.
How do we accommodate utilities?	We need to consider ways to direct readers from the first or last page to the interior pages of the supplement.
Are there any covenants on the deeds?	We need to establish policies for the general look and content of each ad in the supplement.

Formulate Creative Solutions. The last step in a creative forced analogy is to reflect further on the target problem side to formulate possible solutions. ET's executives and category managers were inspired by the idea of using their supplement space as if it were valuable real estate. The analogy suggested new and different ways to allocate space based on fairly assessing impact.

In general, two factors cause forced analogies to succeed or fail in triggering new creative thoughts. An analogy succeeds when it causes the problem solver to examine relevant information and ideas that otherwise would not have been considered. And it succeeds when the problem solver then uses the insights to develop and refine proposed solutions.

Synergistic Techniques

Synergy suggests that, creatively, a team can be more than the sum of its creative parts. But how can a team of problem solvers capitalize on synergy?

By sharing insights, team members generate more creative power than they individually command. Teams can discover options that have eluded members working alone. Teams can also rely on a suite of tools; probably the best-known of these are brainstorming and devil's advocacy. The more diverse the team members' skills and backgrounds, the more creative energy can be brought to bear.

Yet synergistic creativity depends on open minds. It depends on all team members listening and considering suggestions without immediate judgment. Suppose two strong-willed senior teammates had censured Gerald as he tried to explain his odd idea? When conflicts do occur, listening to and treating colleagues equally can help resolve the conflicts more productively, preventing valuable insights from getting smothered or lost along the way.

Increasing Intrinsic Motivation

If creativity really is as arduous and fleeting as we believe, why bother? Why not just settle for a *good* solution and save the effort a *great* one may take? Our answer is that, psychologically, *we must motivate ourselves and others not to settle.*

In her extensive research on the social psychology of creativity within large organizations, Teresa Amabile argues that creativity depends mainly on three factors: expertise, the ability to imagine and think broadly, and intrinsic motivation.[1] Although senior managers can—with diligent long-term effort—improve the first two of these, Amabile argues that increasing intrinsic motivation is a much faster and more effective lever.

In most organizations, employees may want to find creative solutions but find they must overcome significant internal barriers along the way. Leaders may call for innovation even as they inadvertently crush creative efforts. Calls for ever-increasing output and management control have that general effect. Some better balance must be struck with at least five areas of potential improvement:

- The staffing of work teams
- The amount of challenge provided to teams
- The degree of freedom each team receives regarding choices of process
- The resources, time, money, and other support given to creative processes
- The nature and level of organizational reward for creative solutions[2]

At ET, we were fortunate in all five areas. First, our team benefited from recruiting a talented group of colleagues. Nothing is more important than selecting the best, most diverse, most complementary team. Even Gerald the rookie was, finally, a tremendous contributor. Second, our team certainly found the ET problem very challenging, especially because experienced ET marketing managers had not developed a solution despite years of effort. Third, ET senior executives gave our team tremendous latitude to explore possibilities, never being too prescriptive. Fourth, our team had all the resources it needed to come up to speed on the problem quickly and then gather additional needed information. We prioritized a schedule with more than enough time to hold a structured brainstorming session complete with devil's and angel's advocates.

The fifth point was that organizational leaders need to painstakingly foster the context and rewards that can, in turn, breed creativity. Our team cheered Gerald for suggesting his insightful analogy. Once ET senior executives were so taken with our ideas that they decided to sign us on to help them, choosing our proposal over those of two rival consulting firms—then we really celebrated.

The General Manager's Challenge

Creativity is the ability to solve familiar problems in new and appealing ways—that critical 1 percent of genius. Yet many of us feel that, in attempting to find innovative solutions, we struggle against our brain's own thinking processes and against the nature of our organization.

And business settings do often force managers to favor efficiency over exploration. Most business contexts allow few options to be considered, as solution choices are constrained by the needs of technical, financial, or operational feasibility. Furthermore, some people argue that creativity is impossible for them: that their minds do not work creatively, that they are analytical by nature.

We acknowledge that normal cognitive functioning is not particularly well suited to thinking about problems in new ways, and that creativity can be difficult, especially when we have little time. We even acknowledge that each of us may be differently predisposed toward creative thinking.

Still, we believe that with diligence and practice everyone can get better at adopting the different perspectives so essential to generating novel ideas. As antidotes to the usual convergent thinking, we have outlined several practical techniques and tools. Given the increasing complexity, competition, and demands of today's global business, can you as the general manager survive and thrive *without* dedicating the time, resources, and diligence so necessary to searching for creative inspiration?

A Problem Shared Is a Problem Halved

W. Roy Dunbar
Chief Executive Officer, Network Solutions
Former Chief Information Officer, Eli Lilly

Foreign assignments have been hailed as a strategic part of developing well-rounded senior executives. Whether the role is foreign to the executive in its geography or its cross-functional focus, the key to the success of such assignments is to remove executives from what is familiar and comfortable, effectively forcing them to grasp for new skills, dig deeper into themselves, and discover new coping behaviors. For me, the most crucial learnings about problem solving took place just as such an assignment began.

With excitement, I embarked on a new assignment as country manager in the Venezuelan affiliate of Eli Lilly, a large pharmaceutical company. I did not speak Spanish and had never spent time in Latin America. It would be a crash course in the culture, language, and business of this country. Six months into the fiscal year, as I examined the business I was to lead upon my arrival in July, it was evident that the annual business plan had long been forgotten in the face of extreme macroeconomic shifts and aggressive generic competition against our leading and most profitable product. Sales were tumbling and trending below the prior year's results, even though the business plan had called for double-digit growth. Things were bad and were forecast to get worse; for example, annual inflation for 1996 was some 103 percent, and the local currency had suffered a twelve-month devaluation of 100 percent versus the U.S. dollar. Our product costs were in U.S. dollars and our pricing in local currency. To make matters even more challenging, pricing was government-regulated and had not been fully adjusted in line with either dollar-based costs or inflation.

We needed to adapt our business quickly if we were to survive as an enterprise. To signal just how critical it was to stimulate change collectively, I changed the location, audience, and message planned for my team meeting, as well as my own language. While I prepared to present the issues and challenge my new team, my executive assistant and my Spanish teacher both worked tirelessly so that I could deliver my remarks in as intelligible Spanish as possible.

We held the meeting at our manufacturing plant in a provincial city rather than the main office in Caracas. And I made the strategic decision to share the dangerous state of our business with a broad group of managers, not just those who reported to me. Not only was this approach somewhat unprecedented in the affiliate's history, but it also was unusual in the Latin management culture, which in those days was more hierarchical, with decision making and direction always traveling downward from the top.

In early August we had our meeting. As mentally challenging as it was for me to lead a meeting in a foreign language after only eight weeks of study, the feeling of connecting with a team of managers who felt privileged to be trusted with such serious matters and who were being asked to problem-solve and lead solution implementation was exhilarating—and a great reward for the weeks of preparation.

We catalogued a great quantity of ideas that came out of the session. Everyone realized that our ideas had no constraints as long as we remained within our ethical obligations and company policies. These ideas were quickly trimmed to a manageable number that we were able to implement swiftly. Many of the tasks necessitated alignments between key functions that would have taken weeks or even months had there not been the imperative calling all to action. Diverse areas of the organization quickly developed components and delivered interlocking plans in a beautiful orchestration of teamwork.

Reflecting on this experience, it seems to me that although the business results were our most immediate reward for my having stumbled onto the power of sharing the problem with my entire team, there were other, richer outcomes. We were able to stabilize the Venezuela business rapidly with the selected interventions that came out of the group meeting. We not only halted the slide in sales of our most important product, but we actually managed to push it back to growth. We shifted our product mix to better match the socioeconomics of a postdevaluation economy. We adopted tactics that enhanced agility and faster decision making and execution than our competitors', especially in the retail drug distribution channel and to our priority hospitals. The most remarkable outcome was that my entire team now understood both the problem and the solutions in a common way, and so working to win became much easier.

A second illustration from my experience underscores that a problem shared really is a problem halved. When I became chief information officer at Eli Lilly, I had no IT experience, nor did I have much prior understanding of this function and how it created value for the company, other than ensuring that the PCs operated well. Senior-level cross-functional experiences often start with baseline knowledge as limited as this. The challenge is to quickly determine what knowledge is required to effectively lead a new organization—in my case more than 2,500 people—and to have the credibility to develop a following inside the company, as well as sufficient thought leadership of entities outside the company that enhanced the standing of the function and the company as a whole.

Although these were all important and noble challenges, a more immediately pressing question needed an answer: "What is the value of IT to our business?"

The year 1999 was one of those critical years in which the Internet was becoming a phenomenon of business—and driving a stock market bubble that would burst two years later. The year 1999 also preceded the much-feared Y2K, for which essential remediation work on old systems code had to be completed before the start of the year 2000. A chorus of voices warned that even current functionality was in jeopardy and that all hands were needed to fix a problem from the past and ensure smooth sailing through Y2K.

Other, equally loud alarms were warning of the great risks of not embracing the internet era with new web-based business models, lest upstart competitors across the industry value chain do so first and disintermediate the company in a myriad of ways. This fear led to a frenzy of investments in online manifestations of old-line "brick and mortar" companies. We also saw a slew of e-businesses spawned by traditional companies to stake out an online presence.

With guidance from members of the team, we created a broad dialogue among IT leaders within the company to talk about the nature of our specific internal problems and environmental opportunities and challenges. There was a wide chasm between our quite capable IT function and other business functions, such as marketing and research, that did not know how to engage and leverage IT. Because my IT leaders had not integrated themselves into the leadership organizations of their business partners, they were not able to confidently be full partners and to be effective at bringing the right insights and solutions to the decision-making table. Sadly, this problem remains all too common today, even in the best of large corporations.

We needed to build a common understanding among Eli Lilly's leaders of both our internal and our external possibilities, using new web-based technologies to accelerate value in our core business model. My team and I shared the problem with the Eli Lilly operating committee and sought their help and engagement. We needed to establish a systematic and rigorous process to bridge the gap of awareness and communication between IT and other areas of our business about the new realities and the behaviors needed to win in the Information Age.

Our educational process rested on both external insights and internal conversations. We engaged business luminaries who were either thought-leading technologists, such as John Gage, then chief scientist at Sun Microsystems, or individuals who had stellar careers spanning both IT and business leadership, such as Bob Herbold, then Chief Operating Officer of Microsoft and formerly SVP, Marketing at Procter & Gamble, among a number of senior roles. Speakers anchored sessions of joint learning that created great energy and a shared view of the problems and opportunities. Bob Herbold was particularly effective at stating the problems common to major corporations and the uncompromising manner in which management must behave to avoid the pitfalls and to drive the best business value as a team; he later codified these precious lessons in his book *The Fiefdom Syndrome*.

With this improved cross-functional understanding, our IT and operating leaders were now able to talk internally to develop an IT mission that supported and significantly enabled the company strategy. Together we prioritized a manageable number of projects positioned at strategic leverage points in our business where they would make a real difference in our value chain.

Those transformational projects fell into two broad categories: (1) reducing cycle time to cut hours, days, or even weeks out of core processes, and (2) building and improving customer relationships. Over time, we directed a decreasing proportion of our budget to business-as-usual maintenance and support activities, so that we could invest every extra dollar in the strategic leverage projects.

Reflecting on my CIO experience, I see that by engaging on a personal level with every member of the top leadership, we created a common vision and a common purpose. We also reinforced that purpose by restructuring the IT team to allow dual reporting of key members to both a business area leader and to me. I was very proud that my team won many industry awards for the innovation of the IT function and the effectiveness of our e-business offerings. A more enduring lesson from this approach to problem solving was the value of reaching across functional lines and building cross-functional relationships, not only as a matter of urgency at the start of a new assignment, but as an ongoing practice that drives the highest value for a business.

Chapter 5

NINETY-NINE PERCENT PERSPIRATION

. . . and 99 percent perspiration.

—*Thomas Edison*

"Hey there, little lady!" the voice boomed over the phone.

I knew it well. It belonged to Dave, the general manager of a $1 billion business unit of Delta, a U.S. medical products company. Having served Delta over many years, I had deep respect for Dave's organization. Although Dave may be a proud graduate of "the good ol' boy network" school of management (playing golf and driving a Mercedes), no one in the industry knew the customers, their needs, and their aspirations better than he. His team of senior managers was from the same mold.

"We have a problem," he said. "My guys have put together a bid for the Academic Medical Center Consortium contract, but I am not comfortable with it. Can you come and sit with us for a while? See what you can do?"

Under any other circumstances, I would have jumped at the chance to serve this medical products giant again. At the time, however, I was already serving companies in the middle of Michigan and North Carolina, which necessitated four plane trips every week. I had no desire to up that number. Nevertheless, I understood immediately how important the contract was. It was worth a lot of money and was Delta's to lose.

During the preceding ten years, a number of different hospital groups had banded together as group purchasing organizations (GPOs) to consolidate purchasing and negotiate better supplier contracts. GPOs mainly aimed to reduce the overall prices that hospitals paid for supplies purchased from companies like Delta and its rival, Omega. For years, Delta had provided its products to the largest, most prestigious academic medical centers via their GPO, the Academic Medical Center Consortium (AMCC). To Delta, as the incumbent supplier, the AMCC contract would be worth over $100 million in annual sales; stretching for seven years, it represented a substantial portion of Delta's sales and profits.

"When is the bid due?" I asked, hoping against hope that it would be after one of my other projects would be finished.

"In six weeks. Can you be here tomorrow?"

Discovering Pragmatic Solutions

Before continuing this story of Delta and Omega competing in the hospital products industry, we pause to introduce the main lessons of this chapter: how to get the most efficient and effective use of the sweat it takes to discover great solutions.

We argue for three overarching and related questions that problem solvers should always ask:

- How can we create economic value for the customer?
- How can we capture part of that economic value for ourselves?
- What organizational norms and perhaps even personal values might enhance or constrain the potential solutions?

These questions provide the lenses through which one can quickly analyze both the company's competitive position and the industry's competitive dynamic. Along the way, we also suggest other helpful questions and approaches in getting started.

How Can We Create Economic Value for the Customer?

At heart, an organization's strategy rests on choosing what products or services to provide to particular customers. Along the way, the company must develop tailored core competencies to sustain some advantage over the competition. To address these choices, the problem solver should investigate not only how the company chooses its products and customers and how it derives its competitive advantage, but also, and perhaps more important, how customers make their purchase decisions, their buying criteria, and their other alternatives.

Value creation commonly centers on price, quality, service, or some combination thereof. Creating value based on *price* means providing the customer with the lowest initial cost of acquiring the product or service. Creating value based on *quality* of product could involve some product innovation that the customer values, such as longevity, reliability, or lower maintenance costs. Creating value based on *service* means freeing up customers from activities—and their associated cost—that they might have to handle themselves.

Reducing the total cost of ownership is a form of value creation that may be based on a combination of price, quality, and service features. A product may have a lower cost of ownership despite a higher price, because that price may be more than offset by longevity, low maintenance costs, and multiple uses that reduce the need to purchase other equipment. For example, a piece of outdoor equipment that can mow grass in the summer, remove leaves in the fall, and remove snow in the winter promises greater utility than a product that performs fewer functions.

Or consider a U.S. candy company planning to enter the Chinese market by selling only two of its sixteen brands. Regardless of whether it will ship those sweets from Tacoma to Shanghai or will manufacture locally in China, it hopes to create value for a Chinese consumer by giving her sweet tooth more temptations.

The Mississippi BSO—the subject of our turnaround project in Chapters One, Two, and Three—collected, tested, and then distributed blood products to area hospitals. If it had been forced to close its doors, its hospital customers would have faced a set of rather unpalatable alternatives to meet their patients' urgent needs in emergency and surgery blood transfusions: incur the additional costs of collecting, testing, and processing blood donations themselves or take the risk of shipping in blood products from other states. The BSO created economic value for hospitals through convenience and through the assurance of having a local blood supply in case of hurricanes and other crises.

Estimates of potential markets depend on some sense of how customers will value the product or service combined with the sheer numbers of customers. A company's share of the market depends on the advantages it creates for customers versus the competitors' products or other alternatives. The point here is to understand exactly how the customer will value the product or service—low price, innovative value, or service. In some way the deal must appear better than its alternatives.

How Can We Capture Economic Value for Our Own Organization?

It is all well and good for your company to create economic value for the customer; to stay in business, it must capture some of that value for itself. Once again the questions are basic: How and why should the customer pay your company? How is the company better in some relevant way than the competition—in other words, what is its competitive advantage? What core competencies make the company's competitive advantage sustainable? What drives the industry's competitive dynamic, including the competitors' supply cost structures and capacities? How do the structure and conduct of the industry affect the competitors' financial and market performance? Investigating such fundamentals of the industry, and your company's success within that context, ultimately helps define its business model.

By competencies we mean the activities that must be performed by any business in any particular industry to survive and thrive. For example, a nationwide retailer must be able to locate its stores effectively; acquire, distribute, and manage its inventory; merchandise its products; and so forth. Three basic forms of *core competence* can create an advantage in the market: privileged assets, relationships, and capabilities. Most well-run companies differentiate themselves along one of these dimensions. Privileged assets could be a patent, a copyright, or a brand. Privileged relationships provide the company with unique knowledge and access to customers. Capabilities are repeatable processes, such as supply-chain operations or creative software development. The company can gain customers only to the extent that it derives a competitive advantage from its core competencies. It captures economic value to the extent that customers pay for its output.

The Mississippi BSO captured value through the prices it charged for its blood products. Its overall revenues accrued from the quantity of each product delivered and the prices charged for that product. Its prices reflected the demand for each product in relation to supply. For a long time, the Mississippi BSO enjoyed the privileged asset of a regional near-monopoly protected by federal regulations. Its total economic value rested on its revenues minus its costs of blood collection, laboratory testing, processing of products, packaging and delivery of products, storage and inventory costs, and value of expired products.

Because a company's ability to capture value is a matter of advantage, its core competencies have competitive meaning only as compared to competitors' competencies. An industry's competitive dynamic rests on how competitors can and do respond to each other's initiatives to serve customers better. To predict possible competitor moves and what they might mean for one's own company and its economic prospects, one must understand how customers value one's product or service, and just how vulnerable that sense of value is to competitors' moves. Game theory can be used in making such predictions. Solutions become less attractive to the extent that the actions of competitors can block the outcomes that solutions were originally meant to achieve.

As another illustration of core competencies and competitive advantage, consider two mass retailers, SC and MC. Both attract customers by providing an enormous selection of products through their large store format, but they compete and capture value through different competencies. SC has developed a world-class supply chain from Asia; MC leads the industry in merchandising. The supply chain capability enables SC to reduce inventory costs and pass those savings along to customers through lower prices. SC captures value from customers through the sale of larger quantities at lower prices. By contrast, MC uses its merchandising capability to design and sell innovative brands. It captures value through the premium that customers pay for well-designed products.

Firms rarely excel along more than one dimension (privileged assets, relationships, or capabilities) for two reasons. First, it is extraordinarily difficult to be the best in everything. Second, core competencies and basic strategies are integral to one another. SC differentiates itself primarily by the low prices it can charge on commodity-like products. Consequently, its message to customers is, on balance, "lowest prices every day." It puts few items on sale and does not advertise brands. Also, consequently, it does not invest in developing extraordinary merchandising capabilities to bring consumers to the store. Rather, it invests in logistics, reducing transportation and inventory costs to maintain its lowest prices.

Beyond identifying sustainable competitive advantages— let alone core competencies—it is also critical to investigate the entire industry's competitive dynamic. We suggest beginning with a few additional fundamental questions and analyses.

The microeconomics of an industry depend on the costs and capacities of the main competitors to supply products and services to a particular market. Estimates of fixed versus variable costs and productive capacities balanced against total customer purchases are indicative of the entire industry's supply-and-demand situation, which then provides insights into current and future pricing.

Examination of industry structure and conduct can help predict the competitors' economic performance. Industry structure can vary from intense fragmentation, with thousands of similarly sized suppliers of a particular category of products, to the concentration of oligopoly with a handful of competitors. Customers may switch frequently between suppliers, based on the lowest prices, or they may loyally purchase from one competitor that provides the most innovative products tailored to unmet needs. How these competitors conduct themselves in the market—ranging from fierce competition for each customer to long-term contracts that maintain price stability—will have direct implications for their financial and market performance.

The discipline of applying Michael Porter's "Five Forces" model can help explain complicated market dynamics. Systemically examining both the concentration of suppliers and customers and their resulting power over market transactions, as well as the threat of substitutes and new entrants, can provide some sense of the intensity of industry competition. We suggest beginning gradually, just asking how you and your competitors capture economic value from your customers. Reading industry analyst reports or even conducting a basic strengths/weaknesses/opportunities/threats (SWOT) analysis can also help in getting started. We illustrate more specifically how to employ such analyses for problem-solving purposes when we return to the Delta versus Omega case a bit later in this chapter.

Determining sustainable competitive advantages—let alone core competencies and the entire industry's microeconomics and competitive dynamics—can be difficult, especially while also actually competing day to day. But these analyses are indispensable. To sum up this section, economic analyses are part of the logical foundation for solving most business problems. The analyses suggested in this section seek to understand how profits are made in an industry. In other words, how will the organization extract for itself some of the economic value it creates for its customers? Understanding this requires a thorough understanding of how its costs and revenues accrue from the delivery of its products.

What Organizational Norms or Personal Values Might Enhance or Constrain Potential Solutions?

We now address the third basic question that a problem solver needs to consider. In Chapter One we suggested that it is simply not possible to evaluate a course of action without knowing what organizational norms and personal values it is intended to serve. By values here we mean the human or company values that could go beyond extracting profit from the business. We suggested that the definition of a problem depends greatly on those values. Let us extrapolate from that to say that an acceptable *solution* to the challenge of creating and capturing economic value is fundamentally enhanced or constrained by the leaders' values and organizational norms.

Suppose we return to the retail industry. MM, a publicly traded mass merchant, competes and provides value for its customers through the breadth and depth of product choices at low prices; at the same time, MM differs from its competitor in that it provides its employees with generous health care benefits. The CEO argues that to reduce health care and other benefits in the interest of harvesting more economic profit would be shortsighted and would violate MM's core norms about fair treatment of employees. To Wall Street criticism of MM's higher labor expenses, the CEO defends his decision by arguing that it both raises the quality—and thereby the productivity—of its employee applicant pool and also lowers costly employee turn-over. In facing the retail industry demands, the CEO continues to make strategic choices (not necessarily bad ones) that main-tain his commitment to values-based norms—looking after employees' health.

Especially in discovering solutions, a company chooses an ultimate course of action based on the values it wishes to rein-force. Companies may vary widely—even wildly—on the norms that guide them. In making critical strategic and operational decisions, one must discern the relevant norms and make disci-plined choices that serve them to the desired degree.

The Art Part of Solving Problems

Beyond the three basic questions just posed lies the art of choos-ing a problem-solving methodology or framework that will truly illuminate the scene. By *framework here we mean a basic frame of reference (say, marketing, finance, or operations) or a basic concep-tual structure of ideas or analyses (say, potential market estimation, discounted cash flow valuation, or process flow description)*. Asking questions regarding economic value creation and capture, and the values underpinning potential solutions, deepens appre-ciation of the specific problem at hand. That in turn allows an appropriate choice of framework. And an appropriate choice of framework can, in turn, help break the problem wide open.

Problem solvers can choose from hundreds of analytical techniques and frameworks; you probably already know quite a few. Rather than attempting to cite them all, the next part of this chapter illustrates a general process in which they are applied. We return to the case of Delta versus Omega compet-ing in the medical products industry, focusing on how our Delta team asked itself questions about economic value creation and capture and the company's norms and then applied suitable frameworks to lay out a viable path forward for Delta with its AMCC bid. Some of the frameworks we describe are specific to a business function—marketing, finance, operations. Keep in mind, though, that rarely does a problem respect functional boundaries. Problems are simply not that well-behaved. More often, problem solvers must integrate insights from various functions and frameworks.

Delta versus Omega for the AMCC Contract

Getting started quickly was critical to our team's success. As we began our work for Dave regarding the AMCC bid, our team formulated hypotheses for solutions after our first week on the job. Our team's iterative approach combined the best of deductive and inductive reasoning. It depended on deductive logic in our first few days and week, to develop our hypothesis statement, or Week One Answer. Our early guess about the potential winning bid for Delta then guided our subsequent search for information that would test, support, or refute our hypotheses. With these hypotheses in hand, our team quickly shifted to inductive methods, ultimately deriving our conclusions from the results of collecting and investigating more data. In the following sections, we illustrate this fundamentally iterative problem-solving framework through how our team discovered the best solution for Delta.

Week One: Getting Started on the Delta Bid for AMCC

As we started investigating the background of the AMCC bid, we noted that the U.S. medical products industry consists of three major suppliers and thousands of hospital customers. A quick examination of the structure, conduct, and performance of the industry led our team to a few early observations. Dave's company, Delta, currently served 50 percent of the market, Company Omega served 40 percent, and Company Gamma served 10 percent. Because the hospital customer base had been fragmented for many years, the three companies enjoyed strong pricing power, which underpinned their strong financial performance. Applying Porter's Five Forces model, our team uncovered several other salient factors regarding industry competition. With hospital customers facing few viable substitutes for their medical products, the three companies also benefited from significant barriers to entry for new domestic or international competitors: immense up-front manufacturing costs; high, fixed distribution costs; and strict FDA regulation.

However, as we noted earlier, in recent years hospital group purchasing organizations (GPOs) had grown up, governed by respected administrators from their member hospitals, to consolidate purchasing across hospitals—especially around products that, for lack of recent innovations, hospitals now perceived as near-commodities. The GPOs used their buying power and threats of switching to negotiate steep discounts with the largest medical products suppliers. Among GPOs, the AMCC had a reasonably strong record of negotiation.

To further increase their negotiating power, GPOs were beginning to merge. In fact, the Catholic Hospital Association (CHA) GPO was merging with the AMCC. Although Delta held the old AMCC contract, Delta's rival Omega held the old CHA contract, worth about $450 million in annual sales and valid for another three years. Amid the CHA-AMCC merger negotiations, the AMCC GPO had sent requests for proposals (RFPs) to Delta, Omega, and Gamma for new AMCC business. (The official CHA-AMCC merger would take place after and apart from this new round of contract negotiations.) The complicated contract RFP encompassed hundreds of product categories with thousands of stock keeping units (SKUs). Contract purchases would total about $100 million per year for seven years. The RFP required a straight price per unit for thousands of products. The RFP instructed each company to submit a single, secret bid.

After a quick kickoff meeting and an initial round of interviews with senior Delta executives, our project manager Jeff and the team quickly defined the problem, its background, and its component issues. To get started, we asked the following:

- What aspects of the GPO bidding process will be key? How will the GPO award the contract?
- How will the bid affect the AMCC hospital customers?
- Can all three companies (especially Gamma) put forward credible bids?
- What is the best bid that we (Delta) can put forward and still break even?
- What is the best bid that rival Omega can put forward and still break even?
- How will the bid affect Delta's other significant customer accounts or "book of business"?
- How will the bid affect Omega's book of business?
- If Delta loses the AMCC contract, how much in sales and profit does it really stand to lose?
- If Delta loses, how might it minimize the downside impact?

Figure 5.1 shows how we began to organize such analytic questions in an issue tree.

Dave's management team consisted mainly of former sales executives. Over the years they had cultivated long-standing relationships with the key decision makers in their major customer accounts. In previous bids with AMCC and other GPOs, their winning strategy had been to make the best bid possible and then leverage their strong relationships.

At the beginning, our team investigated potential solutions along similar lines—aggressive pricing backed by influence with the key decision makers in the new CHA-AMCC GPO. But we quickly abandoned that notion when we saw the list of the new board of directors. The CHA (with which Omega held the old contract) had used its size—quadruple that of AMCC—to

Figure 5.1. Issue Tree for Delta Bidding

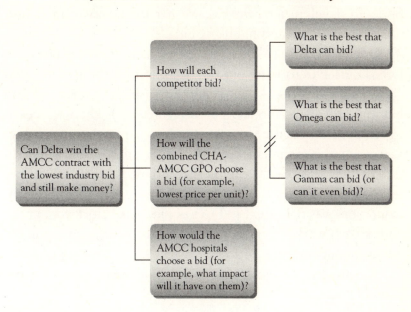

dominate the new board, and many of these CHA directors were long-standing friends and customers of Omega.

That disappointment still left us the option of simply submitting a better bid than Omega or Gamma, thereby creating more economic value for both the GPO and its constituent AMCC hospitals. Because the GPO board's own internal governance structure and procedures required it to recommend a bid choice to the entire hospital membership for final approval, Delta might win the contract with a bid that member hospitals considered advantageous.

The nature of the problem—a competitive bid with a finite number of competitors and equal access to the public financials of each company—lent itself to an industry microeconomic analysis. Within this framework, our team created the first draft issue tree shown in Figure 5.1 and then prioritized issues and developed the work plan. We also began to consider strategic implications. The principles of game theory encouraged our team to ask, "If Delta bids like this, how will the competitors bid?" To develop our own bid, we needed to understand how Omega and Gamma would likely bid.

Fully expecting to change it as we learned more, our team forced ourselves to write out our day-one hypothesis statement: "Can Delta win the AMCC contract with the lowest industry bid and still make money?" (See Figure 5.1.) Then we began to refine it, articulating our assumptions, strengthening weaker aspects of the argument, and identifying remaining issues. In this particular project, keeping the current working hypothesis in constant sight was also essential for communication—our team room was right next to Dave's office. Like clockwork at the end of each workday, he would wander into our team room and ask us for our current solution.

We divided the work plan into manageable chunks for our team of five:

- Jeff, our project manager and experienced problem solver, whose years at West Point and in the Army had taught him to drill our team into an effective unit
- Walter, an MBA from Kellogg, also well seasoned
- George, our likewise veteran Delta sales executive
- Ray, an M.D., freshly graduated from the University of Pennsylvania medical school a month earlier
- Yours truly, directing the overall project

All were eager to help wherever needed. After some discussion, we settled on three main tasks.

Task one: Walter would work with one of Delta's dedicated finance people to develop the microeconomic models for Delta and Omega, which would underpin our team's estimates about each of their best bids. At the time, our team hoped that Gamma was too small to make a credible bid for AMCC's enormous volume of purchases. If subsequent evidence disproved this assumption, Walter would have to expand his models to include a Gamma bid.

Walter and his counterpart in Delta's finance department would develop a perspective on the competitors' fixed versus variable cost structures and the capacities of their manufacturing plants. Based on these cost and capacity calculations, Walter would approximate how much profit would accrue to Delta and Omega over the lifetime of the contract. Because pricing on the contract might also affect prices to Delta's and Omega's other customers, Walter needed further input from Delta's internal marketing analysts about how the new contract might impact Delta's book of business. He would compare that with what was known publicly about Omega's customer contracts. As his Delta counterparts helped him refine these microeconomic assumptions, Walter would feed them into his model of each competitor's best bids.

Task two: We asked George to lead a specially commissioned Delta sales and manufacturing team to see whether Gamma could really bid. Gamma currently served 10 percent of the market ($100 million annual sales). An AMCC contract would double its share. Could Gamma's single manufacturing plant double production so fast? Our work plan needed an answer: if Gamma could not compete, we could run game theory scenarios on only two players, greatly reducing complexity.

Task three: Ray would study how the customers would value the bids. This question was complicated. Delta's customer was technically the AMCC GPO, but AMCC's customers (individual hospitals) would be both involved in supplier selection and directly affected by the result. We had to know how Delta could create economic value not only for the GPO but also for the hospitals.

Ray organized hospital staff interviews, starting at his own medical school alma mater, to inquire how the bid process would work from their perspective—who the decision makers would be and what criteria they would use. Because the new GPO would most likely be run by CHA executives (long-time friends of Omega), this indirect approach of interviewing the hospitals seemed our best way to penetrate the nuances of the bid process. At the hospitals, Ray would also try to understand the direct financial and operational impacts of the bids. The hospitals' costs of switching from Delta's to Omega's products would not be trivial and might favor Delta.

Ray would, in addition, seek perspective on potential "price spillover." In other words, if AMCC pricing came in below current industry averages, how much of that lower pricing must Delta and Omega extend to their other customers as immediate price reductions? Finally, Ray would work with Delta sales executives on a worst-case scenario: How much in sales and profit could Delta actually lose if it lost the AMCC contract?

Week One Answer: "Delta Is in a Tough Spot"

From the internal interviews and external hospital customer visits we conducted within the first week, a fairly unpleasant story emerged for Delta based entirely on the economics of the GPO and Delta's competitors.

Walter and his Delta finance teammate determined that, in terms of potential sales and profits, a "hospital bed" was worth more to Omega than to Delta. Why? The basic answer was pull-through. In this industry, a hospital would choose a supplier for its basic medical products, usually from a competitive bid. Then, due to the high costs of training nurses on two different systems of medical products, that hospital effectively became that supplier's hospital. With the core contract secured for the basic medical products business, the supplier could then sell the hospital its higher-value specialty products. This pull-through could enable a supplier to bid lower on the base contract, enhancing its profits later through specialty product sales.

Unfortunately, because Omega's recent R&D efforts had been superior, its specialty medical products offerings were

Figure 5.2. Hospital Purchases: Value of Hospital Bed Greater for Omega Than for Delta Due to Specialty Product Sales

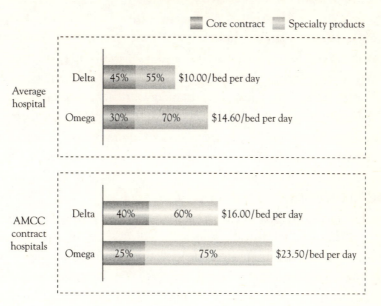

broader and deeper than Delta's, so Omega had much greater pull-through potential. Figure 5.2 shows that this difference between Delta and Omega sales potential per bed per day was even more pronounced in AMCC hospitals, where patients were sicker on average and required more intense and extended care. This big difference alone enabled Omega to bid lower than Delta for the AMCC contract.

How did Walter and his teammate complete this analysis in a week? By choosing just two pairs of hospitals with staff members accessible to Delta: (1) a pair of average size, in similar geographies, one served by Delta, the other by Omega; and (2) a pair of average academic medical centers, one Delta's, one Omega's. Walter made very sure that Delta executives would consider the four hospitals representative of their categories. The executives' agreement on this would help to legitimize the subsequent findings in their eyes. That these four hospitals were considered representative of others in the market was also vital due to the analytical risks associated with drawing conclusions from such a small sample size.

Working with friends in the hospitals' accounting departments, Walter's crew obtained purchase records of basic and specialty products from Delta and Omega and harmonized them with estimates of sales per bed per day (see Figure 5.2). The differences in sales performance were so stark that, even if the analysis was wrong by 50 percent, Omega's recent superior R&D initiatives still implied a serious competitive advantage. The fact that Omega had developed such differentiated medical devices, which addressed previously unmet patient needs, meant it could command significant price premiums.

Furthermore, we began to understand why the negotiating approaches of Delta and Omega had differed over the preceding five years. Delta had pledged "best pricing" to two of its biggest GPO accounts—First GPO ($600 million annual sales) and Sunshine GPO ($150 million). Regarding possible price spillover effects, Ray and his crew had found that Delta's current AMCC pricing was above its pricing for First GPO and Sunshine GPO. If Delta won the next AMCC contract with prices *below* these other contracts, Delta would be contractually obliged to reduce the prices for First and Sunshine hospitals to the same level. This further limited Delta's ability to bid low on the AMCC contract and still break even.

By contrast, Omega had negotiated "no cuts" and was not legally obliged to reduce pricing to its CHA hospitals, even if its winning bid on the AMCC contract was lower than current CHA pricing. The CHA-AMCC merger would not formally take place for some time, so these contracts would not be harmonized now. So complex and large were such contract negotiations, they might not be renegotiated and harmonized across the entire new GPO until the CHA contract expired, three years forward.

Still, Omega's pricing for the AMCC would be transparent to all CHA hospitals, and some on our team argued that although Omega would not be legally obligated to do so, it would be under tremendous pressure to reduce CHA prices, because CHA hospitals would be part of the same GPO in the future. So price spillover might limit Omega's bidding as well.

We briefly speculated why, strategically, Delta and Omega had adopted such different contracting approaches. Was it because Omega's R&D had launched so many superior products? If so, Delta would have to make concessions on price to maintain its market share. But we dropped this speculation fairly quickly in order to refocus on the immediate task of devising Delta's bid.

The details behind the Week One Answer—"Delta is in a tight spot"—were bleak. Modeling the potential profit contribution over the seven-year contract for both Delta and Omega, we used our best current assumptions: similar price spillover for both companies, similar fixed-versus-variable cost structures, and Omega's superior overall sales per bed per day. Results suggested that Delta's breakeven bid price could be up to 12 percent lower than in its current AMCC contract, but Omega's could be 20 percent lower. Figure 5.3 displays the breakeven analysis

Figure 5.3. Omega Can Bid More Aggressively Than Delta

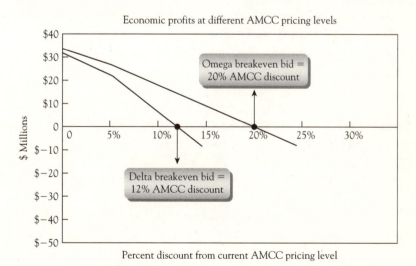

Economic profits at different AMCC pricing levels

Percent discount from current AMCC pricing level

for both, assuming that Omega would have to extend similar pricing to all of its CHA hospital customers. If that constraint were released—if Omega could legally and morally enforce its "no cut" contracts—it could bid even lower. In short, absent new information and other factors, our economic analysis indicated that Delta could not win the AMCC contract, within the current bidding process.

At the end of Week One, Ray and his sales force teammate contributed Delta's one bright spot. From spending time with hospital executives and physicians, Ray knew they were reluctant to change medical products suppliers without significant financial incentives, and Ray's hospital interviews uncovered why: significant nurse retraining on new medical products. Nurse retraining cost dollars as well as morale among an important hospital constituency.

Fortunately, although the GPO executives negotiated the supplier contracts, they still needed to take into account pressures from their hospital members. No one hospital could sway the entire GPO decision-making process, but a coalition of hospitals certainly might be able to. Nurse retraining on the competitor's products meant significant, quantifiable switching costs, which could help incumbent Delta. By integrating the implications of our microeconomic and marketing analysis, our team determined the next jugular question in our problem-solving efforts: Would customer switching costs cancel out the projected price differential between Omega's and Delta's bids?

Week Two Answer: "Delta Could Win on the Total Cost of Ownership"

After the first week, our team shifted priorities to (1) understanding the switching costs from the hospital perspective and (2) developing ways to encourage price spillover to Omega's other customers. Still working on the economic model, Walter continued to refine its competitor cost and capacity assumptions and to lead our team in brainstorming ways to increase Omega's potential price spillover. He also spent time with George and Delta's manufacturing team as they analyzed Gamma's manufacturing capacity. Meanwhile, Ray and his sales teammate went back to interviewing hospital physicians, administrators, and nurses.

Through in-depth interviews, Ray's crew not only quantified the switching costs for hospitals but also identified another piece of good news for Delta: stark differences in hospitals' total cost of ownership of these medical products. Omega provided its basic products at lower prices to hospitals, but because of the way Omega products were engineered, old products were discarded and replaced by new ones as a patient moved from the emergency room (ER) to the operating room (OR) to the intensive care unit (ICU). By contrast, Delta's basic products were engineered to move with the patient throughout the hospital. Delta created economic value for the ultimate customer, in that a hospital needed a far lower *quantity* of Delta's products to manage patient care, thereby leading to overall cost savings compared with Omega's products (as indicated in Figure 5.4).

Figure 5.4. Delta Can Provide an Overall Total Cost of Ownership Advantage for Hospitals

	Dollars per bed per year	
	Delta	Omega
Core contract – Basic products	$2,200	$1,200
Specialty products	$2,800	$3,000
Base contract	$5,000	$4,200
Additional basic products needed due to Omega technology	$0	$2,100 ⬅
Total annual cost to hospital	$5,000	$6,300
Hospital annual total cost advantage if it uses Delta products ($ per bed per year)		$1,300

By contrast, there was no such engineering difference between Delta's and Omega's specialty products. Because current reimbursement practices forbade hospitals' passing along Omega's higher total product costs per patient to payers such as insurance companies, hospitals would have to swallow these additional costs.

Week Three Answer: "Omega Has Delta in a Corner"

The third week started with good news for Delta: George and the manufacturing engineers determined that Gamma could *not* credibly bid. Poring over public plans of Gamma's manufacturing plant and interviewing manufacturers that supplied and installed its equipment revealed that Gamma simply did *not* have the capacity to scale up rapidly enough to serve the AMCC contract. The plant was already working six days, two shifts a day. So it was a two-competitor race for the contract, making the game theory modeling for our team that much more simple.

But the good news did not last through the third week. The first bad news: the GPO bid was structured such that Delta could not demonstrate its advantage to customers in total cost of ownership per medical product. Ray's subsequent interviews with hospital administrators indicated that there would be no way to alter the GPO's RFP requirement that the bids be submitted on a price-per-unit basis. The RFP specified hundreds of products and thousands of SKUs. This reluctance to change may have manifested because the new GPO board's CHA members had historically (with Omega) mainly judged bids by price per unit. And they may have been skeptical of the total cost per unit argument, because many hospitals could not then track purchases in such a way. In turn, some of our team were a bit skeptical of the GPO's intentions. It normally earned 3-percent revenues for itself from the total purchases made by member hospitals—and thus had no incentive to manage total costs of ownership.

All of this was bad news not only for Delta but ultimately for the hospitals as well. If they switched to Omega, even at a lower price per basic product unit, their overall expenditures on medical products could increase, using more units per patient.

Other bad news for Delta: Walter's refined microeconomic model did not change the Week Two Answer that Omega could bid much lower than Delta. Each evening Dave wandered into the team room asking what the current working answer was, and each evening his expression grew grimmer.

Week Four Answer: "Make an Alliance Among Delta and Its Customers' Customers—The Hospitals"

With our more detailed understanding of the current market conditions, industry microeconomics, and competitive dynamics, we now turned to ways to salvage Delta's bid within the RFP constraints. We leveraged many sources to create options: seasoned Delta executives' deep experience in the industry, analogies from other industries, recent competitor moves, and creative brainstorming amongst ourselves. A classic game theory approach enabled us to return to the bid issue tree of Figure 5.1 to structure and then assess the potential outcomes of each option for Delta and Omega. We first attempted to generate options that would leverage Delta's advantages as the incumbent, such as lobbying to dual-source the contract to Delta and Omega, so that Delta would still get the lion's share of the business; or extending the existing AMCC contract for a few more years.

We also tried to come up with options to attack Omega weaknesses. For example, we tried to escalate the threat of price spillover to Omega's existing CHA hospitals, as their CHA purchases would not be specifically included in the new contract. One idea was to announce publicly and credibly that Delta would match any offer Omega made to AMCC. This would reduce Omega's incentives to bid low. It would also increase

Delta's chances because, if prices were equal, switching costs would encourage hospitals to stay with Delta.

We also announced that Delta would send its offer to all AMCC and CHA hospitals to ensure transparency. Our purpose in this was to encourage a hospital push for fair bid evaluation and to make CHA hospitals lobby for the same prices. Our team spent an equal or greater amount of time brainstorming Omega's options, to ensure that Delta's strategies could address potential threats from Omega.

Nearly all scenarios ended in the same result: maintaining current GPO rules and decision-making procedures, assuming a customer value-maximizing bid from Omega, the GPO's best choice lay with Omega. Delta would lose the $100 million annual contract with the AMCC.

We could now see the consequences of Delta's previous strategy and investments. After many years of underinvestment in R&D, Delta had launched fewer innovative specialty products. Yet elsewhere in the industry, hospitals were partnering with suppliers to address major unmet needs, such as patient infection rates or medication errors. Delta had ignored this trend and was now reaping what it had not sown. Its products could not command the price premiums earned by Omega's products. Delta's competitive disadvantage would continue with each new GPO bid until its strategic priorities shifted to investing in much more productive R&D efforts. But redesigning Delta's R&D processes was a longer-term issue, and thus not the current priority of our team.

"But Why Bid on AMCC?"

"Why do we have to bid anyway?" asked Ray in the middle of the fourth week, as we all sat in the team room. Senior Delta executives and other teammates sat in silence, staring in disbelief. All anyone could think was that since the emergence of GPOs, it had become customary for every supplier to bid for these large long-term customer contracts. Contracts for basic products were necessary to provide the fertile environment for company sales forces to sign up purchases of higher-value specialty products. The conduct of medical products suppliers rested on these assumptions. Perhaps not altogether surprisingly, it was the youngest, newest member of our team who asked the breakthrough question:

"But why bid on AMCC?"

Just like that, everyone could recognize his question's implication: take the contract directly to end-user hospitals; bypass the GPO. By doing so, Delta could make its case directly to the hospitals and maybe get them to sign bilateral deals that benefited their bottom lines by lowering the total cost of ownership of medical products. Also, hospitals would not anger nurses by forcing retraining on new products and procedures, and they would avoid all switching costs. Because Delta almost certainly would lose the AMCC bid, the direct contracting option could be better than the earlier "worst-case scenario."

There were so many risks. Would the hospitals even be able to see the total-cost-of-ownership benefit that Delta offered, especially using their antiquated internal cost accounting systems? Would they be willing to forgo GPO negotiations on their behalf, perhaps even going against GPO recommendations? Many of these academic medical centers had helped found the AMCC. Would they now take part in dismantling it? If Omega got wind of Delta's strategy, how might it retaliate? How might this approach affect subsequent GPO negotiations? And did Delta even have the sales and marketing resources to approach hospitals and then negotiate the contracts? Figure 5.5 begins to identify the critical issues and their implications through a systematic decision tree.

Although many of the answers were not immediately known, we put together a work plan to figure them out during the fourth through sixth weeks of our project. After much analysis, modeling, and debate, it was clear to Dave and the Delta team that

Figure 5.5. Delta's Bid Decision Tree

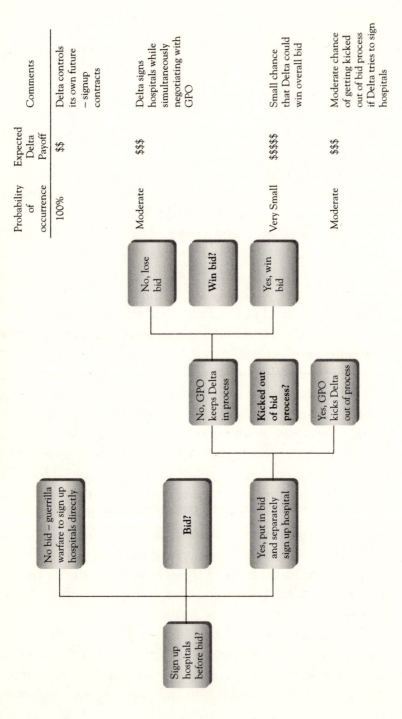

	Probability of occurrence	Expected Delta Payoff	Comments
No, lose bid	100%	$$	Delta controls its own future – signup contracts
Win bid?			
Yes, win bid	Moderate	$$$	Delta signs hospitals while simultaneously negotiating with GPO
	Very Small	$$$$$	Small chance that Delta could win overall bid
	Moderate	$$$	Moderate chance of getting kicked out of bid process if Delta tries to sign hospitals

No bid – guerrilla warfare to sign up hospitals directly

Bid?

Yes, put in bid and separately sign up hospital

No, GPO keeps Delta in process

Kicked out of bid process?

Yes, GPO kicks Delta out of process

Sign up hospitals before bid?

their only recourse was fast and stealthy guerrilla warfare to sign up hospitals before the bid process ended. At this point, the analysis turned from economics to tactics and capabilities. We developed a detailed implementation plan and a series of contingencies to address identified risks associated with attempting direct alliances with the hospitals. We evaluated Delta's ability to go directly to the hospitals, deliver the message of lower total cost, and sign them up. Delta did not actually have the direct-selling and contract-closing capability this required, so we quickly rebuilt one by tapping recently retired Delta sales executives. They knew the industry, knew the products, and, most important, knew the customers. We hastily lured these veterans out of retirement as a direct-sell, contract-closing force.

Live to Fight Another Day

In the end, from its guerrilla signings of direct bilateral hospital contracts outside the GPO bid structure, Delta gained in three ways. First, it salvaged some near-term sales. Second, it clarified focus on its longer-term priorities of designing more innovative products. Third, it created a breathing space to fight another day. Perhaps the ultimate retention of only about $38 million of quite profitable sales disappointed some external observers. Yet Delta's leader, Dave, had reframed the situation such that those who foresaw Delta's imminent loss of most of the $100 million in annual sales understood the real achievement. And Delta survived.

Delta used its second chance wisely, reducing expenses across the board to fund more R&D ventures. Delta engineers worked with AMCC hospital customers to create truly differentiated products that better addressed significant, unaddressed medical needs. If successful with these R&D initiatives, Delta could expect to create and capture more economic value by commanding new price premiums and increasing its market share. Perhaps most important, these efforts returned Delta to its original organizational values built up over fifty years: those of assisting physicians, nurses, and pharmacists in saving and sustaining patient lives.

Where Sweat Really Pays

The problem-solving methods discussed here rest on a mindset of fact-based inquiry. The main benefit of hypothesizing a solution early in the process lies in efficiently organizing subsequent data-gathering, creativity, and analytical efforts. Note that our Delta team constantly altered the working solution to fit the emerging facts, rather than the other way around. Indeed, our team went from guessing, in our first week, that Delta could win with the most aggressive bid and still make money, to despairing that under no scenarios could Delta win the AMCC contract through a direct head-to-head bid against Omega. How did we determine that? By analyzing as exhaustively and comprehensively as possible the underlying economics of Delta, Omega, the GPO, and the hospital customers.

The science of problem solving naturally begins with diagnosing a problem and hypothesizing a solution. From there it relies on superior understanding of the strategy, economics, and priorities of the customers, the competitors, and the company itself. Discovering solutions depends on insightfully integrating analytical frameworks from multiple disciplines and perspectives. Superior solutions come from thoughtful, disciplined, and repeated combinations of analysis and creativity. And sometimes insightful questions or solutions come from the mouths of "babes."

To begin to develop one's own rigorous habit of probing and analysis, this chapter has suggested asking several basic questions: How do you create economic value for customers? How do you capture some of the economic value for your own company? What organizational norms and personal values might enhance and constrain potential solutions? Even if one has spent many years at the same company and in the same industry, it is important to periodically reexamine answers to these questions. Such reexamination of trends in industry structure, conduct, performance, new entrants, and substitutes can help you cope with potential changes in government regulations, consumer behavior, technology, and the competitive dynamic.

Solving the Problem Backward

Mike Nevens
Director, McKinsey & Company

I became a much better problem solver when I learned to solve problems *backward*. This backward approach helps me avoid the five most common traps while solving problems. Shortly I'll get to those five fatal traps.

Never forget that in business the sole objective of problem solving is to improve performance. There are no awards for style, elegance, thoroughness, or cleverness. Good answers well implemented are the gold standard.

So work backward in the sense of always starting with a clear outcome that you want to achieve. How will the business be better if you and your colleagues solve the problem? Will you be able to get a decision on launching a new product, expanding capacity, making an acquisition, exiting an unprofitable distribution channel? Will you have lower-cost operations or a better customer management model leading to more repeat purchases?

Once you know what you want to accomplish, you can figure out what has to change. Do you need to persuade people of the value of a new technology or of the viability of a new process? Do you need to get agreement to take a write-off now to improve profitability next year?

Answering these questions requires that you understand the decision criteria and biases of the decision makers and those who can facilitate or block action. Besides top executives, they often include supervisors and frontline workers who have a stake in the outcome and whose commitment is vital to success. They can often be people outside the company—suppliers, customers, partners, and regulators.

Now you are ready to think about what you will need to know to get those changes made—in other words, to persuade the decision makers, implementers, facilitators, and potential blockers. To get this right you need to spend time listening to those constituents and so learn their bottom-line needs.

Now you are almost (not quite) ready to begin to define the analyses you need to do to convince others of the changes needed to get to the result you desire. You still need to figure out what meets each constituent's "standard of proof." In most situations, you and others already know a lot about the situation, and rediscovering it is a waste of time and resources. Now you can begin your analytic work.

With this approach, you will do the minimum amount of work required to achieve the necessary result. You will also spend most of your time working on the *answer* rather than most of the time working on the problem.

And that is the first trap to avoid. All too often, inexperienced problem solvers spend 80 percent of their time "proving the problem."

The second trap is analyzing the available data rather than finding the data you need to crack the problem. Figure out what data are needed to get the result rather than what data may be at hand. Usually, if all the facts and data are at hand, you have been diverted to resolving an issue that may not be the primary problem.

The third trap is working in an unconstrained solution space. There are theoretically perfect answers, and then there are real-world constraints—time, money, talent, appetite for risk.

Defining the outcome you want and testing to see that it is both feasible and good avoids that wild goose chase.

The fourth trap is using the most familiar and comfortable problem-solving tools. Discounted cash flow and market segmentation are often useful, but sometimes are not a good path to an answer. Solving backward forces you to realize when you need to either learn something new or find others who have the skills to apply different techniques.

The fifth and most common fatal trap is forgetting that ultimately problem solving is about persuasion. The backward approach puts persuasion at the heart of the matter.

The objection to the backward approach is that it takes too long to get started. If you agree with that perspective, you do not understand the problem . . . really.

Chapter 6

HOW TO TELL THE STORY

Why write a story? By *story, or storyline, we mean a logical argument that marshals compelling evidence to test the comprehensiveness and coherence of a proposed solution*. Without doubt, the disciplined habit of writing a storyline can be difficult and time consuming. But its importance to major business decision making cannot be overstated. Taking time to reflect and view the problem and its potential solution from multiple angles can be damned by some as mere dithering. It is not. Rather, it is a way to avoid the worst business mistakes. With the story, you convince yourself of the solution's validity.

Further, elegant solutions have little impact when senior managers remain unconvinced. The upheaval wrought by change is never trivial. Neither are the communication requirements of driving change through an organization. Convincing others to embrace the proposed solution remains the challenge. And for that, you once again need to develop a persuasive story.

We hope this chapter will bolster your habits of clear thinking and effective communication. We begin by describing how to write storylines to convince both yourself and others of the solution. The process of rewriting the story helps pinpoint potential weaknesses in the argument and then focus activities and analyses to address these potential logical gaps.

We then proceed to discuss ways of both identifying and reaching key audiences. By returning to the Delta versus Omega case presented in Chapter Five, we introduce practical tools to develop compelling storylines. The chapter closes with a few reflections of why the telling of stories—similar to the process of discernment described in Chapter One—is so critical to making good business decisions.

Storylines: *How* to Write Them

Developing a well-evidenced argument, or storyline, starts with your one-sentence hypothesis statement and cuts to an outline of the critical evidence needed to support its solution. As explained in Chapter Two, a team begins by diagnosing the problem from its symptoms, then goes directly to a hypothesis statement of the solution, problem background, and context description, and then an issue tree. After some very preliminary data gathering and analysis to solidify its diagnosis, the team proceeds to write the storyline of the entire proposed solution. This version of the story is like a skeleton to which the team will add more analytic flesh.

The team uses the skeletal story to solicit input early in the process from teammates, senior managers, colleagues, and industry experts. These early discussions help plan work and prioritize (and reprioritize) activities and analyses. As the team discovers new information and gains new insights, it updates the storyline. This may mean modifying the solution or even tearing up the original story to devise a new one to fit the emerging facts. Problem solvers should never love their hypotheses so much that they cannot let go of them; so, too, they should not look for supporting evidence for the storyline early in the process, but rather stand ready to transform the story as more information is discovered. Project managers usually draft the storyline as part of their responsibility for integrating all aspects of process and content.

Much advice is available on how to write and communicate well in business.[1] The following steps focus specifically on how to develop and shape the storyline:

1. Define the problem and understand the context (this should come directly from the hypothesis statement and the problem context description).

2. Write down the "one-sentence answer" (based on the hypothesis statement).

3. Group supporting points around major points (these supporting points should come directly from the issue tree).

4. Divide the story into situation, complication, and resolution (in other words, redistribute the substance of steps 1, 2, and 3 under the headings of situation, complication, and resolution).

5. Test the storyline.

Step 1: Define the Problem and Understand the Context

Diagnosing the problem and hypothesizing a solution basically precede writing the storyline. The team then asks further clarifying questions, such as these:

- What are the objectives of this effort?
- Who are the decision makers and the broader set of stakeholders?
- What are their issues and motivations?
- What information do they already know and what would be new to them?
- How might they react to that new information and why?

To illustrate from this point, we continue the Delta hospital products case from Chapter Five. Recall that Delta was bidding against Omega for a multihospital customer contract—the Academic Medical Center Consortium (AMCC). Our team quickly discovered major internal and external factors affecting how each company could bid. One factor was that medical products companies must perform extensive R&D to design, engineer, and gain regulatory approval for their products. Another was that manufacturing plants were built with enormous capacities, which meant significant fixed production costs. Variable costs, by contrast, were relatively small. Consequently, companies were always trying to gain customers and market share, to achieve superior economies of scale and reduce per-unit costs. Another factor was that Delta's ultra-competitive management team had spent many years fighting Omega for customer contracts. The combination of industry economics and management mindset would predispose both Delta and Omega to bid very aggressively for the upcoming major contract.

Step 2: Write Down the One-Sentence Answer from the Hypothesis Statement

Again following our earlier problem-solving steps, once the context is clear, the team should brainstorm to write down the problem in one sentence and answer it in another. Once again, the hypothesis statement can provide a reference. After identifying a potential answer, the problem solver asks what reasons will support it. Do not structure the reasons yet; just catalog them so that the team has as complete a list as possible. To illustrate, here's the one-sentence problem for Delta:

> "How should Delta optimize its potential profits through the bid for the large, multiyear contract to serve the Academic Medical Center Consortium (AMCC) hospitals?"

Our team could now adopt one of many possible one-sentence solutions. For example:

> "Delta can win the AMCC contract with the lowest industry bid and still make money."

> Or

> "Delta can win the AMCC contract and make profits with a bid that is nearly as low as that of its main competitor, Omega."

Now the team starts to create a reasoned, logical argument (storyline). It proceeds by grouping major supporting points and laying factors out in terms of the situation, complication, or problem and the current proposed resolution. Over time, as the team gathers new evidence, the one-sentence answer may turn out to be exactly wrong, but the process ensures that the team will have even more information to go on in reformulating it. In the Delta case, our team's working solution in the first week of the project—"Delta can submit as low a bid as Omega for the AMCC contract, win it, and still make money"—turned out to be wrong. Faced with Omega's superior cost structure and specialty product line, Delta could *not* submit as low a bid for the AMCC contract as Omega could and still make money.

Step 3: Group Supporting Points Around Major Ones

Upon closer inspection, some reasons you list in support of the hypothesized solution will appear more encompassing than others. Reorganize them, placing lesser ideas and details in support of the larger ones. Why do this? By grouping supporting points, the team can quickly identify where its argument is already strong, and likewise quickly assess and focus on gaps where it needs more evidence.

Step 4: Divide the Story into Situation, Complication, and Resolution

A convincing storyline usually first describes the current situation, then assesses the complications, then leads into the solution. This approach is certainly not the only way to tell a story, and it may not even be the most persuasive way given your particular circumstances. To its credit, though, it presents several benefits. First, this straightforward sequence makes the argument clear. Second, it quickly surfaces areas in which there may be disagreements among decision makers. It begins with what should be common ground. For instance, the situation section of the storyline may investigate aspects of the industry, the company, the competitors, or the customer base—all matters about which there needs to be substantial initial consensus. If everyone cannot agree on a fact-based description of the situation, the team faces a whole other layer of difficulties. It would need to return to problem diagnosis, the initial hypotheses, the scope of the work, and the constraints on the solution space—among other matters—to work out where the potential disconnects may be.

That being said, we must remember that storylines, although they may be arguments, are also stories. They persuade in different ways. Sometimes the most analytical ones do not persuade as well as one based on analogies or other approaches. We return specifically to this point of persuasion in Chapter Seven. Right now we focus mainly on developing the storyline to test the solution for ourselves. Is it consistent? Coherent? Well-evidenced? Logical? Comprehensive?

Suppose that at Delta our team's potential one-sentence answer was, "Delta can win the AMCC bid and make profits by submitting a bid nearly as low as that of its main competitor, Omega." The storyline could flow as follows:

Situation: Both companies are likely to bid aggressively. The AMCC represents a sizeable customer among U.S. hospitals. Because it is expected to award the contract to a sole supplier of hospital products, it represents a tremendous opportunity for both competitors, Delta and Omega. The high fixed-cost/low variable-cost structure of the hospital products industry combined with the competitive nature of Delta and Omega senior executives (drawn from the sales force ranks) will drive both Delta and Omega to bid aggressively to capture the very large (and incremental for Omega) volume of AMCC purchases.

Complication: Unfortunately, there are two reasons why Omega will probably be able to submit a bid lower than Delta's. First, Omega has the competitive advantage of a superior product mix (higher-priced specialty product lines) and experience in pull-through sales of these higher-margin products. Thus, by accepted industry metrics, each "hospital bed" represents more profit for Omega than for Delta. The second reason is that Delta's bidding is handicapped by "spillover" contracts worded such that potentially lower AMCC prices must be extended also to Delta's other large hospital customers. Omega's "no cut" contracts do not require it to reduce its prices to other customers.

Resolution: Delta must therefore convince AMCC member hospitals that other issues should overcome the expected price differential between Omega's bid and its own bid, in order to make Delta the preferred option. For example, the AMCC hospitals would face significant nurse retraining costs if they chose Omega, which could be a barrier to changing medical products suppliers. The threat of these switching costs might help Delta retain the AMCC business with a bid at prices nearly as low as offered by its main competitor, Omega.

One way to think about the storyline is as a pyramid (see Figure 6.1). The one-sentence solution is at the top and rests on the situation-complication-resolution argument. Having created the basic structure of the argument, one can group the main points together and then fill in supporting subpoints.

Each section must have its own strong support, and the sections must be linked in a logical sequence. In our case, the major complication that Delta faces lies in Omega's superior competitive position. The resolution rests on the complication's implication that Delta cannot make as aggressive a bid for the AMCC business as can Omega. Absent that complication, the resolution would fail the test of logic. Therefore, our team was particularly careful in collecting sufficient evidence to solidify this critical point. This included sales data reflecting the profit value of a hospital bed to both Omega and Delta. Other, more detailed proof included a list of additional products that Omega sells, their prices, and their projected higher gross margins. Further team efforts profiled Omega's R&D programs over the last several years, which had obtained FDA approval for numerous specialty products.

Step 5: Test the Storyline

At this juncture, the problem solver should pause to scrutinize the storyline. One should ask probing questions about its logic,

Figure 6.1. Early Situation-Complication-Resolution Storyline for Delta

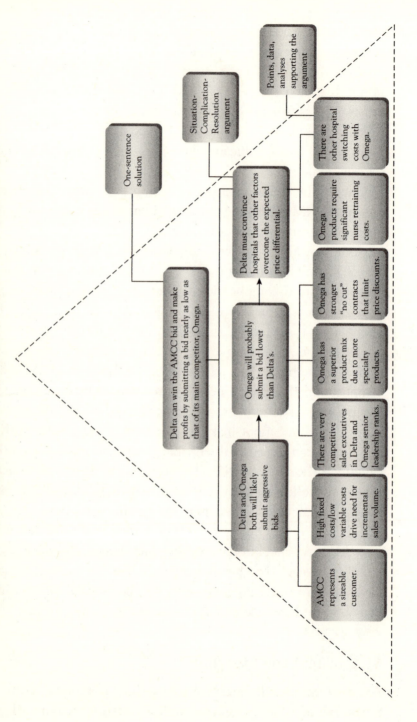

its supporting evidence, potential opposition to it, and other possible solutions. For example:

- Do all the major ideas support the one-sentence answer?
- Are all the major ideas of similar importance?
- What objections might arise?
- Does the argument address the objections?
- Has the team exhausted all other possible solutions?
- Does the storyline convey the fact that the team has exhausted all other solutions?

Our team tested its Delta storyline (argument) in multiple ways. Were any of the supporting points or data controversial? Would Delta managers debate those points or data sources? If they opposed any of them, they might oppose the entire storyline and subsequently the recommendation. In fact, some of our findings were controversial. Many Delta executives remained skeptical of our analysis that indicated the greater value of a hospital bed for Omega. Only a detailed assessment of Omega's industry-leading R&D programs developing new products and their successful launches finally convinced Delta managers of their disadvantage in the market. Only then did they begin to understand the complication that, regrettably, Omega could significantly underbid Delta.

Once we calculated that Omega could lower its prices by 20 percent below current AMCC pricing levels and still break even financially, whereas Delta could lower its prices by only 12 percent and still break even, the jugular question quickly became "Can the hospital switching costs make up the 8 percent difference in prices?" Given an average hospital's annual medical products purchases, the 8-percent price difference translated into possible annual savings of tens of thousands of dollars. Unfortunately, the conclusion to our question, based on extensive customer interviews, was that hospitals might indeed switch medical suppliers for far less than the potential 8 percent price differential between Omega and Delta bids. The evidence forced our team to reconsider whether our one-sentence answer was correct. Maybe Delta simply could not win the bid and still make a profit. Because that was indeed the case, our team was forced to develop a new storyline to fit the emerging facts.

Overall, our team tested itself, its data sources, its storyline, its process, and the proposed solution by constantly asking, "How wrong could we be?" and "How could new evidence change our answer?" The iterative problem-solving methods introduced here depend on a habit of fact-based inquiry. Remember, if the data and analysis do not prove the storyline, then the solution and the story need to change to correspond to the data.

Storylines: *With Whom* to Communicate Them

No recommendation succeeds unless senior managers adopt it. Writing a quality storyline and developing a compelling solution is only half the battle in making this happen. The storyline is a tool to help the team address *what* to communicate; the team still needs to sort out *with whom* and *how*. Here, we provide a quick overview of the parties with whom the team should communicate.

Convincing key decision makers to agree to controversial recommendations requires knowing who within the organization really decides or influences the decision. Usually that is the general manager. Yet it is also important to know who else wields formal and informal influence within the organization.

Authority and influence arise from multiple sources. Some people are influential because they control resources such as the budget or direct reports. Authority also can rest on tremendous depth and breadth of experience, critical skills, or access to essential information. Some managers command widespread respect through extraordinary integrity, whereas others are sought out for intelligent or expert advice. During the course of a project, the team will interact frequently with a wide range of managers. It should use those interactions to uncover formal and informal patterns of influence. Then the problem solver can consciously work out how to gain their input, buy-in, and support.

Clearly Dave would be Delta's eventual decision maker, shouldering the responsibility for the course of action. But a more interesting question remained: To whom would Dave turn to discuss his final decision? We needed to spend time with those influential managers. In the end, we found three whom Dave trusted enough to talk with extensively (two of them had no direct responsibility for customer contracting): Delta's R&D director, for his extensive industry experience and perspectives; its CFO, for his keen intellect, integrity, and financial outlook; and Delta's long-time VP of sales.

Storylines: *How* to Communicate Them

Moving senior managers toward controversial or difficult conclusions can be a grueling journey. The road is frequently long, with many little steps. The team needs to interact often with critical decision makers to solicit their guidance, address potentially divisive issues, and review progress—all with the ultimate goal of swaying the audience toward adopting the recommendation. Meetings with senior executives to review progress need to be managed carefully. We suggest some reasonable tactics.

Foster Common Ground and Prepare

By fostering common ground with senior executives throughout the process, the problem-solving team can more likely reach desired conclusions. Often, common ground rests on a shared understanding of the issues at hand. To prepare the way, establish the context by referring to prior discussions, meetings, and how the objectives of this particular communication fit within the overall project process and goals. Communication must overcome psychological and physiological noise—including the demands of day-to-day operations, customer needs, and competitor moves. Constantly checking for feedback helps ensure that a message is getting through. You may be thinking about the problem at all hours of the day and night, but the general manager most certainly has other skillets on the grill.

Some commonsense observations about presentations also bear mentioning. Try to interact with senior colleagues as often as possible, to convey emerging findings and solicit their feedback. For slide presentations, ensure that each slide reinforces the storyline, makes only one point, and uses active language. Slide titles should convey the "So what?" of each aspect of the argument. Make the argument even more compelling by going back and attempting to tell the story with half as many slides. Ten key slides are better than thirty of varying value. A several-page memo is usually better than a longer one. Perhaps most important, avoid the common pitfall of developing or conducting a presentation based on your team's interests rather than on audience needs.

Although this may seem counterintuitive, the most successful progress reviews with senior managers are also the most boring. By *boring* we mean lacking in uncertainty, tension, and emotion. To make sure this happens, the team should never walk into a review *without* previewing the material with key decision makers prior to the meeting. These one-on-one premeetings foreshadow the discussion, obtain input and buy-in, identify potential concerns, and may even cushion an unpleasant message. The team will gain a sense of who will actively champion or oppose its ideas, who may passively resist, and who waits on the fence.

Right Media and Style

Communication requires selecting media that enable an audience most easily to understand the message. Each organization or function has its own communication style. On joining a new department or team, one should determine senior managers' desired communication styles in order to accommodate them. Some managers may want to join ongoing brainstorming sessions; others prefer to wait for notification of more solidified conclusions. Some need frequent informal voicemail, email, or in-person updates; others prefer more formal presentations. Some comprehend written memos best; others need to participate in a debate.

The problem solver needs analysis and logic to test the recommendation, but may need to discard these tools to convince senior colleagues. Some managers will be persuaded by a data-driven, logical argument supported by critical analyses. Others will be influenced more by stories, analogies, or testimonials. Others will judge a recommendation according to the educational backgrounds, personal experiences, or motivations of the recommenders. In the end, listening can become the most effective form of communication of new solutions.

Prepare for Opposition

Even when the problem solver has thought through and tested a solution and communicated it well in a document or scripted presentation, senior executives may still not be convinced. Whether the audience embraces the recommendation depends on the quality of answers to tough follow-up questions. As Aristotle observed, "There is nothing so convincing as a reasonable man."

Do not under-rehearse a presentation—particularly the responses to potential questions. To prepare for the inevitable grilling, brainstorm what the most difficult questions might be. Anticipate positions each senior manager may hold, and prepare most for the controversial or divisive topics. Writing out the questions and answers can help. So can practicing them out loud.

At Delta, we knew Dave's senior managers would doubt Omega's advantage associated with the superior profitability of its specialty products. So our team spent well over half a day practicing answers and deciding ahead of time who among us would handle particular questions. We practiced describing different successful Omega R&D efforts and product launches. Our extensive preparation paid off, as Delta's current difficult competitive situation began to dawn on the executives.

Stories, Discernment, and Better Decisions

The essence of leadership is discerning the right decision when faced with tremendous uncertainty. How rigorously and systematically you think about a problem and its possible solutions has the potential to make you ultimately a sought-after leader. Developing a fact-based story to support a potential major decision, then testing it deliberately, from multiple angles and perspectives, can help in that process of discerning the right decision alluded to in Chapter One.

A long-standing client of mine, the CEO of a major financial institution, described how he avoided the savings and loan (S&L) mess by just such a process. His management team was pushing two S&L acquisitions as a way of capturing potential market opportunities. He spent an entire evening with a glass of wine, staring into the fire in his fireplace, and contemplating these potential acquisitions and what he would have to believe to justify them. He tried to develop a story behind the factors that were driving the S&L boom. Through developing such a story, he tried to discern the right decision for his bank. At the end of the evening, he held an imaginary debate with his demanding finance professor from his business school alma mater. He concluded that he could not defend, let alone explain, the economic assumptions—cost reductions, revenue synergies, strategic opportunities—needed to justify the S&L acquisitions. He passed on the deals—to the loud criticisms of Wall Street analysts and even his own team. He eventually bought the assets of both S&Ls a few years later for a fraction of their peak value. Deliberate reflection on major decisions and the stories one needs to tell to believe in them can help business leaders make the right decisions—and avoid the worst mistakes.

When offering potential solutions, good communication enables problem solvers to anticipate and listen to overall concerns on the part of the broader organization, to empathize with those concerns, and to help others find the courage needed for future success. Communication is always important, but particularly so when recommendations vary starkly from the current way business is conducted. Both individual general managers and problem-solving teams should employ good storylines to discipline their thinking in solving the problem at hand. Resolutions must be logically tested over and over before a general manager decides to move forward. Over the years, managers may have earned considerable success by conducting their business as usual. As a result, it can be a controversial decision to change how a business is run. Senior managers will need fortitude to try new approaches, which may require vastly different skills and competencies. Well-written storylines can help in that decision-making process. The next chapter discusses the business case—another particularly helpful tool to test recommendations.

Communicating How to Always Do the Right Thing for the Right Reasons

Richard C. Notebaert
Retired Chairman and CEO, Qwest Communications
Chairman, Board of Trustees, University of Notre Dame

What a mess. My third time as CEO was, without doubt, my biggest leadership challenge. Qwest employees, particularly those who served customers, were ashamed of their company. They would travel to and from work in street clothing, changing into their uniforms only during work hours. At social and family events, bad-mouthing the company was commonplace. As a consequence, Qwest performance ranked dead last on virtually every industry indicator of customer service.

If that was not enough of a challenge, Qwest was also under close legal scrutiny. At the time I accepted the position, the Department of Justice, the Federal Communications Commission, and the General Services Administration as well as the local authorities were investigating our operations. Things were so bad that we had been summarily thrown out of the Better Business Bureau. We were under a constant cloud of suspicion. Reading our press clippings, everyone expected that it was only a matter of time until we suffered ethical and legal implosion. In spite of my usual confidence, I felt nervous. But I had learned from years of experience that if you don't feel a bit edgy when you take on a tough task, you probably are not fully prepared for it.

I will cut to the chase: Within the subsequent five years, our J.D. Power rankings on customer service rose from last to first, the ranking of our board audit committee went from the bottom to the top five in a field of three hundred, we satisfied the various entities that had been investigating us, and we built our market capitalization from $2 billion to $19 billion. We achieved these results by thoroughly understanding the factors that had led to our customer service and ethics problems and then systematically addressing them.

Generally, both problems were a result of Qwest's dominant culture. Historically, the company had been technology- and engineering-driven, and major decisions were not necessarily considered from a customer perspective. This needed to change. To a large extent, ethical and reputation slippage resulted from a kind of technological arrogance that assumed that we, as the technological insiders, were better judges of what was "right" than any outside agent, including our customers or regulators. We cared little about our impact on those we served. This also needed to change.

Without doubt, communication was the key to our strategy of change. We did not dwell on the past. Going forward, we needed to foster new ways of thinking about the business. We also needed to provide our thousands of employees some simple guidance on how to handle customer issues and ethical behavior problems. That guidance was to "always do the right thing for the right reasons." We needed to execute against that guidance from the top management team to the front line. My team frequently and consistently communicated the message that customers = work and work = jobs. So pervasive was that message that the union leadership adopted it as a kind of mantra. All new spending had to be tied explicitly to addressing a customer need or concern.

Communication needed to go both ways. I encouraged all employees to contact me personally if they ever had a question about "the right thing to do." I answered every email message within twenty-four hours, and there were literally thousands during the first few months of this transformation. In every case, my answer was tied to serving the customer.

It did not take very long for this theme to be heard and to resonate throughout the company. We further instituted a pattern of frequent communication within the company, with messages of the general form, "Here is something I am thinking about; tell me what you think." As a result, our workforce became better informed about what we were doing. A sense of ownership for our actions prevailed and our accomplishments spread well beyond the upper levels of management.

On the Labor Day after a particularly long effort to fix some customer problems, I sent a message to all employees thanking them for their contributions and asserting that "[w]e are the spirit of service." The union provided a wonderful response by making the words replace our former catch-phrase. Over the next five years the company sold thousands of shirts to our employees with "The Spirit of Service" embroidered over the pocket. I often wore that shirt myself at work.

Beyond institutionalizing a new customer-oriented focus, we also needed to address the ethical climate of the business. At the heart of this effort was what I call the "newspaper test." We asked all employees, whenever making a hard decision, to imagine that the facts of that decision would be written about in the local newspaper, and to consider whether they would be comfortable with the report. If not, we had a problem. We selected an employee whose reputation was beyond reproach to oversee corporate ethics. We adopted a policy of zero tolerance for ethical breaches, and we offered complete support, including the payment of any legal fees, for whistle-blowers. We also offered our full cooperation with any outside party that was investigating us, and we sought to settle fairly any claim that we benefited through illegal or unethical business practices.

Admittedly, the problems that faced me as the new CEO of Qwest were serious and difficult to solve. But I approached them with a sense of excitement, because I love a challenge. Plus, I had nothing to prove personally, as I had already succeeded as CEO in leading Ameritech and Tellabs. Consequently, there was never a question about protecting my personal reputation at the expense of doing what was exactly right for our customers. I felt prepared. I had spent thirty years in the industry starting as a truck washer. I knew how the business worked from the bottom up. I felt confident that if I acted in accordance with our credo, "to do the right thing for the right reasons," I would be able to hold my head high regardless of what might happen. Of course, I also had more than a suspicion that by doing the right thing for the customers, we would build a very strong and successful company.

Part Two

MOVING FROM ANALYSIS TO ACTION

Chapter 7

THE BUSINESS CASE

The Call to Arms

When confronted with huge, complex problems, people act rather less as the models and theories predict they will and more like, well, people. They move along what looks like the safer path, continuing to gather data, conduct analyses, and avoid making an irrevocable choice. In fact, behavioral economists have examined systemic biases that prevent people from making optimal decisions, including a stronger aversion to losses than a preference for gains; favoring certainty over uncertainty regardless of potential gains; rarely treating opportunity costs (appropriately) as the same as out-of-pocket costs; and focusing on sunk costs that should just be disregarded. Perhaps even more important, people systematically delay too long in making decisions, fearing possible regret.

Most often, the demands of business more than exceed our common capacities to cope with uncertainty, formulate solutions, and make the right decisions at the right time. Part One of this book was about discovering solutions. The call to arms of Part Two is "Help the problem solver get to a decision!" This chapter explores how developing a structured business case can reinforce decision making; the next chapter presents a framework to measure trade-offs between conducting even more analysis and taking action sooner. Good problem solvers must build their own intuition about when to move from gathering more data to deciding on and implementing a solution.

Dark Days in Capri

Nothing quite equals the happiness and relief of finishing a successful project for an appreciative boss or client. But with that elation comes exhaustion. My team had just completed a grueling three-month campaign and looked forward to some well-earned time off. Alas, consulting is an exciting profession, but it does make large and unpredictable demands on one's time.

"I need your team to take on this challenge," our senior partner, Lenny, told me. The CEO of a major casual apparel retailer, Capri, had just left his problems on Lenny's doorstep. My team, with its significant retail experience, was the one most qualified to help and could be on the case immediately. I was excited and honored to get a chance to serve Capri—half my closet was filled with its outfits—but my team was tired and would need to dig deep.

Capri was a force in the casual apparel industry. Growing explosively in the 1980s and the 1990s, it had virtually created "casual clothing" for younger shoppers as we know it. As Y2K loomed, however, the honeymoon was over. High levels of brand awareness no longer translated into success at the cash register. In retail language, Capri still had customer traffic but that traffic did not convert into profitable sales. Conversion was the key industry performance metric tracked by everyone—Capri managers, competitors, and Wall Street analysts. And it was dropping. Our task was to figure out why.

Capri had started with good-quality, casual cotton clothing—jeans, T-shirts, khakis. From my own shopping sorties throughout the 1990s, I knew it had broadened its offerings to include more eclectic pieces—feather boas, long cashmere coats—hoping to appeal to the ever more fashion-conscious. I was not sure either my friends or I were Capri's target audience, but I knew this design shift was not quite for me. Perhaps it was one of the factors lowering the rate of conversion?

The Business Case—A Tool for Pressure-Testing Solutions

By business case, we mean rigorous financial and nonfinancial analyses that assess the need for and justify potential alternatives to resolving a business problem or strategic opportunity. We build directly on the storyline tool introduced in Chapter Six. The storyline ends with a resolution, but the decision to adopt that resolution still weighs on a manager's mind. Much time, talent, and resources have been invested in finding the right solution. But have they been enough? The business case provides a systematic way to pressure test that decision. Developing the business case employs lessons learned in Part One about diagnosis, hypothesis generation, creativity, analysis, and communication. In general, the business case addresses several straightforward questions:

- What should we do?
- What will it cost?
- How will we benefit?
- How do we make sure that we are successful?

Problem solvers use the discipline of business cases to weigh financial, operational, and strategic benefits and costs. A business case should be not as precise as a budget, nor too high level to provide helpful, specific impetus to making the final decision. Yet a word of caution: any analysis is only as good as its assumptions. For example, projecting future revenues from an as-yet-uncreated market is an inherently uncertain undertaking. In such circumstances, problem solvers must scrutinize their model's assumptions from different angles and perspectives. Good business cases also address nonfinancial implications of major decisions, such as an organization's skills, capabilities, and morale. Rigorous business cases are particularly valuable when a great deal of uncertainty, significant risk, or substantial investments are involved.

Even the most carefully developed business case may meet resistance. People naturally prefer the status quo. They feel more aggravation about possible losses than pleasure from a potential gain. Because of this normal opposition, we will also describe how to tailor the business case into a strong, well-crafted message to decision makers. Tailoring the business case to organizational and personal values and aspirations is particularly important when the decision is difficult but action is imperative.

Five Steps to a Business Case

Once the storyline has been written, the business case further frames and tests a proposed solution. Among countless ways to develop a business case, our experience favors five general steps or parts, as shown here and in Figure 7.1:

1. Define the problem and articulate critical assumptions.

2. Determine the overall financial benefits and costs.

Figure 7.1. Framework for Business Cases

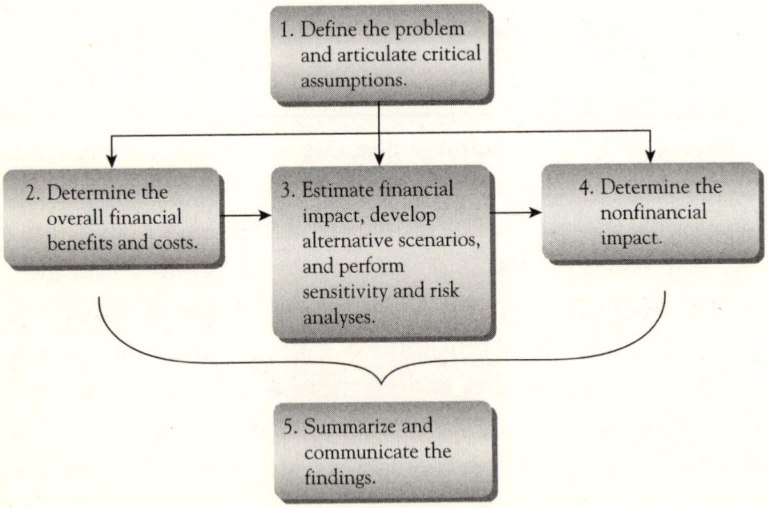

3. Estimate financial impact, develop alternative scenarios, and perform sensitivity and risk analyses.

4. Determine the nonfinancial impact.

5. Summarize and communicate the findings.

Step 1 builds directly on the problem context, hypothesis statement, and storyline. The problem solver needs to understand the project's purpose and assumptions, the data-gathering and analytical challenges, and the degree of certainty required for a decision to be made.

Step 2, determining overall financial benefits and costs, depends on both sound analyses and creativity. Benefits based on cost *reductions* are usually straightforward, but creativity and finesse are often needed to assess benefits such as price *increases* or market-share shifts. Up-front and ongoing costs of investing in the solution must also be factored in.

In Step 3, with a cost-benefit modeling baseline, the team performs sensitivity analyses on factors that could swing the ultimate decision—commonly, these are estimates of market size and growth, but also competitive dynamics, market-share shifts, up-front investments, and the projected profitability of the existing business as it is currently operated, as the business case should capture the incremental performance improvement associated with the solution. The team should also analyze the risks of different investment and return scenarios.

Step 4 depends on identifying nonfinancial impacts, a process that often relies on judgment and less obvious factors. Critical thinking regarding the market, competitive, and execution risks posed by the venture can make or break its business case.

Step 5 summarizes and communicates the business case. Ignore it at your peril: without it, you and your organization may never get to the business decision needed.

At this point, some readers may protest that they already know how to develop an effective business case. In our experience, however, most companies conduct such business case preparation badly. Some make it a game between general managers and finance staff, competing for investment dollars with models that mathematically—and at times magically—hit acceptable targets for either internal rate of return (IRR) or return on invested capital (ROIC). Others fail to complete the work of identifying and systemically testing jugular assumptions. Still others leave unfinished both assessments of the probability of success and the difficult planning of ways to mitigate the inevitable risks associated with a new venture.

Then the frustration starts. Managers are frustrated when the CEO or the board of directors does not approve their investment plans. CEOs and boards are frustrated both that the business cases they see are weak or incomplete and that managers would not know how to improve them. In the end, some CEOs and boards are too polite to provide the harsh feedback—so proposals for investments, new ventures, even acquisitions remain in limbo.

Therefore, at the risk of being prescriptive of business case elements, we will do three things: first, outline a checklist of questions to ask while preparing a business case; second, illustrate those critical elements through the Capri case; and third, comment on frequently committed errors.

A comprehensive business case depends on unassailable assumptions about incremental financial benefits and costs. Beyond rigorously estimating future market size and growth, this implies an in-depth understanding of the value created by the new venture above and beyond the current, probably adequate alternatives. Assumptions on pricing, quantities sold, and market share depend on being able to tell yourself a story as to why customers will switch despite the inevitable reactions by competitors. The potential costs to serve a new market depend on approximations of economies of scale, competitor capacities, fixed versus variable costs, and initial investments versus ongoing costs. The business case must show the incremental cost/benefit improvements represented over the existing operations—the "as is" scenario. Plus, its returns on invested capital (ROIC) must exceed the weighted average cost of capital (WACC) of the company to warrant the investment.

Just a few examples of sloppy analysis include ideas for terrific value creation with imperfect business models to actually capture some of that value, limited opportunities to build a sustainable market position such that competitors can easily eat up market share, and insufficient estimates of the costs to enter a new market. Analysis of future market size and growth drivers can rest on flawed scenarios of technology evolution, regulatory change, or consumer behavior.

A compelling business case also depends on exhaustive investigation of the strategic, operational, and execution risks involved with the new venture. Competitive advantage must rest on some meaningful business aspect that your company can achieve better than others—speed to market, superior cost position, innovation. This valuable, rare, and not substitutable competitive advantage must rest on some core competence. More than likely, your company will not possess all the competencies needed to capture the new opportunity; the question then becomes how to acquire them: hiring new talent, making an acquisition, entering into a partnership? An analytical way of characterizing such risks relies on breakeven calculation—the extent of the market you need to capture, for example, to pay off the investment costs.

Examples of common errors include insufficient clarity regarding "what you would have to believe"—in terms of your customers, competitors, and your own position—to invest in the opportunity. This could include overly rosy assessments of current capabilities—such as design, manufacturing, marketing. Other common errors are overestimating synergies in potential acquisitions to break into a new market, and paying inadequate attention to how to reduce up-front costs and risks—perhaps by making some of the venture self-funding.

As mentioned in Chapters Five and Six, with regard to pressure-testing the business case, always ask yourself, "How wrong could we be?" and "How might new evidence change the answer?" You will instinctively look at a business case differently if the major assumptions—market size, growth, pricing, competitive dynamics, market shares, costs, timing—could be wrong by 50 percent, rather than only 5 percent, and still justify the investment decision. At that point, the investment decision must be a strong one indeed.

My team came very close to failing Capri, not once but twice. As you will see, we first stumbled in the analysis of various future scenarios that would justify our recommendations, and then again in communicating our findings. We hope you will take our near-failures to heart as lessons and not repeat our mistakes.

Step 1: Define the Problem and the Assumptions

Poor conversion of store traffic into actual sales in recent years hinted at a disconnect between customers' expectations and Capri's ability to deliver on them. After analyzing market and company data and speaking at length with many consumers and store managers, we understood how consumers viewed Capri. More important, we began to understand how customer needs were changing. We also quickly hypothesized that the root of Capri's problem lay in its inability to understand and serve those needs.

Nor did Capri understand how those needs were evolving. When many firms adopted the new dress codes of "casual Fridays" and "business casual," many employees were confused and ill-equipped. Previously, many people had purchased two sets of clothing—one for work and one for the weekend—and nothing in between. Capri, one of the main originators of "weekend casual" back in the 1970s and 1980s, had now provided neither clothing nor guidance to meet the new challenge. We thought this largely accounted for the declining conversion rate.

On hearing its customers' criticisms, we initially feared that Capri might need to radically change its value proposition—the types of designs and services it provided in stores. But, as any retailer knows, the brand is the privileged asset, built up over years in customers' minds. One does not take brand-changing lightly. Overhauling the brand requires high levels of market certainty and significant investment. We would not recommend changes that risked the brand unless we had exhausted alternatives and had copious evidence on our side.

Laying out the context, we prepared a scenario that can charitably be called "as is." If Capri continued on the same path, with no relief from competitors or improved understanding of customers' needs, where would it end up? In other words, we estimated the best performance trajectory that was currently possible. The notion was, where would Capri stand if nothing changed? This sobering, necessary "as is" analysis painted scenes of ever-deteriorating market position and profits. It was necessary to give us something against which to compare alternative strategies. Any alternative would need to significantly improve on the "as is" scenario in order to salvage things at Capri—and would have to do so within three years.

Next, we diagnosed the problem and created an issue tree (as detailed in Part One) to make sure we covered all bases, generated hypotheses, and selected the one that looked most promising. We hypothesized that Capri might have to shift customer focus and offerings. We held other hypotheses in abeyance—for example, that revenues were dropping because of inadequate service in stores. We brainstormed ways to test our hypothesis about shifting customer focus. Over time, we developed an early picture of what the repositioning might represent in the future, if Capri could implement it.

The task of projecting the future retail market evolution, Capri's share, and thus Capri's financial performance was fraught

with pitfalls. Many Capri executives disagreed with the assumptions behind our team's "as is" model, believing instead that
they were only one hit fashion season away from a return to
glory. Sadly, the market indicators did not agree. But I made sure
that my team did not proceed with our problem solving until we
reached some consensus on the severity of Capri's market position, knowing full well that, had we not invested in agreeing to
these assumptions, our future business case would rest on a weak
analytical foundation.

Step 2: Determine the Overall Financial Benefits and Costs

We invested heavily in understanding how changes in customer
and apparel focus might increase revenues and margins. We also
examined whether Capri could sell other merchandise at better
margins. We brainstormed how to overcome the markdown
phenomenon that had trained customers to purchase clothing
only when it was on sale.

Our best insights came from studying customer segmentation
at Capri. Rather than segment its customers demographically
(say, by age or gender) we did so with psychological questions:
For what occasion are you buying clothes? What kind of
shopping experience are you looking for? How interested are you
in fashion? Three segments emerged: Apathetics, Fashionistas,
and Stylists. Among them we hoped to find profitable customers
with whom Capri could reconnect.

Apathetics were customers who were largely ignorant of—
and unbothered by—fashion trends. They wore comfortable
clothing in combinations that would be deemed by Capri's
designers as fashion crimes. Not uncommonly, they wore
short-sleeved T-shirts over long-sleeved T-shirts, or even last
season's double-pleated trousers instead of the flat fronts now
in style. Their purchasing priorities were comfort and convenience, and they chose long-lasting, basic items. In other words,

Apathetics wanted a fast, easy shopping experience and did not want to stand out in appearance. They were also extremely sensitive to clothing price. Apathetics contributed about 30 percent of Capri's annual revenues.

Fashionistas inhabited the opposite end of the fashion spectrum, relentlessly hunting the newest "it" thing. Members of this segment, which was skewed toward teenagers and young adults, were influenced most by their friends' styles. Never loyal to one retailer, they stalked the mall for the trendiest look. Fashionistas were somewhat sensitive to price because they bought a lot of clothing, adding about 20 percent to Capri's annual revenues.

Stylists wanted to look current but not trendy. As "business casual" grew more popular, Stylists sought retailers who would help them make sense of the new dress codes and assist them generally in everyday dress. Still, they did not want to look like everyone else at work. They needed help expressing their personal style with clothing versatile for different occasions. Stylists tended to be brand-loyal and less price-sensitive. From our perspective, the Stylist segment held Capri's largest value creation opportunity, if Capri could design, manufacture, and sell to them. Stylists already contributed nearly 50 percent of annual revenues.

Our next step involved carefully categorizing and estimating the overall benefits of focusing marketing and merchandising efforts on Stylists. No other retail competitor was consciously pursuing Stylists. By targeting Stylists, Capri might sell more clothes—more good-quality clothing at its original price—thereby lifting Capri out of the drain of ever-larger markdowns. Surrendering the other, more price-sensitive segments could further help Capri optimize its sales mix and raise gross margins.

Because our working hypotheses involved narrowing down to one segment, the primary benefits would probably come from increasing revenues. This could be achieved while keeping Capri's business model intact. The designers and merchandisers would create new seasonal collections. Capri's existing manufacturers in Asia would produce and ship through Capri's existing supply chain. Capri would continue selling through its existing two-thousand-plus retail stores.

So much for revenues. What about costs? Capri could probably not expect major cost reductions. In fact, expenses might increase modestly due to the need for higher levels of customer service in the stores. District managers might need to hire more staff. Staff might need training in how to consult with customers, explain current fashion trends, and gently help Stylists put together an outfit. But our estimates of increased revenues dwarfed these incremental costs.

Note that our team exhaustively pressure-tested our analyses regarding customer segmentation. If we were wrong on these assumptions, then the rest of the business case would collapse. Through the lens of alternative market segmentations based on demographics and geographies, we profiled competitor clothing collections and analyzed annual consumer clothing spending. We even imagined alternative futures, in which trends toward casual clothing would be reversed. Our main point was to keep asking how to constructively break down the market and how to locate Capri's sustainable competitive advantage.

Step 3: Estimate Financial Impact, Develop Alternative Scenarios, and Analyze Sensitivity and Risk

In addition to comparing potential revenues and costs, we needed to assess broader financial implications of our current recommendation, then reinforce or modify our argument.

The current storyline *situation* was abysmal: trying to be all things to all people, Capri designers and merchandisers had achieved the opposite effect. In the company's early years, when customers were asked to define Capri, they had immediately said words like *American, modern, friendly, confident,* and *simple*. Over the years Capri had built very strong brand awareness.

Now, in a single season, Capri might offer sexy beaded tops to Fashionistas, sweats to Apathetics, and khakis to the Stylists.

Hence the storyline *complication*: Capri's recent offerings had so confused customers that 40 percent were saying, "Capri is not for me." Through structured problem solving, we had exposed the confusion and, possibly, an opportunity for Capri's designers and merchandisers to focus on the Stylists.

The proposed *resolution* drew strength from the fact that the Stylists were not only the largest segment, but also one open to a loyal, profitable, long-term relationship if Capri provided a relaxed, confident, and effortless shopping experience. By focusing on essential clothing, Capri could earn a bigger share of the Stylists' wallet, while still (though not as a major focus) using its basic products and store experience to meet some needs of the other two segments. Capri would be hip, but not trendy; classic, but not stodgy. By adding a selection of accessories, Capri could also help customers infuse their wardrobes with their own personal touches.

Unfortunately, according to our financial impact analysis, the Stylist strategy would improve current profitability only a modest 20 percent. That represented profits in the tens of millions, but the business case was too weak to persuade Capri senior management to risk their cherished brand. It was even too weak to persuade some members of our team. So we devised and then modeled other scenarios, including a potential focus on the Apathetics or the Fashionistas, but each turned out inferior to the Stylist option on any number of financial measures.

Dismayed by the 20-percent prospect, we resolved to reexamine all of our assumptions—and found a simple but glaring mistake: our business case compared the Stylist option with *current* operational performance. But we had already agreed with Capri executives that current performance was likely unsustainable. Left unchecked, Capri's downward slide would continue. Retrieving our overlooked "as is" scenario, we projected Capri's future performance under the Stylist scenario compared with projections with no change of course. Extending five years, we found the Stylist solution a whopping 50 percent better. Moreover, since rank was such a central concern in the retail industry, we hoped this solution would return Capri to being number one.

Testing the sensitivities and risks of the business case here means understanding which three to five factors would need to go wrong to upset the invested capital needed or eliminate the returns. On which critical factors does the business case's probability of success depend? Our Capri business case, for instance, depended on no other competitor's muscling in on the Stylist segment. And future consumer apparel trends not turning toward more formal attire. And Capri's business model and profits not being wiped out by doubled store labor costs to serve the Stylists with additional frontline fashion advice. The strength of the business case depends on critical thinking regarding the risks and ways to mitigate those risks.

Step 4: Determine the Nonfinancial Impact

Our team now closely examined the nonfinancial benefits and costs. Capri executives were very concerned about factors beyond financials, such as customer satisfaction, the market's perception of their brand, and the morale of their hardworking designers, merchandisers, and store managers. We addressed each concern as systematically as we could, using surveys and focus groups to research potential customer reactions to the Stylist strategy.

Investigation into these nonfinancial aspects of the Stylist business case triggered two major concerns. First, would Capri possess the needed capabilities? If Capri did not possess them, how might they acquire them? A few years earlier, Capri executives had led the company into the higher-end, more tailored segment of the apparel market. But they had done so through a poorly integrated acquisition that left battle scars. Our business case would be severely criticized without credible alternatives as to how to bring the required design capabilities in-house.

Second, an effective business case describes what to do and, perhaps more important, what *not* to do. Capri had gotten into this mess by trying to address the sometimes incompatible fashion needs of all customers. Could we convince Capri executives to focus on the Stylists and walk away from the Fashionistas and Apathetics?

Step 5: Summarize and Communicate the Findings

Although controversial, our Stylist solution seemed straightforward. Capri should target the Stylist with the combined value proposition of good-quality clothing essentials and suitable service levels in the store. Our team members kept asking each other, "How wrong could we be? And how does that change the answer?" But we answered with increasing conviction that the financial and nonfinancial aspects of our business case were sound.

And so, with great confidence, we strode into the boardroom to deliver our recommendations. As usual, we had prepared a document based on the storyline. We had practiced our talking points and answers to expected questions.

Throughout the meeting, Capri designers and merchandisers looked distant, disinterested—even disappointed. Because we were discussing the potential salvation of Capri, we had expected the meeting to be interactive, even contentious, with Capri managers shouting questions, challenging findings, and—as usual with this creative, outspoken bunch—disagreeing among themselves. But when the meeting was all done, we were met with utter, deafening silence. Something had gone terribly wrong.

From Business Case to Decision: Failure at Capri?

Never forget that a good problem solver must also be a sensitive storyteller. In the rest of this chapter, we provide a few philosophical and practical guidelines on how to translate highly logical and analytical business cases into more persuasive communications. From what was—at the end of the meeting—a resounding failure, we can draw some lessons.

Societies are bound by stories they share. In many respects, language itself is the living, breathing chronicle of a culture's history, a society's thoughts and experiences. As the filmmaker Federico Fellini put it, "A different language is a different vision of life." In the business world, many leaders and scholars see shared narratives and language as the glue that binds employees to their company's mission.

In problem solving, stories can become the most powerful means of conveying information. We all still like a good story. The legendary marketing guru David Ogilvy once remarked, "Customers need a rational excuse to justify their emotional decisions, so always include one." He meant that emotion trumps reason and that we use rational arguments to justify what is frequently and primarily an emotional decision.

Certainly one must take into account both the rational and the emotional readiness to accept a portentous message. The Capri recommendations foreshadowed a great deal of change. No matter how compelling the data, a strong negative emotional reaction would probably sink our cause. Our presentation to the Capri senior team had failed at least in part because the emotional message was wrong.

The Gulf Between Business Analysts and Fashion Gurus

Back in our team room we sat, confused and scared by what had just transpired. We tried to make sense of Capri's reaction—or lack thereof.

"They didn't get it, you could tell," said Annie, the business analyst on our team.

We tried to schedule another meeting, confident that the next time we could explain more clearly. This was easier said than done. For the following two weeks Capri's senior managers kept their distance. The year's new fashion season was just starting, and designers and merchandisers were gazing into fashion's future, traveling the globe to runway shows. Attention had fled to the catwalks in Paris and Milan. Fashion Week in New York was nearly upon us. The situation seemed hopeless.

As always when confronted with a major challenge, our team returned to basic problem-solving principles. We attempted to understand and diagnose the problem. Clearly, Capri's managers understood their own place in the fashion universe. They were, for the most part, aspiring fashion gurus who had consummated their artistic impulses in a spate of quirky and eccentric creations—creations that had confused consumers about Capri's position in the market. And the designers were a tightly bonded group. They viewed the world through the lens of fashion and had lofty aspirations for their art.

In a brainstorming session, once again our youngest teammate, Annie, hit the bull's-eye, opining that Capri designers were themselves Fashionistas, happiest creating fashion for their fellow Fashionistas. Blindly, we had marched into the artists' boardroom, telling the gurus—the *garmentos*—that their future paychecks required them to design rather basic clothing for Stylists. We were so focused on the financial implications of the Stylist strategy that we had overlooked the fact that our recommendations amounted to designing plain vanilla clothes. Where was the inspiration in that? No wonder they had seemed so disappointed and unengaged. How could we hope to convince them to squander their talents on clothes for those unblessed with a sense of fashion? Their reaction? "What a bleak future!"

While contemplating the mismatch between our solution and the *garmentos'* catwalk dreams, we hit upon an idea: What if we held our own fashion show? Our team's analytical and data-driven business case had convinced us of the Stylist solution. But our business case communication had been all wrong for Capri. We had relied too heavily on the data's ability to persuade. Capri managers spoke a different language. My team of geeks had to learn to converse with the *garmentos* in a more appealing tongue.

In earlier meetings, Capri managers had commented on our team's fashion sense (or lack thereof). We five spanned all three customer segments. John was the Apathetic—great book inside a bland cover. Annie and Richard were our Fashionistas—seasoned experts on the latest trends from frequent forays to the mall. Nic and I were Stylists—neither hip nor trendy, mindful of our appearance but sparing no extra personal time for fashion. Perhaps our message would be best delivered as a story of five ordinary people with different attitudes about fashion.

"We're onto something here," I thought.

I called my thought partner and best friend among Capri's senior managers, the chief marketing officer. "What's your reaction to our organizing a fashion show?"

She wholeheartedly agreed and organized the meeting under her auspices, granting us that needed second chance. This time, no spreadsheets, analyses, charts. We were going to walk the catwalk to show them where Capri's economic future lay.

"Everyday Cool!"

For our fateful second chance, beyond creating our own fashion show and commentary, we also brought in several racks of clothing. To get the message, Capri's managers needed to identify for themselves which clothing categories should be a part of the future and which should not. Capri would no longer try to be all things to all people. It had to be clear about what it stood for: good-quality, essential, casual apparel for Stylists. So, for example, Capri needed to discontinue an Apathetics' favorite—comfortable 1950s Bermuda shorts. Capri might sell over $20 million of these shorts annually, but they would not be a part of its future.

Discontinuing clothing for the Fashionistas would be more painful, but out went the feather boas.

Although the fashion show was a much better way of communicating our recommendations, I still felt ourselves limping through the meeting. Until one Capri manager exclaimed, "Oh, I get it!"

We trembled in silence.

"You want us to do everyday cool!"

He had translated our stumbling attempts into something more comprehensible. And redefining an entire fashion category— "everyday cool"—was an aspiration most designers could rally around. True, some would never find it sufficiently inspirational; sadly, once Capri repositioned its brand, nearly half its designers did leave—one of the new strategy's nonfinancial impacts. But those who stayed are still going strong, designing for everyday cool.

A Tool and a Caution

This chapter introduced the business case—a powerful tool for testing, reinforcing, and communicating the hypothesis statement, storyline, and ultimate solution. Although business leaders can employ business cases to assess comprehensively and systematically and then convey the financial and nonfinancial implications of a recommendation, regrettably this happens less frequently than we care to admit. Often business case proposals are more revealing of the incomplete reasoning, inadequate assumption testing, and sloppy thinking of those who developed them.

Rigorous, meticulous, thorough are the watchwords of a compelling business case. Adopting exacting standards for investment, good management teams use business cases to check the underlying reasoning and analysis behind new ventures. Problem solvers should not underinvest in practicing the business case methodologies described in this chapter.

But all problem solvers also need to be sensitive to the ultimate decision makers' shared hopes, dreams, stories, and language—all of which affect the value of the business case approach. Gathering data, analyzing, calculating financial impact, developing scenarios, and assessing sensitivity and risk should help convince the *problem solver* of the solution, but they may not be the appropriate tools needed to persuade decision makers. Knowing how to craft and deliver a message is not enough by itself. Strong problem solvers also understand both the potential disruptions of change from the audience's perspective and how profoundly people's willingness to change can be affected by what they hear.

The Distance Between Business Case and Business Decisions

Yvonne Hao
Former VP Global Marketing, Honeywell Security
Executive Vice-President, Bain Capital

I joined Honeywell after spending many years as a management consultant, developing strategies for corporate clients. Although well versed in market sizing, customer segmentation, analytical frameworks, spreadsheets, and PowerPoint presentations, I was not prepared for the distance between business case and business decision.

Honeywell Security is a multi-billion-dollar business within Honeywell's overall approximately $35-billion portfolio. It is one of Honeywell's faster growing businesses, both organically and through acquisitions. As a leading manufacturer and distributor of security products such as intrusion alarm systems, CCTV video surveillance, and access control for homes, commercial buildings, industrial sites, and government projects, we aggressively focus on customers, sales, growth, intelligent risk-taking, and results.

When I joined this entrepreneurial division from outside the industry, my initial responsibilities included leading business managers in the development of a five-year strategic plan. Although most of our current customers were in the United States, market research, customer analyses, and competitor profiling revealed a startling fact: the Asia Pacific region—in particular, China—offered the fastest-growing security opportunity. This should have been no surprise, given China's massive infrastructure investments, such as more than forty new airports needing security systems.

However, with a limited presence in China, we were not set up for success. Based in Australia, our general manager visited infrequently and our main salesperson spoke only Cantonese, creating challenges in communicating with the rapidly growing population of Mandarin-speaking customers in mainland China.

So, with my consulting background, I developed a convincing, nearly obvious, business case for expansion into China. Confidently, I marched into my boss's office, expecting him to agree and to start making decisions quickly.

His reaction? "We've lost money in China before, it's all cheap and knocked off . . . Our strengths are knowing our customers and our markets, and that's in the U.S. . . . . China's a distraction; the majority of our profit is here."

I was shocked, of course. I respected my boss tremendously—he is extremely smart, knows the industry better than anyone [else], and has decades of business experience and success. So I started investigating the business case further—and realized that he was right. We had lost money in China—primarily because of intellectual property issues and local competitors copying our products. And in the United States our success was a direct result of tight personal relationships with our customers. Additionally, we were integrating several acquisitions in the United States, and our focus there was critical to overall growth.

Yet, having thoroughly studied all the facts, data, and evidence behind our business case, I emphatically believed in China's potential. If we didn't move, our competitors would. How could I convince my boss and make the strategic shift?

I got more data from more sources, more case studies—and every time, my boss was polite, but no shift to China. My instinct was to keep showing him the data, hoping it would eventually get him to reconsider, but it was becoming clear that path would not work.

The turning point for me was realizing that where my boss came from directly affected his decisions. Our backgrounds could not be more different. He had started as a salesman going door to door, working his way up the ranks. He is a quick decision maker, using instinct, judgment, *and* facts. So I asked when he had last visited China. Many, many times, he replied. As one of the first American businessmen in China, he had established a factory in Shenzhen in the 1980s, but had not returned in years. Now I understood better where he was coming from. I asked him to do me one favor: make a trip to Shanghai and Beijing. He was skeptical, but agreed.

On the trip, China's remarkable transformation invigorated him: the skyline of Shanghai skyscrapers, the modern airports and hotels, the vast highways and bridges—and most of all, the thriving energy of a country coming to life with capitalism. As an entrepreneur, he loved it and could feel the opportunity.

From that point, it's been easier. We hired a very strong Mandarin speaker to build our Asia Pacific business. We moved our headquarters from Australia to Shanghai. We built the business from virtually no employees to more than three hundred professionals based in China, including the local engineers in our recently launched research center. As a consequence, our business now is profitable and one of the fastest-growing in our portfolio. With many big wins, including airports and large infrastructure projects, we are a recognized leader in security and public safety in China.

However, the biggest thrill for me, personally, is that my boss travels to China several times a year, telling everyone it's his favorite place to go. He tirelessly promotes our local business, with numerous media interviews, customer dinners, and government meetings. Every time he goes, he returns wanting to invest more. He even knows a few words in Mandarin!

The research, analysis, spreadsheets, and graphs behind business cases are relatively easy. The real challenge in making a solid business case persuasive comes in understanding the obstacles for key decision makers and what will help them overcome these and act. In more cases than not, getting minds changed and decisions made depends on factors beyond just numbers. Rather, it is often about the organization, the people, and the implications across the entire business. The good news is, once you determine what really matters, you can work to influence the decision, and then quickly execute—bridging the distance from business case to business decision—as we have in Honeywell Security.

Chapter 8

WHEN GOOD ENOUGH IS BOTH

To Buy or Not to Buy?

Thousands of flying carrots. In the cavernous Las Vegas convention hall, I was watching a huge machine separate edible carrots from rotten ones. The food processors' trade show was abuzz about this breakthrough technology that could relegate manual sorting to history. I stood mesmerized in front of the 40-by-60-by-100-foot piece of equipment. Good carrots and rotten debris streamed in from the left on a conveyor belt. The machine photographed, recognized, and then separated good carrots from decayed ones based on discoloration and ejected the debris with well-timed air jets that flung them into the air.

A small start-up company in Green Bay, Wisconsin, had developed this prototype sorter by combining innovations in material handling, photography, recognition algorithms, and ejection mechanisms. Now the senior management of the global Food Processing Equipment Company (FPE) hoped to purchase not just one or two automated sorters, but the entire Green Bay Sorting Company (Green Bay). After extensive negotiations, the Green Bay founders finally agreed to consider selling their company—and were asking for $20 million. My team was given ten weeks to determine whether this deal was a good one for FPE.

Intelligent Trade-offs Between Analysis and Action

This chapter should help you better decide how much time to dedicate to analysis in solving a problem and, perhaps more important, when to move to action. It builds on the previous chapter's discussion of how business cases can help examine and test a proposed solution from multiple angles.

The chapter describes a framework for deciding intelligently about trade-offs between analysis and action. By intelligent trade-offs, we mean the necessary and difficult compromises of giving up one set of activities, such as continuing analysis, in exchange for another set of activities whose implications may not be perfectly foreseen. Such trade-offs frequently involve choices between the speed of execution (or even the threat of losing the opportunity) and the accuracy of the proposed solution. They also include the more familiar choices between resources, timing, return, and risk.

As we described more fully in Chapter Seven, continuing to gather data and conduct analyses feels safe. But continuing to analyze also entails ever-increasing costs. The general manager must decide whether the incremental costs of continuing analysis do or do not outweigh the incremental benefits of an ever-more-precise solution. This trade-off may feel like comparing apples and oranges: comparing the theoretical incremental accuracy of the solution with the out-of-pocket resource costs and lost-opportunity costs of continuing the search for a better solution. If the costs outweigh potential benefits, it is time to move on to action. The trick is to recognize and seize the moment.

We want to enhance your innate sense of when "good enough" is both good and enough. You may think this is not such a big problem. But consider the manager who always works his or her project team toward the perfect "100 percent" solution. Solutions and the time to arrive at them are almost always inversely related: 80 percent of the time will be spent discovering or refining the final 20 percent of the solution. What might the project team have discovered in other areas of exploration had their manager been content with the 99-percent optimal solution, instead of 100 percent? What about the 95-percent solution? And so on. In the meantime, what other opportunities has the business missed? Good general managers learn to know intuitively where to draw the line. This chapter proposes guidelines that can speed your learning process.

A problem's complexity and uncertainty usually drive these trade-offs. Problem solvers should examine the opportunity cost of continued analysis, the decision's potential impact, and the reasonableness of the proposed recommendation based on industry and other experience. We also encourage them to cultivate the necessary courage to make such decisions. In this chapter, we discuss methods for making such informed judgments, which can often increase problem solvers' comfort with making them. Before discussing guidelines, we detour briefly into economics for some useful grounding.

Marginal Returns

Our approach to "good enough" rests on the idea that incremental analysis may yield incremental insight, which borrows directly from the economics concept of marginal utility. The primary purpose of "the dismal science" is to solve for the problem of *scarcity;* that is, the fulfilling of people's limitless desires with limited resources. The analogy here is to obtain the most accurate solution with limited problem-solving resources. Due to fundamental constraints on their resources, economies can maximize utility only by allocating resources as efficiently as possible. Due to similar constraints on resources, problem solvers also need to allocate resources well to maximize accuracy in the solution.

Utility is a fundamental concept of the laws of supply and demand. It designates the benefit or satisfaction a person receives from consuming a particular good or service. Economic utility is a rather abstract concept; the same is often true of *accuracy* in problem solving. That being said, *total utility* can usefully be thought of as the aggregate sum of benefits a person gains from the consumption of goods and services. Total utility corresponds to the level of total consumption. Usually, the more a person consumes, the more benefits the person receives and, consequently, the larger his or her total utility (satisfaction) will be.

Marginal utility is the additional benefit that a person gains with each extra amount of consumption. Although someone's overall feelings of satisfaction, or utility, may increase as the person consumes more and more, the incremental amount of benefit or utility of each incremental good consumed usually decreases. The decrease obeys the law of diminishing marginal utility: total utility increases at a slower rate with each incremental product or service consumed. People usually have a certain threshold of satisfaction; once that threshold is crossed, they no longer gain the same pleasure from consumption.

Employing these economic concepts as metaphors, problem solving closely replicates the marginal utility curve, progressing left to right on the graph in Figure 8.1: moving from

Figure 8.1. The Problem-Solving Journey: Incremental Analysis Yields Incremental Insights

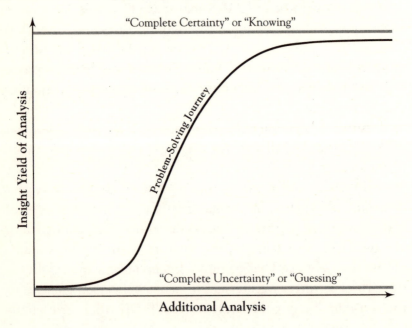

complete uncertainty to complete certainty. In layman's terms, complete uncertainty is *guessing*. At the beginning of most problem-solving efforts, the team may have little expertise in the business issue and may have gathered little data or conducted few analyses. Hypothesizing a Week One Answer requires some informed guessing. Complete certainty amounts to *knowing*. At this point, the solution rests on extensive research, experience, and analysis.

Problem-solving individuals or teams need to determine where they need to be on this curve in order to move forward. They should choose a position on the metaphorical curve that enables them to make the best decisions, given the opportunity costs inherent in more analytical work. One thing is clear: continued analysis is not costless. It incurs costs in the direct expenditure of resources and the loss of opportunities for doing something else. Another thing is also clear: no business decision should be made at either end of the spectrum. For instance, when confronted with a difficult problem, one must move away from merely guessing toward more knowing. Through creativity and well-structured analytical work, one needs to gain enough insight to make an informed decision. The tough question is how to avoid "analysis paralysis"—endless analysis.

Statistics and operations researchers define this as an issue of identifying the *optimal stopping rules*. General managers must choose the optimal time to make a decision so that they maximize expected payoffs and minimize expected costs associated with incremental activities. Many use sequentially observed variables to do this. Anyone who has interviewed for a new job or sold a house can relate to this problem. For a house on the market, the different purchase offers and their associated costs and timing are examples of sequentially observed variables. For instance, offers for your house may come in daily, weekly, or monthly, or even unpredictably. Each offer has a cost associated with it, such as an assessment cost or the continued cost of living in the house. When you receive an offer, you must then decide whether to accept it or to wait for a better offer. The trade-off question you face is this: you are nearly certain that a better offer will eventually come, but will the difference in the two offers compensate for the increased costs of waiting for it? For those who wish to explore more economics, statistics, and the theory of optimal stopping, we have provided an endnote of additional research.[1]

Weighing Incremental Analysis Against Incremental Insight Yield

In problem solving one must move from uncertainty to certainty, although one never truly starts at one end or reaches the other, as shown in Figure 8.2. Three stages of the journey are (1) the beginning, when the problem-solving team is learning a great deal; we call this stage "Increasing Marginal Returns

Figure 8.2. Increasing, Constant, and Diminishing Marginal Returns on Analysis

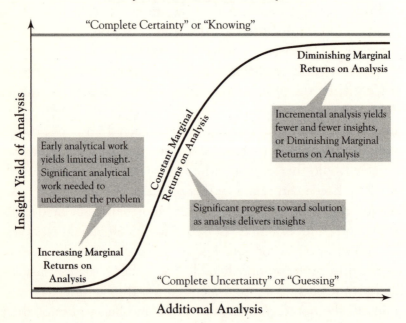

on Analysis"; (2) the longest portion of problem-solving time, which we call "Constant Marginal Returns on Analysis"; and (3) the last stage, when care must be taken not to waste time on additional analyses; we call this stage "Diminishing Marginal Returns on Analysis."

Stage One: Increasing Marginal Returns on Analysis. When a problem-solving effort gets under way, certain amounts of data collection and analysis are needed simply to understand the context, diagnose the problem, and agree on a hypothesis statement. Activities during this stage include data gathering, interviewing, industry assessment, customer and competition profiling, and economic analysis. This initial work helps to develop a quick working hypothesis. Figure 8.2 shows how getting started on the analysis provides slow but increasing marginal returns of insights into the problem.

Stage Two: Constant Marginal Returns on Analysis. Having completed the foundational research, an individual problem solver or team starts to prove the working hypothesis or change it to fit the emerging data. Figure 8.2 also illustrates how the analyses continue to yield insights and provide constant, relatively plentiful marginal returns, thereby yielding the greatest absolute returns. This stage most likely unearths the evidence that leads to the ultimate recommendations. The speed and duration of this stage depend on the uncertainty and riskiness of the problem.

Problems vary, so it is difficult to prescribe which analyses to conduct in Stage Two. But our experience suggests some common topics, listed here and displayed in another form in Figure 8.3, which encompasses more than just Stage Two.

- **Market:** Size in units and prices, drivers of future growth, and overall profitability
- **Customers:** Segmentation, key buying criteria, and purchasing processes that may explain market share shifts

among competitors, and other substitutes or alternatives that address customer needs

- **The company and its competitors:** Descriptions of privileged assets, capabilities, and relationships that underpin sustainable competitive advantage or lack thereof; also the structure, conduct, and performance of industry competitors

- **Environment:** Regulatory, technological, consumer behavior and other changes that may directly impact the market

- **Opportunities:** Value creation through focus on customers, products, and services, as well as pricing and business models that capture value

- **Key success factors:** In-depth understanding of the investments, resources, and skills and capabilities needed to capture the value

- **Potential initiatives and returns:** Economic breakeven, net present value, as well as strategic, operational, and organizational risks

Figure 8.3. Basic Questions to Address in the Problem-Solving Process

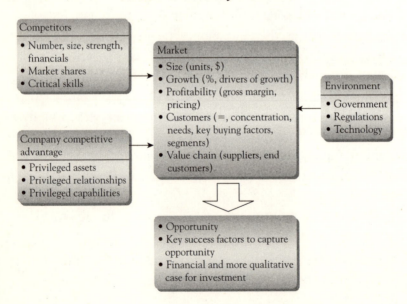

Stage Three: Diminishing Marginal Returns on Analysis.
At some point the marginal returns from the analysis start to
diminish. In other words, the incremental insights decrease,
as shown in Figure 8.2. Additional analyses no longer greatly
change the proposed solution.

At this point it is critical to place the problem-solving effort in
a broader perspective, being sure to include constraints. Ongoing
analyses conducted by limited resources carry their own opportunity
costs in terms of forgone opportunities. The general manager needs
to recognize the point of diminishing marginal returns and make an
intelligent trade-off between the enhanced certainty represented by
additional analyses and the associated forgone opportunity costs.
As mentioned earlier, this trade-off may feel like comparing the
proverbial apples and oranges—an improved decision versus some
additional costs. The general manager must be ever mindful of
the direct and indirect costs of missed opportunities when deciding
whether or not to continue to refine the proposed solution.

The rest of this chapter deals with guidelines for developing
one's intuitive sense for when a problem-solving effort has hit the
point of diminishing marginal returns. We discuss ways to recognize this point in your work, such as questions to ask and dan-
ger signals to watch out for. We demonstrate the guidelines first
through the FPE case, illustrating how, under difficult conditions,
our team evaluated the trade-off between further analysis and
moving to action; we then summarize them in general terms.

FPE and the Green Bay Sorter

And so we return to our tale of the flying carrots. You'll recall
that the senior management of the Food Processing Equipment
Company (FPE) hoped to purchase the entire Green Bay
Sorting Company (Green Bay). After extensive negotiations,
the Green Bay founders had offered to sell their company for
$20 million. My team had ten weeks to determine whether this
deal was good for FPE.

Background on the Food Processing Industry

The food processing equipment industry consists of three global competitors and a fragmented multitude of regional and local ones. As one of the three globals, FPE designed, manufactured, and provided after-sales service to a host of international, regional, and local customers, including Conagra, General Mills, Nestlé, and McCain Potatoes. These customers used FPE equipment in their regional plants to process raw vegetables purchased from local farmers. The companies then sold the frozen or canned vegetables to retailers such as Albertson's, Tesco's, and McDonald's. The long industry supply chain culminated with retailers selling these vegetables to consumers for their dinner tables.

Even though FPE's superior design of conveyor belts, freezers, fryers, and packaging lines had made it an industry leader, FPE had not been able to create an automated sorting machine. But its customers increasingly wanted a completely automated vegetable processing line, so the lack of an automatic sorter left a huge gap in FPE's product portfolio.

To the best of our team's knowledge, Green Bay had placed only four of its sorter prototypes in vegetable processing plants in the Midwest. It charged approximately $250,000 per sorter, which, minus direct material and labor costs, earned it an approximately 50-percent gross margin on each machine. Because the average gross margins of freezers, fryers, and conveyor belts were 25 percent to 35 percent, the Green Bay sorter gross margins were very attractive.

Developing the Hypothesis Statement

As I stood before the sorter prototype, all I could think was, "I do not know anything about processed carrots except that my grandmother liked cooking them for Sunday dinner and I liked eating them. And that my team has ten weeks."

In line with the problem-solving process outlined in Part One, our team began by hypothesizing our Week One Answer—that

FPE should enter the sorter market through an acquisition of Green Bay only if it could answer the following questions in a positive manner:

- Was the sorter market large, growing, and attractive?
- Did the Green Bay sorter represent—to the best of our assessment—the optimal technology?
- If we made reasonable assumptions about risk and return, did the sorter opportunity justify the proposed acquisition price of $20 million?

The combination of these questions became our hypothesis statement. Figure 8.4 expands the hypothesis into a basic issue tree, identifying a number of the jugular issues.

Stage One: Early Research (Increasing Marginal Returns on Analysis)

At first, we had trouble even comprehending how the sorter worked, let alone its current and potential applications. It turned out that by modifying the computer algorithms based on color, the Green Bay sorter could differentiate not only good

Figure 8.4. Issue Tree for FPE-Green Bay Sorter Case

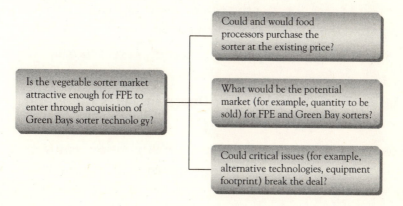

carrots, but also other good vegetables of similar weight—such as peas, corn, and beans—from debris or rotten vegetables. With changes to the conveyor belt and ejection jets, the sorter could be made to handle heavier vegetables such as potatoes. Further, as-yet-untested modifications might enable the Green Bay technology to sort sturdy fruits such as apples, oranges, and grapefruit. Changes to its material-handling aspects could extend it to more delicate fruits and vegetables such as pears and tomatoes, as long as the cameras could detect some level of discoloration. After an initial examination, we concluded that the sorter had a myriad of potential applications.

Each succeeding day our team learned more and more. FPE's marketing, sales, and service managers explained, in rather rudimentary terms, their understanding of the potential sorter market, based on research on overall equipment sales in dollars and units, FPE's own gross margins, its long-standing customers' needs, and their purchasing processes. Nevertheless, we still lacked adequate evidence to support or contradict our working hypotheses. As shown in Figure 8.5, our team was squarely in the first stage of the problem-solving curve, experiencing increasing marginal returns of insight based on our initial analyses.

After about a week, we brainstormed with FPE executives about potential deal-breaking issues. What risk or challenge could derail the entire potential acquisition? For example, we asked,

- Can and will food processors adopt this new technology?
- Is the overall size of the potential sorting market sufficiently attractive for FPE and Green Bay?
- Can alternative superior technologies enter this market?

Stage Two: Developing In-Depth Insights (Constant Marginal Returns on Analysis)

As expected, we analyzed and analyzed. And we constantly gained new insights. Our team process started with the fundamental

Figure 8.5. Marginal Returns on Analysis for FPE-Green Bay Sorter Case

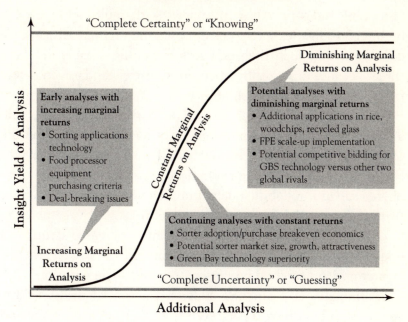

question of how attractive the market for sorters could be. Would food processors even purchase the new Green Bay sorter? To find out, we analyzed customer economics and profiled the introduction of other technologies into the food processing industry. Our numerous interviews with food processors in North America and Europe revealed critical purchase criteria: a new piece of equipment had to first reach thresholds of reliability, safety, and defect rate. Then any new piece of equipment had to fit into existing production lines, as major changes would be too costly. After that, the purchase decision was based strictly on economics. Equipment decisions were primarily left up to the individual plant manager. They would compare the payback on the equipment, calculated over the industry average of seven years, to the next best alternative—in this case, wages paid to seasonal manual sorters. Figure 8.5 summarizes the progress on the entire FPE–Green Bay sorter project.

We also examined the issue of whether superior sorting machines from other industries might migrate into the food processing industry. After interviews with multiple experts in high-tech industries such as electronics and pharmaceuticals, we concluded that such high-end sorters would probably not be a threat because of vast differences in industry standards in defect rate specifications and profitability.

A quick walk through several food processing plants and a study of the engineering plans of others confirmed that the Green Bay sorter could be retrofitted into existing food processing lines without major additional costs. Indeed, the sorter offered superior reliability, defect rates, and space usage over the twenty agricultural workers who currently sorted vegetables in most plants. In addition, the government's increased scrutiny of migrant agricultural laborers would, if anything, provide an even greater impetus for food processors to invest in automation.

Although our team had addressed potential deal-breaking issues, we did not have a perspective on the total market size and the possible technology adoption rate. We solved the adoption question fairly quickly. During harvest season, food-processing plants ran around the clock, seven days per week, to prevent vegetable spoilage. On average, each processing line required twenty employees for sorting. Given the required payback of less than seven years, an average harvest time of a hundred days, and the current sorter price of $250,000, the breakeven wage was about $1 per hour. Then-current agricultural wage rates around the world certainly made investing in a sorter financially viable—and, indeed, attractive in higher-wage areas like North America and Western Europe. By contrast, sorting technology might not make financial sense in Latin America or in Asia outside Japan. In sum, our analysis indicated that North American and European food processors would be inclined to invest in sorters.

But our current state of knowledge was not yet "good enough" to make a recommendation regarding FPE's possible acquisition of Green Bay. We still had too many outstanding issues that could swing the conclusion toward buying or not buying the company. More specifically, we still needed to determine the overall sorter market size and attractiveness, which proved much more difficult. At first, our team tried to estimate the worldwide number of food processing lines because, at one sorter per line, the number of processing lines should approximate the number of required sorters. The analysis seemed straightforward. We planned to combine market research regarding the number of food processors and the number of plants each processor ran with assumptions about plant capacity, and hence estimate the number of lines within plants. The resulting number of lines would be our market estimate for potential sorter sales.

But our team could not obtain the necessary data because much of the capacity in the extremely fragmented market for vegetable processing was still privately held. In addition, plant sizes varied significantly. We had to find an alternative that would give us a more accurate result. After all, FPE executives were trying to determine whether $20 million for Green Bay Sorting was a prudent investment.

After many abortive attempts, our team hit on an idea: maybe we could estimate the total market from the sorter capacity and total tonnage of processed vegetables. This insight was based on the operational assumption that to avoid bottlenecks at a plant the sorter must work at the same speed and capacity as the rest of the food processing line.

We gathered what we knew already. Processing twenty tons of vegetables per hour per line was the industry standard. The Food and Agricultural Organization in Rome provided the total tonnage of processed vegetables by type of vegetable and country of origin. Customer interviews indicated the number of days of harvesting and processing per year per type of vegetable. Potato chip and french fry operations harvested and processed potatoes far longer during the year; in contrast, peas, corn, and beans had a much shorter harvest and processing season. Plants processed vegetables close to the fields, because delivery costs prevented the shipment of unprocessed vegetables over great distances. Our calculations revealed that the total market for sorters could go well into the thousands, about half of them needed in high-wage countries. Once again, creativity and persistence overcame theoretical and empirical challenges.

At the current price for sorters of $250,000, the potential unit demand translated into billions of dollars. Given the opportunity to replace manual labor, adoption of the technology was expected to be rapid. After initial adoption, the market was expected to revert back to a seven-year replacement cycle. And we knew that sorter sales gross margins could be on the order of 50 percent.

Our next question was whether the FPE–Green Bay combination could capture the lion's share of this large potential market. Customer interviews indicated that reliability, defect rates, and economic returns would drive the purchase decision and, thus, market share. Green Bay faced two small, regional, focused competitors—one Dutch, one Belgian—that had sorting technology still in development. Studying their prototypes, our FPE engineering teammates concluded that Green Bay's was a superior sorter because it had benefited from breakthroughs in material handling and ejection mechanisms.

The Green Bay technology did not necessarily represent a *sustainable* competitive advantage, because other competitors might overcome its intellectual property defenses by backward-engineering around Green Bay's patents on material handling and ejection jets. But these innovations did bestow competitive advantage for a period of time that FPE and Green Bay together could exploit in the global race to automate sorting. Furthermore, the two competitors were small, independent, and had limited sales and service infrastructure that reached only food processors in their immediate vicinity. FPE could reach around the globe in commercializing the Green Bay sorter technology. Figure 8.6 outlines the more comprehensive issue tree and problem-solving effort.

Figure 8.6. FPE-Green Bay Sorter Case: Issue Tree

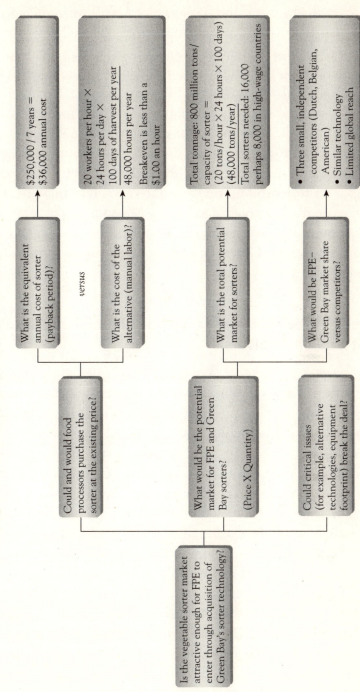

Six weeks into the project, and still gaining constant marginal returns of insights from all of our analyses, our team began to draw some tentative conclusions. Under almost all sets of assumptions, the potential sorter market was sufficiently large to warrant FPE's investment. Moreover, Green Bay might not have priced the sorter appropriately. Once FPE owned the technology, it might raise the sorter prices to reflect its value to the customer more closely. With the sorter's current price around $250,000, the payback period for such an investment was just over a year, depending on wage rates, whereas most food processors normally would accept a seven-year payback on their investment. Figure 8.7 summarizes our team's recommendations to FPE: purchase Green Bay and its technology at the negotiated price. And buy it fast!

Stage Three: Optimal Stopping (Diminishing Marginal Returns on Analysis)

Our team still had four weeks until our original deadline and a number of outstanding questions, including additional sorter applications and acquisition integration. With engineering modifications, the machine could potentially sort other products such as rice, woodchips, and recycled glass. For implementation, FPE would need to scale up sorter production in its existing operations, as the potential Green Bay acquisition did not include scaleable manufacturing facilities. As with any acquisition, there would be execution challenges associated with merging the organizations, harmonizing processes and technology, and retaining the best talent.

Despite still having four more weeks, our team had two main reasons to conclude that we had reached a point of diminishing marginal returns (as shown in Figure 8.5). First, uncovering sorting opportunities for other products would simply improve the economics of the acquisition, which were already positive. Second, given FPE's good record with acquisitions, FPE could,

Figure 8.7. Overview for FPE Entrance into the Vegetable Sorter Market

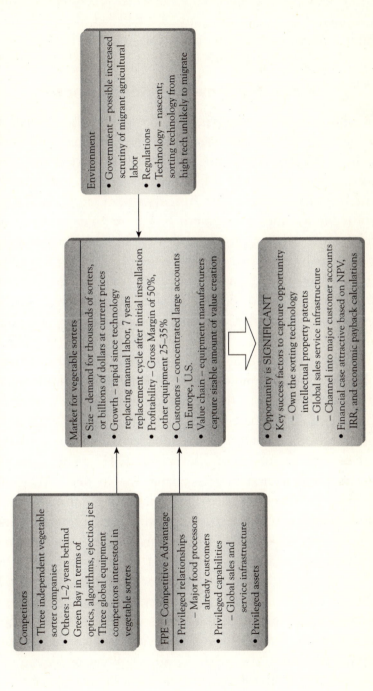

in all likelihood, employ its established processes to assimilate the small Green Bay company. We decided to present our recommendations to FPE's senior management without delay.

Yes, But How Do I Really Know?

We hope this case gives you a better feel for the types of trade-offs that a general manager or problem-solving team needs to make between continuing analytical activities and moving toward action. The key at FPE was our ability to recognize when the marginal returns—or insights—from additional analyses started to decline. We certainly had more time: an entire month left in the original schedule. We could have completed additional analyses to gain greater certainty regarding the potential market, customers, competitors, and environment. Indeed, we had even generated ideas as to what those analyses might be: estimating the market for sorters in other applications such as rice or developing the scale-up manufacturing plan for FPE.

So with more time left for the project and more analyses already planned, how did our team decide to stop early? How did we instead get to the decision to present our recommendation that FPE purchase Green Bay without delay? We placed our problem-solving efforts in the broader context and asked ourselves, "How wrong could we be?" and "How might the results of these incremental analyses change the answer?" Some unforeseen critical issues might still derail our recommendations, but up to that point, in extensive discussions with potential customers, industry experts, and FPE executives, we had uncovered no such deal-breaking issues. Nor had we unearthed other issues that might shift our positive assessment of the acquisition. If we decided to continue to analyze the situation and its issues—for example, with further customer interviews or with an analysis of the next generation of sorter applications—we would probably simply confirm further what we already knew about the market opportunity. If anything, we would most likely make the already large and attractive market even larger and more attractive. FPE's history of successful acquisitions and launches of other innovative new food processing technologies led us to believe that it could succeed again.

Moreover, there was a great opportunity cost to spending further time analyzing the recommendation. FPE and Green Bay had signed an exclusive negotiating agreement for a certain period of time. Once that agreement expired, Green Bay could have auctioned off the sorting technology. To the best of our knowledge, FPE's two global rivals were unaware of Green Bay's potential sale. However, if they entered the fray, the ultimate price that FPE paid for the sorting technology could increase. Alternatively, FPE might even lose Green Bay to a higher bidder and suffer the negative consequences.

A simple thought experiment can further clarify these guidelines on stopping analysis and moving to action. Let us take two challenges that could emerge after FPE acquired Green Bay: first, introducing Six Sigma processes into sorter manufacturing to drive out unwanted variations; second, using its complete portfolio of food processing equipment to diversify beyond equipment to actual food processing. The problem's complexity or uncertainty has a significant effect on when problem solvers will experience diminishing marginal returns on the effort. The more uncertain and risky the issue, the longer it may be before reaching that point. Figure 8.8 modifies the margin curve to reflect each challenge for FPE. Because FPE engineers had extensive experience with Six Sigma processes, their department would not need much effort to apply this process once more, to sorter manufacturing. In Figure 8.8, the curve shifts to the left because the engineers would be working on a problem with greater certainty and less risk.

However, FPE's expansion beyond its core business of equipment design, manufacturing, and service to become an actual food processor would represent a fundamental change in its strategy and business model, and hence a highly uncertain,

Figure 8.8. Problem Solving Under Greater or Less Uncertainty

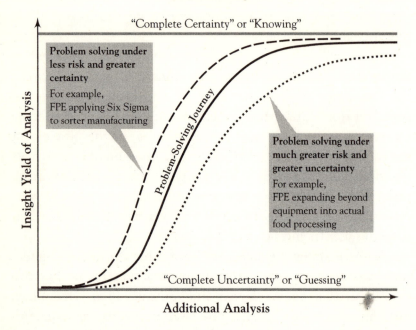

risky move. Changing a company's core focus should never be taken lightly. FPE's equipment design and manufacturing and its global reach in terms of sales and service infrastructure underpinned its current competitive advantage. To move from there into actual food *processing*, FPE would need to build additional and different core capabilities, such as merchandising and consumer marketing. Such a decision would have to be based on much greater analysis regarding the potential resources required, risk, and returns. Again, Figure 8.8 plots the effect on the marginal analysis-insight curve.

Persevering Through the "Wallow Curve," and Other Advice

A few words of caution based on experience. Throughout Parts One and Two, we have presented the problem-solving framework as a journey from uncertainty to solution. We have argued that success rests on disciplined habits of mind in probing a problem from numerous angles, deductive logic to determine a hypothesis of the solution, fact-based inquiry, and pressure-testing of assumptions. But success also rests on persevering in the process, because the problem-solving journey is never linear. In fact, along the way you will inevitably encounter what we call "the wallow curve," a period in which you and your colleagues will despair of arriving at any answer. Trusting the problem-solving process as outlined here is essential, yet it can also be very difficult to do if one has not had practice. Our advice is to trust it, tough it out once or twice, and then know that it will get easier with experience.

Having toughed out the process and arrived at a compellingly evidenced solution, you may still encounter another common problem. The boss dithers away by asking for more analysis, which you perceive as unnecessary. Or a powerful internal opponent to your recommendation stalls the decision by requesting the same. Given how common this problem remains in corporate life, we offer a few tactics for handling your response. First and foremost, the solution must succeed against your own very exacting standards of scrutiny. Once the business case is bulletproof, carefully place the proposal in the broadest possible business context. Then characterize the (negative) consequences of not making a decision. Courage and integrity are the necessary ingredients in mounting an effective response to such opposition.

Although this chapter has frequently focused on speed and timing, the decision to move to action rests chiefly on the magnitude of impact and some judgment of the intuitive reasonableness of the recommendation. The greater the financial risks and other resource investments required for implementing the solution, the greater the analytical certainty required. Furthermore, the test for the reasonableness of the recommendation is a practical one, based primarily on industry and other experience. With regard to FPE's potential entry into the sorter market, the verdict on the acquisition would still be positive even if our team had been 10 percent, 20 percent, even 50 percent off in its estimates of either potential market size or breakeven economics for the food processor or the competitive advantage of Green Bay's technology. Prudent managers never settle for inadequate answers. As with breaking the problem wide open, knowing when to stop is—by its nature—an art.

We end this chapter with an instructive case in which the general manager tried his best to solve the challenges facing his international organization, and kept on trying, long beyond the point when judgment would indicate that good enough was indeed good enough. He has generously shared his experience of what was, in the end, a heartfelt failure, as well as the lessons he learned from it, in the hope that readers may be better attuned to the "good enough" indicators in their own problem-solving efforts.

The Changing Dynamics of a Strategic Alliance

Dr. Abraham F. Lowenthal
The Robert F. Erburu Professor of Ethics, Globalization and Development
University of Southern California

By the late twentieth century, the West Coast had emerged as a substantial center of demographic, economic, political, techno-logical, and cultural power. Given the West Coast's importance, it seemed time for an independent nonpartisan leadership forum on international policy to develop in California, the largest pop-ulation center on the Pacific Coast. Such organizations had been established on the Atlantic Coast of the United States right after World War I and had quickly become important as sources of insight and centers for exchanging ideas and information and for informing decision makers and opinion shapers. So much of this country's role in the world involves West Coast firms, nongov-ernmental organizations, and citizens that it was anachronistic to think that the "national interest" of the United States could still be defined in the Boston–New York–Washington corridor, without perspectives and participation from California and the other western states. This concept motivated a group of leaders from the West Coast to launch a new international policy organization in the mid-1990s.

Those who founded the new forum faced an immediate strategic decision: how to relate to a very well-established national foreign policy organization, based in New York, with some members and programs on the West Coast, and long-announced aspirations to grow in both respects. The new forum's initial core group included several people who, as members of the national organization's board or on its behalf, had earlier endeavored without much success to develop a strong western presence for the New York entity.

The founding core group saw three options: to compete with the national organization explicitly on the basis of our West Coast roots, to suggest to the national entity that we become a regional subsidiary, or to incorporate independently while seeking close cooperation with the New York organization. After careful reflection, we decided to establish an independent entity but also to propose a unique strategic alliance with the national forum. We understood that at first we would gain more from such an alliance than we could offer: instant prestige branding by association and immediate access to the national organization's western members, in exchange for our promise to provide augmented programming for this membership and to help identify additional national membership prospects. But we were also conscious that the New York organization's western members had been complaining about infrequent programs—some were even resigning as a result—yet the New York forum's management appeared unlikely to invest the substantial resources that would be required to build a strong regional presence. We suggested that it would be far more effective for a West Coast–based organization to import the national organization's products and personnel than for the New York entity to continue to rely on somewhat anemic outreach. The argument resonated with those in New York best informed about the West Coast.

The New York organization's management and board and the steering committee of the new West Coast entity in gestation soon agreed on the following:

- The new forum should be "established in cooperation" with the New York organization.
- Acknowledgment of this link would be made on the new entity's letterhead, at all of its meetings, and in the New York organization's and the new entity's annual reports.
- All members of the New York organization residing in the West would be offered immediate membership in the western forum without paying any additional dues.
- The New York organization would share with the new West Coast center the dues it collected from such joint members, thus providing revenue—at first amounting to nearly 10 percent of the new organization's budget—for the enhanced programming.

It was also agreed that the New York organization would be represented on the new forum's Board, and that I, as the new organization's president, would become a vice president of the New York organization and regularly attend its board meetings.

However, what began as a carefully constructed and very promising strategic alliance, mutually crafted to meet each organization's needs, turned out over time to be difficult to manage and sustain. Different opinions emerged within the national organization's staff and board about the convenience of close association with the fledgling enterprise. Some argued that the senior organization was not receiving sufficient recognition for its role;

others reported that its West Coast members were enthusiastic about the alliance and wanted it strengthened. Some operational problems emerged while I was on a sabbatical in 1999–2000, leading to questions about the new forum's dependence on its founding president, and concerns arose in New York about being linked to a possibly weak offshoot that might not survive. At this stage, a member of both organizations' boards persuaded his colleagues in New York to (1) invest in enhancing the strategic cooperation, (2) redesignate it as a "partnership," (3) secure the New York organization's further help in strengthening and solidifying the new West Coast effort, and (4) work out the details for ensuring adequate ongoing credit for the national organization's growing contribution.

During the succeeding years, as both organizations expanded, their respective capacities to deliver value to their members were rapidly enhanced. The West Coast forum, from its incipient concept, grew steadily in membership, numbers and quality of programs, budget and staff capacity, and institutional solidity. Meanwhile, however, the New York organization, already well established, very significantly further enlarged its budget, staff, publications, technological infrastructure, and capacity for outreach. Thus the gap between the two organizations' profiles and power grew, despite the new enterprise's progress. Opportunities for cooperation expanded, but so did frictions between midlevel operating personnel in the two organizations. Differences on mundane details became occasions for bickering. Some competition developed for the primary loyalty of members and for funding from members, corporations, and foundations; this was particularly true in the San Francisco Bay Area and in Seattle, where both organizations were operating from some distance.

I was aware of these frictions, but clung to the belief that because the fundamental case for strategic cooperation was powerful, the leadership of the two organizations would overcome what seemed like surmountable differences. I failed to anticipate how much the dynamics of a strategic alliance can shift over time, particularly when the parties are themselves changing significantly.

The New York organization's calculus about close engagement with the Los Angeles–based forum shifted, as some of its personnel and leaders came to believe that the association was diluting its brand and co-opting its membership. As the new organization grew, it could offer greater value, but it could also be perceived in New York as more threatening in terms of regional market share. As the national forum's resources and profile enlarged, it became harder for some of its key leaders to see the advantages of close association with a much smaller, less visible, junior partner, not in its league in terms of products or prestige. At the operating level, mid-level staff with responsibilities for managing the week-to-week relationship stood to gain in autonomy and influence from institutional separation—a point I probably underestimated—while those in the New York organization's leadership who had been most involved in crafting the partnership retired from active service, and new leaders, personally uncommitted to the partnership, took their places.

I am not sure, even in retrospect, of the relative weight of these (and perhaps other) factors, but some combination of them led the New York organization to end the full partnership—an outcome for which I did not adequately prepare. On the contrary, in the face of growing doubts, I repeated the arguments for strong partnership to the point that ultimate rejection of that course felt at the time like a personal defeat.

In truth, the eventual termination of the alliance, handled quietly and gracefully by the two organizations' boards, probably did not significantly hurt either organization, and it may have helped both in some respects. Neither party needed the other by this stage as much as both had at the outset. The new Los Angeles–based forum has become recognized on the West Coast as the region's leading international policy center, has successfully managed leadership transitions on the board and staff, and has consolidated a core annual budget, of which the national organization's dues sharing—still being provided to this point as part of the separation—now amounts to less than 3 percent. The New York entity, meanwhile, has developed enhanced national program instruments—including an annual conference, frequent telephone conference calls, and regional task forces and book clubs—that keep its distant members somewhat engaged. Each organization can now proceed without the complication of satisfying another party with somewhat different objectives, constituencies, membership criteria, and metrics for evaluating success.

I may well have been wrong to resist the pressures for separation; I was certainly wrong not to anticipate their sources and strength. Closer consultation in the second phase of the alliance might have produced more substantial and better-integrated joint ventures, and both parties might have gained, but it is by no means clear that greater investment in bolstering the relationship would have paid off over time. It would have been useful for both organizations to agree more explicitly on the metrics for evaluating the alliance's progress, rather than to operate without a clear understanding of each partner's expectations. But the main lesson may simply be that the strategic alliance was based on a temporary confluence of interests and constellation of personalities, and that it was misguided to try so hard to maintain the partnership after some of these interests diverged and its original architects disbanded.

I believe the effort to construct a strategic alliance at the outset was a creative and effective response to the West Coast forum's need to bootstrap itself into rapidly establishing convening power and credibility. The alliance worked well at first mainly because the national organization thereby served its far-flung members better at little cost, while rethinking how it could become a more truly national effort. But it also succeeded because of extraordinarily trustful relations among many of the key players—a serendipitous product of long-standing relationships.

To keep the alliance working well over time, as the two entities changed and their needs diverged, would have been challenging in any case, but it became more difficult because insufficient attention was paid to broadening and deepening the personal relationships on which cooperation ultimately depends. Strategic alliances are hard to construct, but even harder to maintain, and mutual confidence remains as important in later stages as at the start.

Part Three

DRIVING THE SOLUTION THROUGH THE ORGANIZATION

Chapter 9

FRAILTY, FORTITUDE, AND A LEADER'S COMMITMENT

"The best laid plans of mice and men go oft awry."
—*Robert Burns*

"*No, no, no.* We are not going to proceed with the plan," declared Jack, in an uncharacteristic outburst. Jack was the general manager of a $2-billion-plus division of MedTech, a global manufacturer of medical devices. Although normally reserved and gracious, now he was visibly upset.

Shock and silence lay thick in the packed conference room. I can still remember the shape, color, and make of the florescent lights in the ceiling as I prayed for divine intervention. None came.

For my consulting career, this could become a disaster of epic proportions. My project manager, Steve, and I stared at each other in disbelief. Six months of painstaking work to develop a new strategic direction for MedTech had come to this rejection. All I could think was, *How did we get to this point?* and *We have to sort this out—and fast—before all of our best-laid plans are lost.*

At its heart, change is about people. It was only after years of serving some of the most successful and aggressive senior executives that I suddenly realized these extraordinary leaders were as human as I was, with dreams, fears, desires. Senior managers had always seemed different to me because they controlled extensive resources, had armies of employees reporting to them, and were responsible for company-changing decisions. However, they worry, as do we all, about barriers to progress and career: success, failure, professional reputation, personal risk, work politics, personal rivalries, talent, culture, organization, processes, technology. And without their vocal and public commitment, no significant change is possible. This may seem obvious, but obviousness has not prevented many recommendations from gathering dust in corporate corners.

Moving from Problem Analyst to True Problem Solver

Up to this point in the book, our objectives have been to develop elegant solutions and build judgment as to when to stop analyzing problems to move toward action. Part One concerned the process of identifying challenges, diagnosing problems, discovering solutions, and testing and then communicating them. Part Two concerned building one's intuition about when to move from further analysis of a proposed solution to taking the decision to start enacting it. Now, in Part Three, we turn to tailoring our solutions to the organization's needs—its norms and its unique readiness for change. Who cares about the elegance? The solution needs to *work*. In the most successful transformations of companies, the pattern is iteration between problem solving and implementation. Part Three concerns ways to overcome the inevitable and potentially enormous issues associated with enactment.

Implementing solutions is possible if critical issues are addressed. First and foremost is getting the senior leaders who are affected by a solution (either as implementers or as recipients of its consequences) to commit to it. This chapter concerns how to assess managers' commitment and, if necessary, encourage them to commit further. Chapters Ten and Eleven will outline systemic ways to overcome the other principal barriers to change in an organization.

A word on perspective: first, our viewpoint in Part Three is that of persons who are already convinced of the solution's value and whose current goal is its successful implementation. It matters not whether the problem solver is an outside consultant or an inside manager. The advice remains unchanged, as does the enormity of the task. Without doubt, implementing a solution is much more difficult than developing it in the first place. But it can also be that much more rewarding. If formulating a solution to a business problem is part science and part art, implementing it is almost all art.

Second, we contend that the role of organizational and personal values in implementing new solutions has been underrated. Not only must *what to do* be consistent with company norms, but *how to do it* must be as well. Most effective and lasting business transformation begins with leaders inspiring their employees to focus on their core values.

A word of caution as well: those who successfully drive change through an organization do not become great overnight. They work at it. And they share similar personal attributes: the never-give-up temperament of Prime Minister Winston Churchill in the midst of the bombing of Britain, the foresight of General George Marshall in understanding how the complex dynamics of post-war Europe would evolve, and the face-to-face leadership skills of General George Patton, who could consistently motivate his troops in the trenches to take on nearly impossible missions. If that seems like a tall order, it is. Transforming an organization can be overwhelming, so we start, step by step, with the personal side of implementation: confirming or encouraging senior manager commitment.

Why is commitment so important? Leaders, and particularly senior managers, must be committed to the desired solution. They must possess the fortitude to risk potential failure. They must overcome their own very understandable aversion to such risk, in order to drive change. This hard reality is informed by years of experience and observation: without visible, explicit, public commitment to change from those who will be critically involved with implementing a solution, the team of problem solvers might as well go home.

Assessing a Leader's Commitment to a Proposed Solution

Recall our mission for this book, outlined in the Introduction— to present a set of outstanding habits of mind in solving complex business problems. To assess a leader's level of commitment to new plans, we recommend the habit of gentle, conversational probing, through a series of diagnostic questions. Consistent, persistent probing can unearth sources of unease or even outright resistance. Shortly, we will also consider how to conduct tough discussions with managers who are unwilling to support and assist with a solution.

As we shall describe, such conversations start with empathy with the manager's aspirations and fears, as their role and way of conducting business may be about to change beyond all recognition. Creating the right environment for a probing discussion is half the battle. It requires trust, tact, and finesse in a relationship that may take a long time to develop. It also requires understanding the specific challenges facing the manager. For example, on what criteria is he or she evaluated? What are his or her particular areas of strength and weaknesses? Motives and interests? How does this manager's job interrelate with those of other managers, and how might the solution affect those relationships? For the most apparent obstacles, the problem solver should craft solutions in advance. Managers may, quite reasonably, still resist the solution. And that can shake the problem solvers' confidence in their recommendations and their willingness to persist in the face of initial adversity.

The conversation should begin as broadly as possible and then move to more specific issues. It can help to ask three diagnostic questions shown here and in Figure 9.1:

- Do you really believe in the threat or opportunity? Is there a need to change?

- Do you think that the benefits associated with the opportunity outweigh the costs?

- Do you believe the organization has, or can quickly acquire, the skills needed to capture the opportunity? In other words, can the organization do it?

In what follows, we refer back to earlier cases and to our unresolved challenge at MedTech to illustrate how one might use these questions to surface submerged barriers.

Figure 9.1. Diagnostic Questions to Assess a Leader's Commitment to Change

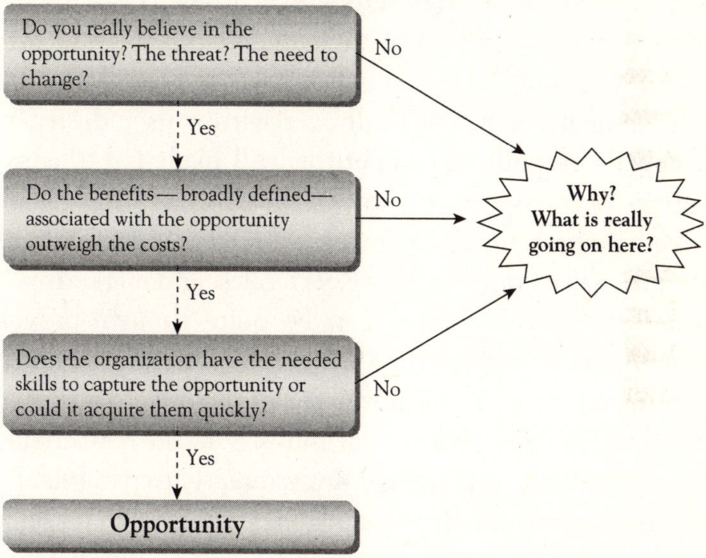

Do You Believe Change is Needed?

Persuading managers of a threat or opportunity often depends on skills described in Parts One and Two: effective problem solving and compelling business case development. One of the most straightforward ways is benchmarking performance against that of competitors. If another company in the same industry, serving similar customers with similar products and services, has already achieved a higher level of performance—say, in R&D productivity or sales force effectiveness—then it is difficult for managers to debate whether more aggressive goals in R&D or sales are appropriate and achievable. Although they may question how the results can be accomplished, they should agree that others have proved it is possible to achieve them.

The initial discussions with Capri executives (described in Chapter Seven) illustrate this point. Our team profiled Capri's casual clothing competitors. We benchmarked Capri's retail store performance on leading indicators such as comparative sales growth per store, labor costs, conversion rates, and inventory turns. After seeing that their stores measurably underperformed competitors, Capri senior executives began to discuss seriously a major overhaul of their merchandising and marketing strategy to turn the business around.

If a company is a real trailblazer within its industry, glowing comparisons with its competitors will likely fail to convince executives of further opportunities. In this case, the team may describe how best-practice companies in *other* industries perform across critical functions such as R&D, sales, and marketing. Such cross-industry benchmarking can be quite thought-provoking, as it amounts to arbitraging expertise from one industry to another to create and capture incremental value. In the 1990s, for example, the pharmaceutical industry faced new challenges as it began to brand and market drugs directly to patients. Before FDA deregulation of direct-to-consumer advertising, pharmaceutical sales forces mainly sold new medications to physicians who then prescribed the drugs to patients. After deregulation, many industry insiders saw building relationships directly with patients as a tremendous untapped opportunity to drive drug sales further and increase compliance. Pharmaceutical executives looked to the consumer products industry to see how leading companies had built strong relationships with loyal consumers through their global brands. To capture the new opportunity, industry leaders such as Pfizer, Eli Lilly, and GlaxoSmithKline hired marketing and branding talent from Procter & Gamble and Unilever to launch their direct-to-consumer initiatives.

The problem solver must address the unique concerns of the particular manager or group of managers. Suppose a manager leads a sales organization, but the solution works predominantly by increasing product margins through reducing production cost. Implementation of the solution may well require effort from across functions in the organization, including the sales force, so the sales manager reasonably asks, "What's in it for me and my folks?" Depending on the company's norms, the answer could range from a simple appeal to the manager to improve the company's overall performance, to an explicit, negotiated plan for sharing any gains generated by the solution among all those who helped make it work.

Do You Believe the Benefits Outweigh the Costs?

No matter what the opportunity, managers must also believe that benefits outweigh the costs, in order to commit time, resources, and talent. In Chapter Seven, we advocated defining potential benefits as broadly as possible in generating business cases. Benefits include (1) those evidenced by financial estimates; (2) market impact, such as increased market share or improved customer satisfaction; and (3) internal operational gains in productivity or efficiency. Less measurable, nonfinancial implications include, for instance, employee morale or momentum in the marketplace.

Costs must be even more broadly defined. They begin with the financial business case investments as outlined in Chapter Seven. Managers must also assess internal nonfinancial costs, including disruption, loss of focus, and even the lost-opportunity costs associated with implementing the new program.

The Food Processing Equipment Company (described in Chapter Eight) delayed a significant reorganization, intended to enable it to focus on major global customer accounts, until after it acquired the Green Bay Sorting Company. The organizational change was going to significantly increase FPE's upselling of food processing equipment. Although FPE managers believed in the opportunity, they consciously weighed the costs and benefits of the proposed change, then delayed its implementation because they wanted to minimize disruption and loss of focus during the Green Bay acquisition and integration.

The benefits and costs just described are organizational. When dealing with individual decision makers, we suggest being very mindful of personal benefits and costs. In our observations, many individual motivations boil down to desires for more power, prestige, money, impact, or perhaps the desire to leave a lasting legacy as a leader. Successful transformation of a business can also transform the leader into a hero.

But one should remember that supporting a change entails a risk of personal failure. Empathy with the fear of this risk is crucial for the problem solver. Risk and fear are often the elephants in the room, and they must be acknowledged rather than ignored or swept aside. What matters is not the actual probability of failure but the manager's perception of it and the possible consequences associated with failure. An individual's failure may damage part or all of the company's initiatives and can lead to personal loss of position, promotion, raises, and even profession reputation. Some organizations make change even harder if they prize never being wrong and never changing one's mind. Sometimes characterizing the consequences of *not* attempting the change can increase the impetus to do so.

Can the Organization Do It?

Even if they believe in the opportunity and benefits, business leaders must understand the skills required to capture the opportunity. They must then soberly assess their organization's competence. Does the organization have—or can it quickly acquire—the necessary skills? If the company's capabilities are weak on essential dimensions, managers need to create a plan for obtaining the skills, be it through training, acquisition of other companies, outsourcing to other suppliers of such skills, or perhaps even hiring new managers. Ideally, the business case estimates not only the costs and benefits of a proposed solution, but also its probability of success, which depends on market factors and the company's existing and needed capabilities. In essence, the problem solver must be a master of clarifying the path to the goal.

As mentioned earlier, leading pharmaceutical companies recruited marketing expertise regarding direct-to-consumer advertising from powerhouse brand-builders like Procter & Gamble and Unilever. As another pharmaceutical example, most research and development of new drugs has historically focused on small chemical molecules. When new scientific breakthroughs shifted R&D focus to biologic compounds like proteins and other large molecules, most pharmaceutical companies lacked this expertise. When pharmaceutical industry executives determined that biotech drugs represented a tremendous opportunity to transform medicine, to be able to participate they needed to quickly acquire new skills. Many pursued a double strategy, hiring eminent biotech scientists into their own research programs and acquiring smaller biotech firms.

Next, we investigate how the three diagnostic questions came in handy at MedTech, where general manager Jack had stopped us cold with his "*No, no, no!*"

The Challenge of Change at MedTech

MedTech was a leading innovator in orthopedic implants and heart devices. MedTech's products helped crippled patients walk again and gave patients with severely damaged hearts a new lease on life. Historically, its manufacturing plants could barely meet hospital demand. Its highly trained sales force would frequently accompany their cardiac surgeon customers into the operating room to explain new surgical techniques or the intricacies of a new device.

Although still enjoying strong growth, MedTech had begun to face pressures on pricing and market share. Global competitors with comparable devices were beginning to challenge its technological superiority. At the same time, insurance companies and other payers began to limit medical cost increases and reduce reimbursement to hospitals for surgical procedures. To address these challenges, MedTech senior management (including Jack) had asked my team to work with MedTech colleagues to look hard at the environment and devise a sustainable strategy for growth.

As in many disciplined problem-solving efforts, one could say that our team stumbled onto the central insight inadvertently—yet not entirely by chance. In our experience, accidental insights happen far more often during well-structured inquiries. In this case, within the first two months, during a series of hospital interviews, our team discovered a critical opportunity. Many hospital customers wanted to consolidate their institution's purchasing process. Currently they bought different medical devices from two, three, or even four manufacturers. Most tertiary care hospitals that performed cardiac and orthopedic surgeries with MedTech-type devices wanted to simplify their purchasing processes to just one manufacturer. In contrast, the country's leading academic research medical centers would continue to purchase devices from all suppliers so that their surgeons could experiment with the latest technology innovations.

From this insight, our team gradually developed a growth strategy. MedTech should continue to lead the industry, launching cutting-edge innovations into major academic medical centers. At the same time, it should also help tertiary care hospitals consolidate all of their purchases with one broad-based supplier:

MedTech. Our team spent another four months developing the comprehensive, systematic business case and implementation plan to divide MedTech sales force to serve these two distinct customer segments and their vastly different needs.

But Jack's outburst during our progress review presentation meant that "the best laid plans of mice and men . . ."—our whole proposal might soon be toast.

After the meeting, Steve and I took a deep breath and made the long trek to Jack's office. Jack was not there, but his very nice assistant, Patty, made an appointment for us the following morning—at 8 A.M. That evening, in a little Italian diner, Steve and I mulled over how we would handle the next morning's conversation with Jack.

I had always held Jack in the highest regard. When I first met him, he had managed businesses on three continents for more years than I had been alive. Tall, straight, with grizzled, close-cropped hair, he reminded me of a knight of the Teutonic Order. Born on a farm in North Dakota, with a tremendous work ethic, reserved, but never too busy to say "thank you," Jack had always been one of my favorite clients. Through my many years of working with Jack, I had come to understand the true meaning of leadership: inspiring ordinary employees to achieve extraordinary results, year after year.

Probing the Causes of Jack's Opposition

How should we respond to Jack and his opposition to the plan? After strenuous debate, Steve and I agreed on a few basic principles. First, we still wholeheartedly believed that MedTech could realize enormous growth by refocusing its sales strategies at the two distinct customer segments. The research, data, interviews, analysis all pointed in that direction. Second, shame on us for not staying closer to Jack during the course of the project. Although we had dutifully kept him informed of our progress and solicited his feedback on the major initiatives, his very public rejection proved that we had not communicated sufficiently with him. Third, we would ask Jack three simple questions to try to diagnose the reason that he was opposed to the plan:

- Do you believe in the opportunity to drive incremental sales by focusing on key hospital customer accounts?
- Do you think that the magnitude of broadly defined benefits associated with this opportunity outweighs the costs?
- Do you think MedTech has, or can quickly obtain, the skills and capabilities required to capture the opportunity?

From his answers, we should begin to understand his resistance.

We did not underestimate the seriousness of the situation. If we could not unearth the reasons for his opposition, and if that opposition persisted, then our only option was stark indeed. No movement forward would be possible without Jack's active support. We would need to let the opportunity pass. We would need to walk away—both literally and metaphorically.

Waking up the following morning, I had that sinking feeling in the pit of my stomach. I used to suffer that feeling in elementary school when I was sent to the principal's office. In recent years, I had suffered it when I needed to go to the dentist.

Steve was already waiting for me outside Jack's office—looking not much better than I was feeling.

Jack's Initial Response

In response to our questions in the meeting, Jack convinced us that he really did believe in the opportunity. In his judgment, its magnitude outweighed the potential financial disruptions and other costs associated with capturing it. He also feared that without quick action, MedTech might lose the competitive advantage to its aggressive global competition: others might move quickly to capture incremental sales in the tertiary care hospital segment.

His reservations, he said, lay primarily in his fear that his sales force and marketing function did not have the right skills to capture the opportunity. Historically, the marketing department planned product launches for R&D innovations. It designed programs to train physicians on the features and benefits of its new devices. MedTech's sales force was terrific at educating individual surgeons about recent innovations on a one-on-one basis, thereby generating sales. MedTech's salespeople built such strong relationships with the surgeons that they vacationed together and were godparents of each others' children. Yet neither the marketing department nor the sales force were the "executive types" that could explain to hospital executives the financial benefits of consolidating purchasing to just one manufacturer. Jack feared that even MedTech's best employees would never be able to manage the chief financial officer of a major hospital network, let alone a CEO. He worried that he was setting his division up for failure.

Steve and I tried to reason with Jack, arguing that he could hire additional senior salespeople to manage key accounts. Both the CFO and president of MedTech would even step in to help Jack personally manage the largest hospital accounts. Yet Jack still looked unconvinced.

"What Is Really Going on Here?"

At an impasse in the discussion and personally at a loss for words, I suddenly had an inspiration. I remembered a similarly awkward discussion that I had witnessed, as a junior-tenured consultant, between Mike (a very seasoned senior partner of my consulting firm) and a troubled CEO. Mike was a legend in our firm—gruff, loud, demanding, a devout Catholic who swore like a sailor. I felt safe around him only when I was with his assistant, as she was the only person who actually yelled back at him.

His towering intellect and even higher professional standards were housed in a brusque exterior that intimidated colleagues and clients alike.

Yet some senior executives responded warmly to him. I think the smart ones intuitively saw beyond the stern exterior. For Mike had a huge heart. His empathy and compassion were disarming. He defined his role as helping others to be more successful, regardless of whether they were trying to overcome problem-solving challenges or find the courage to make difficult decisions. He had spent years building trust with his clients and colleagues—and he knew when to use that trust. He was a master at asking the perceptive, extraordinary, blunt question and then turning quiet to listen.

I recognized that I was no Mike—the master of the tough, yet heartfelt discussion—nor would I ever be. However, I quickly inventoried my options. The current conversation with Jack was going nowhere. Therefore, there was little risk in trying alternatives.

Next, I surveyed the nature of Jack's and my relationship over the years of working together. Jack recognized that I was deeply familiar with his business, customers, and especially "his guys." As a matter of fact, he frequently thanked me for working tirelessly for their benefit. I also believed that he acknowledged my intelligence and objectivity and that my main motivation was to make him and his team more successful. I concluded that my long-term relationship with Jack was one of the most trust-based professional ones I had.

Then, half intuitively and half consciously, I ran through a mental checklist of the things I had learned from observing Mike in such tough conversations. I checked whether Jack's office door was closed. By protecting him from an audience, we might increase the likelihood that we could discover his reservations. I made sure Jack and I were at the same eye level. It may seem simple, but people are less likely to tell you what they fear if you are looking down on them. Finally, I edged my chair around a bit so that Jack and I were on the same side of the conference table and both looking forward together. Perhaps that might make him feel, however unconsciously, that we were in this situation together.

Over the years, I had been proud of my tact and diplomacy. I had brought finesse and structure to many chaotic and difficult circumstances. Now, however, I let go of those skills. With significant discomfort, I set aside my documents and worked on complete instinct. I looked at Jack, took a deep breath, and asked, "Jack, what is really going on here?" Then I kicked Steve under the table, signaling him to keep quiet, and I bit my lower lip to keep myself from filling the inevitable silence with my own chatter.

"Well," Jack finally began.

We waited silently.

"I am more worried about something else." He quietly admitted that he was not worried about "his guys" or even the potential failure of his division in implementing our proposed conversion of major hospital accounts. He agreed that a number of targeted, talented hires could help execute the compelling economic value proposition to the largest tertiary care hospital accounts. Over time, MedTech could implement an overall account management system.

I knew we had begun the conversation that we needed to have.

What Jack feared was that he personally might not be able to manage the transition. Because he came from the manufacturing organization, Jack possessed a great facility with the intricacies of medical devices. By spending extensive time with customers and studying in an executive MBA program, he had taught himself basic skills in sales and marketing. But the new growth strategy required tremendous depth and understanding of finance, sales, and marketing, which Jack feared he fundamentally lacked.

At this point, I still sat quietly to hear what Jack would say next. I needed to determine quickly whether Jack would respond better to sympathy or to problem solving at this moment. I was ready with both. Fortunately, one look at Jack's face showed me that he was hugely relieved by his confession, and the old Jack was back. He was not looking for my empathy so much as seeking my abilities as a thought partner. We were back into problem-solving mode.

After a pause, we all began to brainstorm how to overcome Jack's very legitimate concerns.

The result? After eighteen months of hard work, MedTech has now signed up many of the critical accounts, driven incremental sales, and built tremendous momentum in the market. Jack is a hero at MedTech for driving this transformation.

Risk, Frailty, and Empathy

Let us say it again: change is difficult, especially for those who are asked to lead others through it. We trust that the habits of probing and the diagnostic tools outlined here, as well as Jack's story, will help whenever you are called to take up the challenge of driving change through an organization and you face either outright opposition or passive-aggressive resistance to new solutions.

The three diagnostic questions help both to identify the rational objections that senior leaders may harbor toward a change plan and to assess the overall strength of their commitment. But never underestimate the emotional objections that may accompany the rational ones: fear, defensiveness, inertia. Managers must possess tact, trust, and courage to deal with the emotional barriers to change. Perhaps more than anything else, empathy— this sensitivity for others' feelings—is essential. That larger-than-life, gruff senior partner, Mike, had empathy in spades. And in my relationship with Jack, I learned how I could show my own innate empathy for others' concerns in a professionally appropriate manner.

If you are the manager charged with both finding the solution to a problem and executing the solution, you will need to reflect on how strongly you believe in that solution. The three diagnostic questions presented here can help you do that. You should take the time for such reflection; we guarantee that your colleagues, subordinates, and superiors will be waiting and gauging your visible commitment to (or reservations about) the changes needed, in order to decide about their own.

Although this may be perceived as controversial advice, in our experience, if senior leaders are not committed to needed changes, then both problem solvers and the subordinates who will need to work hard as agents of the implementation should metaphorically walk away from the initiative for a certain period of time. No substantive change is possible without the explicit support of management. Given their control of resources, direct reports, budgets, and responsibilities, obstinate business managers are nearly impossible to work around.

Continuing with our investigation of ways to drive implementation of new solutions throughout a company, Chapter Ten addresses other potential barriers to change such as misaligned organizations, entrenched processes, inadequate technology, and opposition or insufficient talent among employees. Chapter Eleven describes a pragmatic approach to launching an implementation process that builds momentum within an organization toward the solution. But the main message here is that risk and fear are often at the heart of human frailty when bold action is required. It is not every day that one encounters senior leaders with the fortitude to conduct their business in the future very differently from the way they conducted it in the past.

An Engineer's Paradise

Shona Brown
SVP, Business Operations, Google

In business, most problems can be classified in one of two ways: *What should be done?* or *How should it be done?* In my experience, most people overinvest resources in the former and underinvest in the latter.

The solutions to the "what to do" problems are usually driven by data. Sometimes data are mixed or conflicting, so it's important to learn to triangulate, test assumptions, and search for more evidence in order to reach reasonable conclusions. And solving "what to do" problems can be so broad and fraught with uncertainty that data limitations become a severe handicap. It may be necessary to attack the uncertainty through scenario analysis, analogies, stories, and small pilot experiments. Having understood the scope of the issue, you can proceed to financial analyses (expected value calculations, net present value, and cash flows) to frame a recommendation and mitigate the associated risks.

The problem may be so complicated that it requires major computing power to work through the numerous constraints to deliver the optimal solution. But in the end, you will arrive at a solution with some prescribed specificity and within some acceptable margin of error and risk. Academic training in professional degree programs (for example, MBA, MD, JD) offers the diagnostic skills for these types of problems, as do engineering and other applied sciences.

"How to do it" is a much more complicated and difficult aspect of real-world problem solving—one for which most academic programs do not provide good training. Organizations are filled with people who are not necessarily the rational actors that economic textbooks often describe. Instead, their aspirations, emotions, fears, and petty rivalries can fundamentally complicate the problem and its potential solution. Other factors—geographic dispersion, cultural differences, linguistic challenges, functional divisions—can complicate simply trying to get groups of people to *do something*—let alone getting them to do the right thing. The fact is, to effectively address the most challenging problems may require changes in human behavior. Yet inertia can be an incredibly powerful obstacle to getting large groups of people to change ingrained habits or thinking.

It is also noteworthy that the problems of "what to do" and "how to do it" are rarely independent of one another. Diagnosis and implementation may be two different processes, but you'll need to consider their interrelationship when addressing hard questions.

At organizations, such as Google, that are growing rapidly and focused on innovation, often the most difficult business problems emerge when figuring out "how to do it." And as these organizations grow even larger, it becomes more difficult to optimize innovative behavior, because the more people there are, the greater the complexity of finding solutions. (Of course, it's essential that the people doing the problem solving are brilliant and innovative, but this alone is not sufficient.) Once large numbers of people are involved, the perfect plan will never be implemented exactly as imagined. As the character Ed Finnerty said in Kurt Vonnegut's novel *Player Piano*, "If it weren't for [people], the world would be an engineer's paradise."

Chapter 10

BULLDOZE THE BARRIERS

Submariners Under Attack

"We have this operation on the East Coast that we've neglected a bit. Any chance you guys can take a look at it?" The request came from Mac, the North American general manager of Global GasCo, both an international oil exploration company and a leader in roadside gas-and-convenience stores. The situation with its chain of gas stations, although not yet dire, was certainly serious. Global GasCo station franchises dotted the highways of the Eastern seaboard, among other U.S. regions. But recently Global GasCo had grown very little in sales per store and in number of new stores. Competition was squeezing the franchises' margins. "These franchises of ours are tough to control," Mac admitted.

Global GasCo senior management was dominated by ex–naval officers, a high proportion of whom had been submariners. Submariners, by their very nature of their work environment, are generally both short in stature and disciplined in leadership. Former submarine captains Mac and his boss Brady ran Global GasCo as a tight ship, with a clear hierarchy, clear responsibilities, and command-and-control management practices. Discipline, order, and authority were essential characteristics of the Global GasCo organization.

Global GasCo had indeed neglected its East Coast gas stations—it had not updated the good, but rather basic, franchising offer in many years. Our mission was to find a way to improve near-term profitability and drive significant future growth. And to do it in a way that harmonized Global GasCo's more military management culture with the diverse needs of hundreds of rather noncompliant franchisees. It was a tall order indeed.

Major Barriers to Implementation of Solutions

The quest for effective change starts, but does not end, with the business case for the proposed solution, which we discussed in Part Two. The business case reflects the costs, benefits, and expected net value of a new solution, the latter not always being sufficient reason to implement. Companies must assess, and be prepared to deal with, many and various obstacles to change. Even if senior management is committed, the organization may not be. The solution and its implementation must be consistent with company norms. It may need to be altered to fit its more general readiness and ability to change. The problem-solving process must always iterate between discovering solutions and modifying them in line with frontline possibilities.

In the previous chapter we addressed leaders' commitment as the first and most important success factor to drive change. Other potential obstacles stand in the way. This chapter describes them and suggests ways to cope. Many of the most inspiring corporate transformation efforts have foundered and sunk on the rocky shoals of cultural and operational resistance to change.

As a general metaphor, imagine what happens when you try to crush a plastic milk container so it takes up less space in your recycling bin. The bottle usually resists being crushed as completely as you would like. If you do not push quite hard enough on at least two sides simultaneously, the container has a tendency to expand back to something that vaguely resembles its original shape. Business organizations and milk containers respond to change similarly. Organizations can be incredibly resilient in regaining their shape in the days, weeks, and months following attempts to change them. Why this resiliency in organizations?

To drive efficiency and effectiveness and so produce reliable, predictable levels of performance, organizations commit as many business activities as possible to routines. Several factors reinforce the general resistance to changing these routines. First, organizations are made up of people with their own frailties and fortitude. In the previous chapter, MedTech's general manager Jack harbored no doubts at all about his ability to manage the *current* business, in which similar efforts yielded similar levels of performance. But the new strategy of driving growth by consolidating the purchases of major hospital customer accounts entailed many unknowns, and Jack did have doubts about his ability to manage the *future* business. The same feelings were likely held by his engineers, marketers, and sales force. Such potential change instills fear in those charged with accomplishing it. When pushed to change, but given the opportunity to spring back to their original shape like the milk container, members of organizations return to the comfort associated with the usual ways of conducting business to escape the fear represented by the unknown.

Second, the actions of employees within a business are fundamentally interdependent. The auto mechanic who slips the brake disk onto an axle depends on another worker to have mounted and attached that axle securely. The waitress who delivers burgers and fries to her customers depends on the kitchen staff to maintain a sufficient inventory of burgers and fries. The insurance agent who sells a policy to her neighbor depends on the underwriter to assimilate the information collected by the agent and to price the policy quickly and appropriately. Change the routine of any actor in an organization, and all other actors must change theirs. So not only do individual members of an organization want to return to the status quo, but their colleagues who are also reluctant to alter their own ways push them back. Like the plastic milk container, the interconnected and systemic nature of organizations makes them particularly resilient. Given even the smallest opportunity to resist newly imposed changes, they will tend to revert. To deal with this, the problem solver must focus on how behaviors are learned and rewarded, how they are interdependent with other actions, how they are aligned within an organizational structure, and how consistent they are with organizational practices. Although the elasticity of the plastic milk container analogy may have reached its natural limits, organizations also face a number of additional obstacles to change, including how well these changes are supported by technologies and whether the organization's own employees may be up for the challenge. These are the ingredients for successful approaches to drive permanent change.

We will not say much about finances as a major barrier to adopting a new solution. It is true that a plan's financial costs and implications are critical decision factors, and some finance-related factors can increase the likelihood that a business plan will be approved. For example, detailed analyses of the timing of expenditures as well as cash flows, not to mention self-funding plans, can increase the confidence of those investing. But in our experience, in most circumstances financial considerations are not the greatest implementation barrier. When backed by adequate levels of information transparency, good business cases find funding either internally or from external investors. If the proponents who claim a plan will earn superior returns for investors are having difficulty finding takers, most likely the business case is weaker than they claim.

We will also not say much about culture as a major barrier. Some argue that an organization's culture is a potential barrier, and we actually agree. However, we suggest that problem solvers not take on necessary cultural change separately from the context for the solution. In the end, organizational culture depends on the commitment of leaders; their values and priorities; the structure, processes, and technologies employed by the business; and its essential capabilities. For long-term cultural changes to happen, senior leaders must share consensus about the new direction, adopt common problem-solving approaches, and redesign novel ways for their organizations to be successful. Cultural change always takes longer and can be more frustrating than problem solvers imagined when standing at the outset of a major change effort. But changes in the broader, problem-related context will, over time, create the conditions for cultural change.

The following sections look at four additional principal barriers: organizational misalignment, entrenched management systems and processes, antiquated technology, and insufficient talent and capabilities.

Barrier: Organizational Misalignment

An organization is more likely to adopt a solution when its tangible and intangible benefits are distributed in a way that employees consider fair. Years of research have shown that the perceived fairness (or unfairness) in reward distribution strongly affects employee commitment and satisfaction. A solution rarely lasts long if it relies heavily on one department's efforts in order to benefit another department—the ones doing the work must see benefit for themselves. The question of what is fair is answered by the norm of equity: the more that the benefits that individuals receive reflect their role in producing those benefits, the greater the perceived fairness. General managers must proactively ensure that benefits of a new change are distributed equitably.

Besides inequity, other misalignments of organizational structure can make it extremely difficult to provide individuals with the support, information, and incentives they need to reach the company's goals. For example, at the Food Processing Equipment Company (Chapter Eight), management saw a market opportunity to bundle its entire portfolio of proprietary equipment to sell as a package to some of its global food-processing customers. FPE quickly identified the immediate challenge to the new, customer-focused sales strategy: Who would do it?

The problem was that FPE's organization was structured around business units that focused on individual product lines (for example, sorters, freezers, fryers) with shared regional service support. Under the existing structure, for any big customer account, several product managers (for sorters, freezers, fryers) jostled with each other in negotiating contracts. But to sell a package, someone would need to take responsibility for each global account. Who would do that? And how could sales, profitability, and other financial data be tracked by customer account, when it was currently aggregated by product line and sales region? How would cross-selling be encouraged within customer accounts without fostering unhealthy competition? What incentives would encourage customer-focused behavior?

Making changes to organizational structures should not be undertaken lightly. At worst, alterations can wreak havoc. Still, it is sometimes necessary to realign the organization's structure with the company's new aspirations, strategy, and market position. So, in order to capture its upselling opportunity, FPE dissolved its product-line-focused divisions and adopted a new structure organized around end-user accounts with dedicated marketing and sales resources; the equipment-specific research and engineering departments were consolidated into one support group shared across product lines. Changing the organizational structure triggered a change to its internal culture.

As emphasized in previous chapters, communication is essential to driving organizational change. Broad, extensive, and, at times, repetitive communication facilitates employees' understanding of the need to change and encourages their commitment. Although they rarely do, senior managers should invest heavily in communication to overcome opposition and to build support for the new organizational structure.

Barrier: Entrenched Management Systems and Processes

Management processes fall into at least three areas: (1) strategic planning, which includes strategy formulation, business development, and investment prioritization; (2) budgeting, financial, and operating review; and (3) hiring, development, and personnel review. To drive short-term earnings and long-term growth, these processes should reinforce each other. The primary challenge to this is distribution of information so that good decisions are made: What information does each senior manager need to get? When? What quantity and quality of data do they need, and how often?

There is no denying that management systems and operating processes are often difficult to transform. For example, it is hard for an organization to completely overhaul its internal processes if it regularly uses incremental quality improvement approaches (Six Sigma) to reduce variations in processes. In such a case, it might make more sense for the organization to tailor a solution in a way that harnesses existing management systems than to attempt an ideal solution.

However, sometimes entrenched processes do need to be changed. For instance, existing management processes prevented one high-tech manufacturer from accessing new inventions created by outside smaller entrepreneurs. Through its strong marketing reputation and close relationships with major global customers, the company had an opportunity to drive incremental growth through licensing or acquiring new innovations from smaller start-up companies. But because there was no single hub of business development, each of the licensing functions within its business units bagged little game in the hunt for innovations around the world. Further, once the high-tech company licensed or acquired a nascent technology, the new products were incorporated directly into existing business units that had neither the financial systems nor the operational processes to launch them. To cope with these problems, the high-tech company consolidated and centralized the business development function across all divisions at the corporate headquarters. It also created a central incubator that would foster the growth of new products before they would graduate into the existing business units.

Barrier: Antiquated Technology

Change efforts can also be handicapped by outdated, poorly designed, or inefficient technology. Problems arise when a solution requires new technology that exceeds the capabilities of the people in the organization. In that event, either the solution must be modified to require less demanding technology, or employee capabilities must be upgraded through training and recruitment.

For example, a large industrial company suffered unsustainably high levels of bad debt in its customer base. In the usual course of business, the sales force would book the sale before sending the customer's information to the internal audit department for a credit check. The numerous delinquent accounts were then sent to the customer service department to attempt to collect overdue receivables. The technology solution to this dilemma was deceptively straightforward. Placing credit-checking software on the salespeople's computers enabled them to evaluate a customer's credit quality prior to closing a sale. But the technology solution did have to be reinforced with changes in process and incentives. The sales force needed to adopt new standard operating procedures that required a comprehensive customer credit check prior to closing sales. Also, to further reinforce the new way of interacting with customers, the sales force's bonuses were no longer based on top-line sales but rather on customer account profitability.

Barrier: Insufficient Talent and Capabilities

To drive major change within an organization, senior managers must objectively assess whether they have the necessary skills, talent, and mindset internally. If the answer is no, then part of the solution must address acquiring those capabilities. For example, a major global chemical manufacturer embarked on a growth strategy to increase sales through creating end-use, market-based commercial products, rather than selling commodity chemicals. However, the chemical giant's management team had all been promoted from the powerful manufacturing function and knew little about marketing. To succeed, this chemical company needed marketing expertise to design and launch its new, consumer-focused products. By recruiting marketing veterans from Procter & Gamble, McDonald's, and Coke, it filled these gaps and injected fresh perspectives. In this case, structural and process adjustments were also required so that the new talent received the information they needed, were rewarded appropriately for performance, and could progress along attractive career paths.

There are large hazards associated with changing mindset and behaviors in an organization with a firmly established culture and way of conducting business. Nevertheless, companies can greatly increase their chances of successful transformation if they identify and then make careful plans to overcome the kinds of barriers of implementation just outlined.

The Barriers at Global GasCo's East Coast Operations

Through calculated risks, major acquisitions, and sheer bloody-mindedness, Global GasCo had built a dominant position in oil and natural gas. Its geologists prospected for oil in the Arctic, Central Asia, Africa, and South America, and among the most unsavory regimes. Its downstream operations included gas stations just about everywhere there were cars on the road. Its extraordinary international presence stemmed from the vision, determination, and hard work of its leaders, Brady and Mac. Using practices they had learned in their years in the Navy, Brady and Mac ran a tight ship. With several hundred thousand employees, they had to.

Historically, Global GasCo had been a leading innovator in the franchise offering. Its proven business model offered strong operating margins for both itself and its gas station franchises.

In addition, Global GasCo had gone beyond what was prescribed in its contracts with the franchises to provide ongoing support and assistance on marketing, systems, and operations. Its expertise was recognized; other franchisors had followed Global GasCo's model closely when launching their own franchises.

Over the years, however, Global GasCo's business model had begun to disintegrate as variations proliferated. Within its current East Coast portfolio, franchises varied in terms of asset ownership, operational control, and the royalties paid to Global GasCo. The East Coast operations were a veritable alphabet soup of franchise acronym variations, such as COCO (company-operated, company-owned locations), FOCO (franchise-operated, company-owned), and FOFO (franchise-operated, franchise-owned). For a while, even our dedicated team could not keep them straight. In the end, we developed a simple rule of thumb for deciphering the acronyms: operations came first in the acronym, then asset ownership. So COCOs were under the most direct company control, while FOCOs paid the largest royalties because Global GasCo retained ownership of the assets.

The net effect of the confusion and overall franchise neglect was stagnation rather than growth and overall poor financial returns for both Global GasCo and the franchises. Mac asked for our help in both improving near-term profitability and jump-starting future growth.

Working Toward the Solution

Comparing the financial performance of COCOs and FOCOs with that of FOFOs, especially regarding ROIC (return on invested capital), we concluded that FOFOs presented Global GasCo with a double opportunity for growth and capital efficiency. If we could tap the entrepreneurial drive of the franchises, perhaps they could drive the needed growth. Our team quickly developed a working hypothesis of the solution: Global GasCo's franchise operations should all become franchise-owned.

Yet the path to achieve this goal became an obstacle course. In franchising, economies of scale drive performance. Most operators should own more than one franchise. However, much to our surprise, single-site operators dominated the East Coast franchise network. This was a radical departure from other franchise operations in the fast-food and hotel industries, in which the rule is multisite operations. A high percentage of single-site operators means lower overall performance, because multisite operators often outperform single-site operators thanks to better skills. Our team's analysis indicated that, given Global GasCo's current levels of support to its franchisees, the natural operational breakpoint would probably be a five-site operation. A franchise owner could then spend one day a week at each of his five gas stations/stores. Yet most ran nowhere close to five.

Furthermore, extensive surveys revealed that Global GasCo's long-term neglect had soured relations between itself and its franchisees. An early innovator, it was now far behind competitors in terms of supporting franchises with IT, communications, or marketing. As a result, many franchisees were questioning Global GasCo's commitment to them. One interviewee captured their sentiments succinctly: "The [Global GasCo] district manager for this area is nonexistent. He is not a people person—he comes in only twice a year and that is twice too often."

Given these sentiments and the lack of profitability of current franchise operations, we saw slim hope that Global GasCo could entice franchisees to take on more gas stations. Why would any small business franchisee risk losing money on yet another? Our team would need to turn around the franchise operations first, as the foundation of future Global GasCo growth. I personally harbored another fear: perhaps we faced a more fundamental clash of values. Perhaps Brady and Mac's strict military management style might collide with the more entrepreneurial franchise owners that Global GasCo had to attract.

As if our team did not have enough on its hands, Global GasCo faced problems in places other than its franchise network.

Oil and natural gas exploration was increasingly fraught with geological and geopolitical risks. As a result, investment in upstream exploration was far outpacing investment into downstream retailing. This imposed severe capital constraints on the company. But it was going to have to discover some way out of its multiple dilemmas: fix the franchises, drive growth, and unlock additional capital for fuel exploration.

Faced with this complex situation, my team and I returned to problem-solving basics. We modified our original, simpler hypothesis statement to fit our new facts. The first part focused on the franchises: What should Global GasCo do in the short term to improve operations on the East Coast and thereby increase franchise profitability? The second half examined how Global GasCo could use its franchisees to drive growth and improve ROIC.

After several weeks of hard work on financial analyses, benchmarking against competitor franchises, and extensively interviewing company executives, franchisees, and industry experts, our team arrived at a conceptually straightforward solution regarding the franchise operations, detailed in the following section. As is frequently the case, however, this elegant recommendation was tripped up by operational constraints. Our team spent many more months making the solution work.

Our elegant, yet pragmatic solution had two parts: first, a wide-ranging "operational excellence program" to revitalize the franchise channel; second, a massive decapitalization of the franchise network to unleash further growth elsewhere. This second part required converting all franchise-operated, company-owned stores (FOCOs) into franchise-owned ones (FOFOs). Perhaps some time in the future, if all FOCOs could convert into FOFOs, then Global GasCo could also auction off its COCO stores to the new entrepreneurial franchise owners. But no conversion of FOCOs into FOFOs would be possible without a far more profitable offer to potential franchisees, so part one had to succeed.

The execution barriers were massive.

Reworking the Solution Toward Implementation

In preparing the "operational excellence program," our team turned to estimating how profitable the franchises could be. In other words, we needed to devise the appropriate operational stretch goals for the franchises. To this end, we extensively benchmarked against gas-and-convenience competitors to show that Global GasCo's franchise performance was far from "best in class" on revenue per store, gross margins, cash management, expense indicators such as labor, and many other industry metrics. In effect, we needed to help the franchises improve every single line on their income statement and balance sheet.

In the early "blitz" phase of our operational excellence program, we attacked each issue, beginning with procedural changes to reduce expenses immediately. Our team would help franchises reduce the costs of goods sold by coordinating purchases across the entire franchise network. Global GasCo colleagues would teach franchisees how to use a labor scheduling tool that improved labor management and further reduced costs.

Moving from procedures to technology, Global GasCo would invest in and help roll out new point-of-sale technology that made franchises significantly better at managing their operations. (Unfortunately, as with most new technology implementation, the point-of-sale system cost far more and took far longer than any of us expected.) In addition, new basic supply chain technology would help franchises manage cash better with just-in-time inventory replenishment.

No operational detail was ignored, including previously overlooked factors such as the bathroom cleaning schedule—because customers frequently judge a gas station by its bathrooms. The greatest opportunity, however, lay in improved selling and marketing. Our initiatives would help franchisees increase revenues per store by introducing new product category management, targeting pricing increases, running seasonal promotions, training employees on upselling techniques, and increasing the store's range of products.

With great fanfare and even a franchisee managers' convention, we planned to launch the "operations excellence program." If we could entice the franchises to stick to the program long enough to start seeing the financial benefits, we could ensure that the program built the momentum needed for its success. Our team recognized that Global GasCo's long-term success was intertwined with the short-term turnaround of franchise profitability.

The Long-Term Solution

Simultaneously, we developed the long-term solution: Global GasCo needed all FOCO operators to purchase their store assets. This single decapitalization initiative would unlock significant financial capital, which Global GasCo could then redeploy toward more efficient uses. Global GasCo would provide extensive start-up assistance and even overhaul its real estate department to improve new site selection. But Global GasCo could not simply provide franchisees with a loan to purchase the FOCO assets. Why not? Because Global GasCo's expertise lay in gas exploration and retailing, not in small business banking. Our team decided to put Global GasCo's global muscle to good use on this problem. Brady and Mac would pressure their bankers to introduce a loan program for franchisees to borrow the $1.5 million needed to purchase a station.

Our team developed two detailed and separate business cases for the franchisees and for Global GasCo. For the franchisees, by our team's estimates, if all the initiatives were implemented, the "operational excellence program" could increase profits by 20 to 30 percent—perhaps even 50 percent, on average, per store. For Global GasCo, the net financial impact of the conversion of FOCOs to FOFOs was in the billions of dollars. Our team was confident that both senior managers and franchisees would welcome with open arms what we considered to be a very effective solution.

Overcoming Resistance from All Sides

We were thus shocked, truly stunned, that our recommended two-pronged program ran into serious, entrenched resistance from both franchisees and Global GasCo executives. As with the Capri case in Chapter Seven, the Global GasCo case was, for me personally, another tremendous lesson in how to address potential adoption barriers like the ones just described. The remainder of this chapter narrates how our team systematically overcame them. We begin with equitable distribution of effort and benefits and organizational alignment.

The Distribution of Efforts and Benefits

Without doubt, our team was caught off guard by the franchise opposition. The "operational excellence program" was expected to improve their operating margins by up to 30 percent, perhaps even 50 percent. Although most were supportive of these turn-around initiatives, contrary to our expectations, they did not sign up in masses to purchase the franchise assets. Because converting FOCOs to FOFOs was essential to the goal of redeploying Global GasCo's capital, we had to sort out why the franchisees were reluctant to purchase their franchises.

After serious but quick due diligence, we found that asset acquisition excessively burdened the franchisees. Ownership of the assets and control of the operations meant that franchisees had to put significant personal capital at risk. The program needed to ensure that they also earned substantial economic benefits from their efforts. Even with the successful execution of the "operational excellence program" within the stores, FOFO operators would still earn slim margins. This was due to the royalties payable to Global GasCo. Global GasCo tried to improve the situation by bearing some of the implementation costs; it provided guarantees to the banks for the small business loans and even invested in the point-of-sale technology. Yet these efforts were not sufficient to create a win-win situation for both parties.

In the end, to ensure the fair distribution of effort and benefits, Global GasCo had to make the difficult decision to renegotiate the franchise offer and allow FOFO operators to pay lower royalties.

Organizational Alignment

The short-term "operational excellence program" ran into big challenges right from the start, not only from the franchisees but also from within Global GasCo. Until that point, Global GasCo had used a more command-and-control approach to franchisees. The corporate center frequently issued orders, which franchisees promptly disregarded. The organization was not designed to provide the extensive franchisee assistance and training needed to make the new program a success.

Consequently, Global GasCo's approach needed a thorough overhaul, starting with its values and mindset. It needed to recognize its franchisees as clients and then treat them as such. For instance, our team quickly established a special marketing department at Global GasCo that provided franchisees with initial training and ongoing proactive guidance on introducing new products, category management, advertising promotions, tactical pricing, and cross-selling training for employees. The new marketing department became so detailed that it even suggested which coffees to serve at what markup to maximize profit. Our team also created a special IT department to train franchisees on the new technology investments, such as how to use the new scheduling system to reduce their labor costs.

In another clear value-added service for its franchisees, Global GasCo began to benchmark key performance indicators on a quarterly basis, so that franchisees themselves could troubleshoot issues and identify new opportunities. By working jointly with franchises on their new quarterly operational priorities, Global GasCo managers and franchisees were able to drive lasting performance improvements. Ever so slowly, Global GasCo began to think of and treat its franchisees as true clients.

Targeted Investment in Technology

New technology can often facilitate change, but not always. In our experience, major technology overhauls rarely proceed on time and on budget. Nevertheless, new technology often enables the capture of critical information that underpins good decisions.

Some franchisees took longer than others to adopt the new technology, but all acknowledged that these new systems helped raise their profits. A new inventory management system enabled just-in-time ordering, cash management, ongoing replenishment, stock-out reduction, and overall supply chain management. Data gathered by the new point-of-sale technology led to better decisions about merchandising and targeted pricing. A new back-office system not only simplified procedures for staffing, thereby increasing labor productivity, but also tracked key metrics of ongoing overall store performance. The performance data greatly enhanced the quarterly operations reviews between Global GasCo executives and franchisees.

Technology overhauls are frequently a double-edged sword. They can provide new information that improves management decision-making and overall performance, but as anyone who has changed IT systems can tell you, they are arduous and risky. Given these realities, companies usually modify IT systems only in the most pressing circumstances. At Global GasCo, senior managers demanded well-thought-through business cases, with particular attention to the associated risks and execution plans, before deciding to make any technology changes.

Institutionalizing New Management Processes

Management systems and processes can facilitate needed change, but are themselves among the most difficult *to* change. Employees get used to doing things according to entrenched routines, and changing them can require coordination across vast numbers of people. This was true at Global GasCo.

The "operational excellence program" forced franchisees to develop their own annual budgets, participate constructively in quarterly operations reviews, and execute tighter financial discipline. The new annual budget process was meant to drive a number of other important, closely related changes. As a start, the franchisees were required to create and submit their budgets for the following year. These budgets were based on projected revenue and cost projections for each individual gas-and-convenience store. These projections in turn were based on expectations about the external environment and performance in sales per category, gross margins based on bulk purchasing, and labor and other expenses. Global GasCo then expected franchisees to adhere to their budgets, and the company used the budgets as a basis for identifying, analyzing, and addressing operational variances. Because cash management was also a priority, franchisees were required to closely track inventory and cash position.

Many small franchise owners—especially those who had been running an informal family business—were shocked by these professional processes, not to mention the need to show up prepared for an annual budget and quarterly operational reviews. Many were overwhelmed, simply lacking the skills to develop such a budget. Indeed, these new requirements weeded out the weaker franchisees. Some adopted these procedures only selectively; others took them on and never looked back.

New Talent and Culture

The frontline "operational excellence program" enabled both the franchisees and Global GasCo to increase overall profits and royalties with what became a superior franchise offer. For a franchise, the main benefit of the program was higher profits. For Global GasCo, the long-term solution (made possible by the transformation of company-owned stores into franchise-owned ones) involved expanding Global GasCo's footprint across the

East Coast and extending that new format to other geographic regions in the United States. Global GasCo's *ultimate* benefits came from decapitalizing the franchise network, thus providing significant incremental investment in oil exploration.

Institutionalizing this program, our team quickly addressed many of the practical challenges, such as designing a package of start-up services—training on operations, IT systems, finance systems, and an introduction to marketing. Global GasCo's banks established an attractive loan program for franchisees to borrow the capital to purchase a franchise. However, Global GasCo would never be able to drive retail growth and at the same time decapitalize without a cadre of franchisees ready to sign up for the new FOFO stores. Regrettably, many of Global GasCo's current franchisees were small family business owners and possessed neither the mindset nor the appetite for risk to expand their operations further. We needed to recruit new entrepreneurial flair.

Collaborating with Global GasCo's recruiters, our team defined the characteristics of entrepreneurial "early movers" who would be convinced of the franchise's economic value. Global GasCo located this talent within other well-run franchise organizations: McDonald's, Subway, Marriott. With a thoughtful package of incentives, our team began to lure their franchisees over to Global GasCo. After signing up, these entrepreneurs helped Global GasCo further refine the offer. They applied their experience to increasing profitability of their new businesses.

With hindsight, it is clear that our program did not move as quickly as we could have to remove intransigent managers—both within Global GasCo and in the franchisees—that ultimately presented the biggest barrier to change. Global GasCo needed a whole new mindset about taking risks, providing service, and driving returns. With missionary zeal, these vocal champions of the program gave firsthand accounts of the benefits, thereby enlisting fellow franchisees into multisite ownership. We were fortunate to recruit as many new entrepreneurial franchisees as we did. Without them, the whole plan would never have gotten off the ground.

Organizational Norms, Personal Values, and Resistance

We would like to return to the question of why the elegant multi-billion-dollar solution for transforming Global GasCo and its franchises initially aroused such opposition from all quarters. After the successful transformation of FOCO into FOFO gas stations on the East Coast, Global GasCo directed its winning combination toward an even greater goal: nothing short of auctioning off all FOCOs and even COCOs (company-operated, company-owned) gas stations to entrepreneurs across the country. This program unlocked a tremendous amount of capital—in fact, billions of dollars—that Global GasCo then redeployed toward oil and natural gas exploration and exploitation.

Were there more reasons that franchisees and parts of Global GasCo at first resisted our recommendations, despite clear, extensive benefits for both parties? Much of the answer lies in the organizational values and norms. The successful implementation of the program required two implicit values shifts. We did not begin to see progress until we made these values shifts explicit and began discussing them with all participants.

First, for the franchises, what had been a more family-oriented business model needed to become a more professional, information-driven one. Pricing, purchasing, placement, and even employee scheduling would now be subjected to specific metrics, then tailored to regional competition. Professional annual budgets and operating reviews became par for the course. Timely market and franchise information became an extremely valuable part of examining and then making better business decisions.

Second, Global GasCo's senior management faced an equally demanding change in norms. Starting with Brady and Mac at the top, they had always issued orders to subordinates, who were expected to comply promptly. Collaboration was not part of the internal vocabulary of the place. Yet without collaboration among former superiors with those they had considered for many years to be their subordinates, revitalizing the East Coast franchise network would have been impossible. I spent the better part of a year coaching the two former naval commanders, Brady and Mac, through this difficult change in values.

Be Prepared to Slog

Whether you are a determined manager or simply a dogged consulting team, the Global GasCo case shows you that effective implementation requires much more than a business case that (ideally) projects significant net benefits over costs. Our team moved back and forth constantly between our ideal solution and pragmatic frontline results. We were willing to rework any part of the solution to make it work. At times, like the plastic milk container that resists being crushed, many in Global GasCo wanted to bounce back to their old, comfortable, safe routines of conducting business. To drive overall decapitalization, Global GasCo executives took particular care that significant benefits would accrue fairly to those actively investing time, effort, and resources. Much like a hard push from multiple sides that finally collapses the milk container, Global GasCo's successful and permanent transformation required mutually reinforcing, simultaneous pushes of hiring new entrepreneurs, modifying incentive programs, aligning organizational structure, and instituting new processes and technology. Mac and Brady were constantly on the road, selling their program of change. They even hosted a national conference to educate new owners of the FOFO franchises on what equity their sweat would return.

Our eighteen-month effort to revitalize the East Coast franchises and sell off most of the assets to FOFO owners was a genuine slog. As a bulldozer pushes the dirt to change the contours of a landscape, we pushed at this organization from all directions. With each push, we discovered new hills and valleys that needed to be bulldozed over and adjusted. After the first few months of severe worrying, I gave up pulling out the new gray hairs that kept springing from my head. I just could not keep up. We encountered so many roadblocks along the way, reasonable observers asked why we even tried. Why did we bother?

The answer lay in Brady and Mac's aspirations for Global GasCo. Continuing to be a good oil and gas company of good global size, good profitability, and good operational performance was simply not enough for them. They wanted to transform this good company into a thriving, world-class organization, and they would let nothing obstruct their vision. Implementing large-scale changes in a complex organization is not for the meek or faint of heart.

In the next chapter, we turn our attention to a tried and tested process to build momentum for necessary change in an organization.

Act Now

Bob Parkinson
Chairman, CEO, and President, Baxter International

To revisit an old adage: "One learns more from failure than from success." It's why a commonly asked question in a job interview is "Can you provide me with an example of a problem you were unsuccessful in solving?" And the actual, or implied, follow-on question is "What did you learn about yourself, your leadership style, or your decision making as a result?"

The tendency in responding to such a question is to provide a specific and, perhaps, dramatic example of a failed strategy, a misguided acquisition, or a significant misreading of changing market or competitive dynamics.

However, in reflecting on this question as it relates to my business career, I invariably gravitate to bad decisions that I have made about people. That's not to say that I've made a habit of hiring underperforming managers and executives. Actually, I'd like to think (maybe I'm not being intellectually honest here) that my "batting average" in hiring highly capable executives is quite good.

Having said that, I can say we have all made mistakes in the people we hire. This is inevitable. However, the biggest mistakes I've made over my career have been not addressing problem situations with people in as timely a fashion as necessary.

A good question for any leader to ask himself or herself, as a litmus test, is "Have I ever taken someone out of a role because I felt they were underperforming, only to reflect on the decision six months or a year later and feel I made a mistake in moving ahead too precipitously?" I can honestly say I have never had this experience.

Conversely, I can recall at least five to ten situations over my career for which I can objectively say (now at least) that I should have moved more quickly to deal with a situation that clearly was not working.

There are many plausible explanations for delaying addressing issues of performance; most of them falling under the heading of *rationalization*. "The person is growing in the role." "The individual just needs some more time to come up the curve." "The person's strengths outweigh his limitations." And so on. If we're honest, we would all agree that we've been there.

Yet *why* have we all been there? I wonder why "act now" is such a particular problem on people-performance issues? I would speculate that part of the answer is that the stakes of these situations are fundamentally higher than with other decisions. It may be a strange analogy, but contrast a poorly performing senior executive with reengineering a suboptimally performing piece of equipment in a manufacturing plant—the machine does not get moody, does not create a negative buzz in the organization, does not send out resumes or talk disparagingly about the company to customers, suppliers, and industry observers. When it comes to changing people's roles—or even changing the people themselves—these are all potential barriers to action, as they certainly strike fear in the hearts of many leaders. Thus, within the risk/reward equation, there will always be a readily visible downside to action. Is it surprising, then, that general managers frequently hesitate to act on people problems? Nevertheless, my argument would be that the downside to inaction is inevitably greater.

When it comes to addressing individuals who are not working out, the first rule is to trust your instincts. It is important to force yourself to clearly define where there are specific gaps between actual performance and your expectations. Of course, it's imperative that shortfalls in performance versus expectations be clearly defined and communicated to the individual, and that a fair opportunity is provided for performance to be improved. It is also critical to have trusted individuals on your staff (your HR head, or other trusted members of your management team who have sound judgment) to validate your instincts. And the final thing to remind yourself is that "being nice" invariably does a disservice not only to the organization, but also to individuals who almost always know their performance was not meeting expectations. By not acting expeditiously, you are diluting trust throughout the entire organization, and diminishing your personal reputation as a leader.

Chapter 11

THE TOILS OF SISYPHUS

Back at Capri

"Our sales are going down, our market share is going down, and our conversion rates are going down. We need help to turn this situation around—fast," said James, Capri's COO. Over the years, we had labored together to carry forward the work described in Chapter Seven: refocusing Capri on the Stylist segment of consumers. We had also launched a new retail concept and even taken Capri toward international expansion. The challenge now seemed to be the disappointing performance at Capri's stores.

"I need you to come in to assess the situation," James added, "and then propose how to make change happen in our unique organization. What has your track record been in driving *lasting* change in the retail environment? Good, good. See you next week."

The evolution of the retail apparel industry was making it ever harder for Capri to compete. Savvy competitors were encroaching on Capri's relationship with Stylists. Higher-end competitors expanded their casual assortment, while lower-end competitors gained share by introducing new apparel. Once an industry leader, Capri faced deteriorating in-store performance. With such a dire situation on our hands, our team returned to the basic problem-solving principles and quickly assembled the facts behind the precarious situation.

On a lone positive note, recent market research revealed that Capri had much higher brand awareness than any of its competitors. But despite that awareness, on the main industry measure—comparisons in annual sales growth per store or "comp sales"—the company had been declining for several years and lagged its competitors. Capri's market share was also declining across most of its major product lines. More damaging in the long term, the rate of converting traffic to sales was less than half the industry average, indicating that former customers were simply not returning to Capri's stores and buying again. Capri's stock price was being punished mercilessly on Wall Street.

But these facts still only amounted to symptoms. Our team could not immediately determine the underlying source of the problems. Could it be somewhere in marketing? Merchandising? Perhaps store operations? Capri had just finished a year-long program to revitalize and refocus its product assortment for Stylists. Could this have been the wrong direction? My whole team, which had also worked on Capri's repositioning project described in Chapter Seven, prayed that this was not the case.

Driving Implementations of New Solutions

Chapters Nine and Ten addressed issues of leaders' commitment to executing major change and the values conflicts generated through that execution. Other principal barriers included misaligned organizational structure; antiquated technology; entrenched management routines; and inadequate mindset, talent, and employee behavior. At the end of the day, implementing recommendations that deliberately and sustainably raise levels of performance frequently means upgrading the company's fundamental organization, processes, and, ultimately, talent. This chapter describes a tested, reliable process to do that.

We begin by noting that a very high number of turnarounds and major change programs in business fail. Some estimates run to 70 to 80 percent. Unfortunately, many such programs remind one of the punishment of Sisyphus. In Greek mythology, Sisyphus was a brilliant rascal who sometimes played tricks on the gods to get what he wanted. He even tricked his way past death. Finally, the gods condemned him to the eternal hard labor of rolling a boulder up a hill, only to have it roll back down to the bottom each time he got it to the top. Not only difficult but also frustratingly futile, unrewarding, and repetitive, the "toils of Sisyphus" is a metaphor for all such work.

The pragmatic, hardnosed advice in the following pages may seem counter to our earlier advice to set high aspirations in problem-solving endeavors. We do not think it is. What we mean to show is that practical experience teaches an incremental approach toward implementation, to overcome the business equivalent of Sisyphus' torment. Successful change requires moving the organization to the next plateau of performance and then spending time consolidating gains. Prudence dictates that senior managers pace themselves and their organizations in achieving long-term plans. They need to find ways to keep the boulder from rolling all the way back down the hill. Perhaps they can alter the contour of the hill, or park the rock on a plateau now and then, or even set chocks to prevent a backslide. Senior managers cannot rush out too far ahead of their organization's readiness or capabilities. Courage, stamina, and tenacity are the watchwords of successful implementation. Please read this chapter in that pragmatic spirit.

The Inspiration for Change

As we showed in Chapter Ten, few difficult implementation initiatives are possible without senior leaders' express commitment. Problem solvers must assess the degree to which senior managers are ready and willing to drive a change. If they are not expressly committed to driving change, we suggest that the team, the general manager, and subordinates excuse themselves gracefully and go home. Proceeding threatens to waste everyone's time and money and risk the reputation of the project champion or external consultant.

The inspiration for change can arise from either negative or positive sources. Most often, the current or projected future market dynamics may threaten a company, perhaps its very existence. Greater competition, changing regulations, customer pressure, or technological evolution can create such an increasingly tough environment. For example, the combination of pressures from Japanese competitors, greater customer demands, and ever-rising pension and health care costs have pushed American car makers into an uncompetitive position and forced change on their senior teams. More rarely, absent external threats, a positive source of inspiration may be the leaders' own high aspirations, perhaps as the transformation of an entire industry.

Few institutions cultivate the flexibility needed to drive major change without disrupting ongoing business. In most cases, although senior managers can and do focus, for a short period of time, on developing solutions to company problems, the demands of the business prevent them from sustaining their involvement all the way through implementation. As a consequence, most efforts fall short. A tested process to overcome such challenges is based on the following series of steps (see also Figure 11.1):

1. Set aspirations.
2. Achieve "quick wins."
3. Expand the program in stages to build momentum.
4. Sustain the impact.

Set Aspirations

Leaders must discern how aggressively to set their aspirations, consciously weighing the risks of failure before communicating them broadly. Executives must then translate those aspirations into short-term and long-term goals defined by metrics

Figure 11.1. Driving the Implementation Process

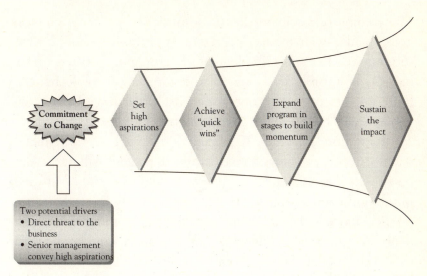

like revenue, cost, and other financially-based and market-based targets. Chapters Six and Seven noted how organizations are bound together by shared experiences and narratives. Thus, beyond describing the goals, executives must also tell a compelling story of why the transformation is essential. Stories are how employees will best understand the need for change.

As we suggested earlier, senior leaders can rarely run the existing business and at the same time dedicate the extraordinary additional time required to implement change. One way to handle this, once aspirations are established, is for general managers to commission a small, high-powered team to shape the solution, drive the program, and become its internal champions. Without such champions, complex solutions of the sort described here are unlikely to be carried out. Once program goals are achieved, team members can be folded back into the organization. In the meantime, the team needs to be freed, at least in part, from day-to-day management duties.

Achieve Quick Wins

Many employees remain skeptical until they see some progress being made, even if that progress may be more symbolic than substantive. For most implementation programs, three to six months is entirely too long to wait for demonstrable impact. Employee attention will not sustain itself that long. Early progress may also be needed to assuage management fears of failure.

In most organizations, 10 percent of the employees will immediately support the new changes, while 20 percent will never support them. The real question is how to win over the hearts and minds of the remaining 70 percent, who initially sit on the metaphorical fence and watch which way the wind will blow. Without doubt, highly visible, confidence-building quick wins are essential to win them over. These can involve customer interaction, organizational changes, or process changes, so long as they indicate both that senior management is serious about the changes and that change is possible within the organization. Quick wins should lead to public celebrations of individual and collective achievement, and problem solvers should explicitly plan and conduct them. Although it is not always possible, quick wins are even more helpful if they bring early financial returns, thus funding further implementation, at least in part.

Appointing outstanding project leaders to the change program is a valuable type of quick win. When respected, high-profile leaders stake their professional and personal reputations on the outcome, the organization takes that as an express signal of commitment. Without doubt, every program needs a strong internal leader with extensive influence and respect in the organization.

Expand the Program in Stages to Build Momentum

Besides assisting senior managers to size up their aspirations, problem solvers must also address other questions of program expansion: How broad should the change program be? Should it target only selected areas to generate impact and credibility early, or should it address challenges more generally across the organization? What trade-offs are best when choosing among speed of implementation, quality of impact, and cost of the program? As mentioned earlier, a focused, dedicated implementation team is best equipped to address these issues.

A large organization can start with a *pilot*—a test case of the changes. Tried out in a small portion of the organization, the pilot should rapidly reveal whether good results are possible. The early quick wins that result from a pilot also build momentum. After the pilot shows success, the program can be cascaded out to the broader organization. When planning pilots or cascading rollouts, be sure to consider potential conflict with organizational norms, possible structural modifications, and needed shifts in mindset and behavior.

Sustain the Impact

If changes are not woven into the fabric of the organization, then when the focus moves to other priorities, an organization can return to its previous suboptimal ways, just as Sisyphus' rock rolled back down the hill. By weaving change into the organization's fabric, we mean incorporating changes in the fundamental business processes of strategic planning, budgeting and operating reviews, hiring, and human resource management. Over time, these changes should become the norm.

Getting to that point depends on first establishing extensive commitment to and momentum for the solution. As political campaigns hang on converting undecided voters, so business change depends on reaching the 70 percent of employees who sit on the fence. Converting them depends on credible communication of aspirations and quick wins. Momentum itself reduces the likelihood of early backsliding. From there, ultimate success depends on how well you have done your weaving.

Implementation Lessons at Capri

Stepping back for a moment from our discussion of the principles of an implementation process, consider Capri's mess: fewer customers were purchasing fewer articles of clothing, leading to declines in profits and stock price. Yet this was merely an inventory of the latest symptoms. What had fundamentally caused Capri's problems? Our team's early research yielded some good news: Capri's brand was always in the shopping consideration set of a vast majority of current and potential customers. Given this level of brand awareness, we ruled out marketing as the main source of the problem. Traffic in the stores had not fallen off dramatically; it continued to grow. Furthermore, survey after customer survey indicated that Stylist customers liked the new product assortment, valued its quality, and were genuinely happy with their purchases when they did purchase. From this we determined that merchandising was also probably not the main problem. Quietly, and just between ourselves, we also sighed a huge sigh of relief at seeing such market validation for our "everyday cool" strategy.

Diagnosing Capri's Latest Problems

If our data and analyses excluded Capri's marketing and merchandising as the main causes of deteriorating performance, then a process of elimination left only store operations. A rapid, six-week diagnosis of ten stores in three regions quickly confirmed this working hypothesis. Customers themselves told us that the reasons for their not making purchases lay within the four walls of the store. They could not find the clothing they wanted in their size or color, and sometimes they could not even find a helpful salesperson. In retail terms, Capri faced serious problems in product availability, salesperson availability and deployment, and the interaction between customers and salespeople.

Our team was quite perplexed with the product availability problems. Every survey revealed that customers were disappointed that they could not easily find their desired product in the store. But according to the new inventory tracking system, the customers' desired items, sizes, colors, and styles were supposedly in stock in the stores. However, after some investigation, our team found that the product was not in its correct place; more often than not, it was in the back storeroom; less often, somewhere else on the store floor.

Salesperson availability problems were easy to see at peak traffic times: there simply were not enough salespeople to assist all the customers, and certainly not enough to provide the level of assistance that customers were expecting. Salesperson deployment issues were also straightforward to diagnose. Customers tended to congregate around certain product areas, but few salespeople were ever stationed there to serve them. Also, in numerous surveys customers said they needed more assistance selecting products, especially newer products like accessories with which they did not have much experience. They were looking to salespeople for explanation, advice, and guidance, yet almost never receiving it. This was where Capri had been meant to shine— providing style advice to the Stylist shopper. Capri had yet to capitalize on this major opportunity. By the end of the initial six-week diagnostic effort, it was clear to our team that these service problems were responsible for Capri's declining conversion rates and lack of comp sales growth.

Although relatively easy to diagnose, the problems would prove very difficult to fix. It would take changing the daily behaviors and mindsets of nearly thirty thousand sales employees working in over two thousand stores. The rest of this chapter first discusses the main challenges to implementing new business practices at Capri, then describes the pragmatic approach that helped drive ultimate change.

Capri's Main Barriers to Implementation

As noted in Chapters Nine and Ten, the primary implementation obstacles lie in leaders' commitment and values conflicts.

Other barriers entail organizational structure; technology; management systems and operating processes; and alignment of employee talent, behavior, and mindset to the challenge. There was no question that Capri's senior leaders were committed to the needed changes. They had already done a tremendous amount of work for the Stylist strategy. Equally clear was the fact that Capri had always aspired to excellence in serving its customers—and these initiatives would further reinforce that norm. Commitment was there, but was the ability to drive the necessary changes also there? Time would tell.

With regard to Capri's organization, our team decided that the current basic structure served the purposes of the improvement program fairly well. Within stores, the salespeople reported to store managers. Within a district, all store managers reported to the district managers. In turn, district managers reported to regional managers, who reported to the chief operating officer. Moreover, the existing management systems—training, human resources, budgets, operating reviews—could be used directly to support the changes needed. Additional investments in technology, such as a staff scheduling tool, were needed, but that was not an insurmountable obstacle.

The real challenges lay in transforming, across the board, the behaviors and mindsets of Capri employees. Some of our suggestions would ultimately fail, as they clashed with Capri's deeply held norms. Other initiatives would force fundamental changes onto Capri. In fact, although we did not recognize this earlier, we were asking Capri to transform itself from a *product company* to a *customer service company*. At Capri that change would require a revolution. But lacking that understanding earlier, we focused first on introducing process changes in product availability and salesperson availability in the stores.

The Implementation Program

Capri's COO, James, understood that Capri needed to sell more products to potential customers visiting its stores. Even modest increases in conversion rates would significantly increase comp sales growth. Our research had revealed that beyond getting the right apparel to the right place in the store, these changes would require more staff in key areas of the store, especially during peak traffic times. Also, staff would need to act differently around customers.

Our team's initial six-week diagnostic in ten stores had provided an overall confirmation of the opportunity, bolstered the business case for the service change, and given James and his colleagues the confidence to proceed. This initial diagnostic had uncovered and assessed the main problems, estimated the improvement potential, and taken a first cut at defining ideal salesperson behaviors. The implementation program, however, needed to address all of these challenges systematically and comprehensively.

Capri Leaders Set the Aspirations. James and Larry, his chief of staff, publicly announced that the organization's single most important objective for the coming year was to improve conversion rates by 5 to 10 percent across all stores, which would translate into a sales increase of hundreds of millions of dollars. James and Larry justified these aspirations first to the Capri's CEO and board of directors, and then to all regional managers, district managers, and store managers at Capri's annual meeting. The pair continued to reinforce these goals in their biweekly conference calls with regional and district managers. They also cleared their calendars; James committed 25 percent of his time to the effort, Larry 50 percent.

It was interesting for me to observe how James arrived at the appropriate aspirations for Capri. He had the input from our six-week, ten-store diagnostic program that had raised conversion rates by 25 percent, but he discounted those results as arising from a level of focus and energy that might not be sustainable across two thousand stores. Also, a failed store program two years earlier had reinforced James's pragmatism. He could not afford another perceived failure. Indeed, several of his best district and regional managers had adopted a mindset of "this too shall pass." After weighing these factors, James set the conversion rate aspirations at 5 to 10 percent—far lower than the results from the diagnostic stores. He reasoned that the overarching goal was for the Capri's field organization to perceive itself as a success. Our team was confident Capri could beat James's goal.

Quick Wins and Credibility. James and Larry faced deeply rooted skepticism. Their employees had survived several waves of change initiatives in the last few years, none of which had achieved widespread impact. To overcome this history, our team worked with James and Larry to accomplish several prominent quick wins to signal the seriousness of the new effort. A first quick win was changing the replenishment shipment process to improve product availability in the stores. Other quick wins involved changing procedures so that sales associate staff could be added quickly, and so that well-respected up-and-comers from Capri's own ranks could staff the implementation team.

Almost overnight, the new product replenishment process was an enormous success, achieving two goals: first, significantly improving product availability on the store floor, and second, substantially reducing the labor costs of replenishment work.

For years, Capri had changed out nearly its entire store clothing inventory every six weeks. After closing time, store managers and employees would simply lock the doors and then pull an "all-nighter" until the work was done. To unpack and shelve or display all the new clothes, each associate would complete the entire process with each item: unpacking, adding a sensor, hanging the garment on a hanger, figuring out where the hanger would go. It was a horribly inefficient process, and staff had to go through it every six weeks.

We completely redesigned this task, transforming it from batch processing to assembly line. In the new, much more efficient process, each associate was assigned an assembly-line role, such as unpacking or adding sensors. The new process could achieve the same results in 60 percent less time. Relatively easy to learn, straightforward to execute, and slashing the time required for an arduous task, the changes generated tremendous positive word of mouth in the organization. Store managers eliminated the all-nighters, proving beyond a doubt that change was possible at Capri.

Keeping labor costs within the budget had been a perennial concern for Capri's store managers because of company strictness on store labor costs. Many levels of approval were required to add any store labor above the budgeted amount. Completing replenishment with a fraction of the usual labor freed up labor dollars. Capri's corporate headquarters did not require that the replenishment labor dollars be cut from the budget, so store managers and district managers could reinvest the savings into additional, badly needed customer contact hours.

In the long term, savings from improving the efficiency of replenishment and increased conversion rates would cover the entire cost of change and more. Yet in the short term, to launch the program and improve conversion, an investment in sales associate time and training was clearly needed. James and Larry decided to budget extra resources for labor in the stores and changed the dreaded procedures for adding labor, putting the decision into the hands of district managers and regional managers working with their store managers. This radical change in procedure strongly signaled their commitment.

James and Larry also made an inspired choice of project leader. They chose Denise, a twenty-year veteran regional manager known for her shrewd and disciplined attention to operational results and her intuitive understanding of customer needs. Respect for her among staff and colleagues was wide—approaching awe. Denise thought long and hard before accepting the assignment. In effect, she staked her twenty-year personal reputation on success. Then she carefully selected a top-notch team of district managers to assist her.

Expanding the Program in Stages to Build Momentum.
Although convinced of the revenue opportunity and secure in
having Denise's highly talented team in place, James, Larry, and
our team still had to translate much of the conversion improvement strategy into recommended actions that made sense to
sales associates and store managers. We would proceed in mea-
sured steps, so as not to get ahead of Capri's ability or confidence
in implementing. We could not afford setbacks. Two "learning
stores" served to refine our program; later, before rolling the program out to the entire store network, we would again test it in a
specific ten-store pilot.

Within the learning store environment, our team attacked
the relatively easiest problem—namely, product availability—
and then moved on to tougher problems. The new assembly line
replenishment process ensured product availability. We moved
on to sales associate availability, then to their deployment, and
then to their interactions with customers. Consolidation of each
change was key. The equivalent for Sisyphus would have been
the chance to park the rock on a plateau so he could sit and rest.

Although the solution to sales staff availability seemed conceptually straightforward—schedule staff when the most customers visit the store—it was quite difficult to achieve. No data had
been collected on customer visits by day, by hour, and by store.
Some stores faced peak customer traffic during the lunch hour;
others peaked during the week in the late afternoon, 4:00 P.M. to
8:00 P.M.; others, in weekend malls, were quiet during the week.
Our team devised simple data-gathering tools to analyze each
store's unique traffic flow, and we combined the results with survey data on customer service expectations to develop the optimal ratio of customers to staff.

We recommended holding the ratio constant during all
opening hours, so that the store would vary its amount of
sales staff according to customer traffic patterns. Even this
proved difficult to do, because stores were only intermittently
using the staff scheduling tool developed by Capri's corporate

headquarters. The tool was complicated to learn; consequently, many store managers employed their own *ad hoc* rules of thumb in scheduling their staff. Our team worked hard to develop a simple scheduling program with a graphical user interface to help store managers staff appropriately.

Optimal staff deployment in the store also proved relatively straightforward to devise: trained staff would be stationed near the most complicated new clothing in the store. Most stores did not have product specialists on staff, let alone the number of them now needed, but our team was on a roll with fixing problems, so this one did not stop us. Collaborating with Capri's human resources department, we designed a crash course on the features and benefits of special products. After thus quickly training specialists, we had to make sure that they were not pulled from their designated areas to other parts of the store. The new scheduling program enabled store managers to increase specialist coverage in high-impact areas of the sales floor during peak hours and protect them from being drawn into other responsibilities, like manning a checkout line or fitting room.

In this way, we were very careful to consolidate gains as we pushed our boulder ever higher on the hill, with each plateau representing millions more dollars collected at Capri's bottom line.

Making the Changes Stick. Better product availability and better salesperson availability and deployment raised Capri sales. Yet the major conversion opportunity was still out there. Marketing surveys revealed that customers would be willing to purchase additional apparel if confident salespeople would help them create an outfit. To capture this upselling opportunity, Capri needed to improve the daily interaction between its sales-people and customers, which in turn implied a change in the skills, behaviors, and mindsets of sales employees. To this end, our team recommended behavioral changes and new performance management systems to reinforce them. Unfortunately, some proved impossible to do.

Once again, it was not hard to see what was needed. Market research revealed that customers did not want to serve themselves; they wanted modest, reactive assistance. At the low end of service, assistance might be simply finding a particular size or color of a garment or getting fitting room assistance promptly. On the high end of service, customers might want explanations of Capri's newly introduced clothing or suggestions on how to coordinate an outfit. In general, customers expected sales associates to pick up visual cues about the service they required.

We need to pause to stress the following: this represented a nearly revolutionary change in Capri's way of doing business. Capri would need to change from a company that designed and produced quality clothing to one that used its products to provide additional services to its customers. Sales associates whose main responsibilities had been the maintenance of a clean and neat store now needed to learn how to sell. They needed to interact at a different level with the customer, picking up customers' signals about what service they required.

Our team devised a substantial training program to answer the selling questions that customers would frequently ask salespeople. We even distributed simple, laminated selling assistance checklists for associates to keep in their pockets for quick, easy reference. Although wholesale turnover of staff was neither possible nor desirable, over time, hiring of new sales staff would emphasize new customer interactions and build a cadre of associates with excellent selling skills.

Despite our progress, late one night in the team room, James and Larry shared fresh concerns with our team. Would these radical changes stick? Particularly after the intense focus of implementation was relaxed? James and Larry feared the gains were not consolidated as we expanded the program step by step. They feared that Sisyphus' rock, parked on ever-higher plateaus, was still precarious and might roll back down the hill—right on top of them. Confronted with these concerns, our team set to work on the incentives, operational reviews, and other systems designed to ingrain the changes.

Inadvertent Conflict with Capri's Norms. On further investigation, we uncovered good grounds for James and Larry's worries. Salespeople were not performing the needed customer services consistently. Yet our proposed solution caused an even bigger firestorm. Schooled in individual performance incentives, our team recommended that Capri modify the program by tracking individual sales results and then compensating employees accordingly. Capri's leaders flatly rejected the proposals, no matter our arguments. Capri prided itself on being run as a family-oriented company, which translated into a policy of bonuses being paid to the entire store team based on its store performance. They simply would not alter this principle. We had to find another way. In the end, driving to maximize their new bonuses, the staff themselves at an individual store level took care of any slacker employees—by chasing them out of their store.

But other aspects of Capri—such as the nature of internal conversations—also had to change to make the program successful. Many of Capri's existing financial, budgeting, and human resources processes did not contribute to the new focus on service and had to be modified. For example, the program required essentially new, unfamiliar interactions among sales staff and managers, based on much more data analysis and troubleshooting. Yet Capri's managers were not equipped to do this well. Only slowly did they begin to tackle topics like customer service levels and conversion rates. Store managers coached associates on the new selling behaviors. They also organized brief daily meetings to announce the goals for the day. To identify ongoing problems in stores and prioritize the topics for their new weekly problem-solving discussions with store managers, district and regional managers conducted daily and weekly audits on specific performance criteria.

For this visually oriented company, our team created a large board for every store's back storeroom, proudly displaying and tracking the action plan. The finance and training departments in corporate headquarters captured relevant data and shared it with store managers to improve lagging performance. All sales-people could then see for themselves their store's targets and their collective progress on critical metrics like conversion, comp sales growth, product availability, and customer satisfaction. They could also quickly see where their store lagged and needed sharper focus.

Difficult Trade-offs Along the Way. At the end of the day, the implementation of most solutions does not proceed as initially planned, which is why successful implementation requires problem-solving instincts as keen as those needed for discovering the original solution. The team on the ground must constantly weave back and forth, modifying both the solution and the way that it is executed, as needed. This process depends on judgment, insight, and experience. It is more art than science.

As Capri moved from the "learning store" phase to the ten-store pilot, the overall program was refined, simplified, and prioritized. Once we got to them, the pilot stores surpassed our expectations for conversions and significantly improved their customer satisfaction levels.

When James and Larry launched the program beyond ten stores at the annual national store manager meeting, several rollout questions lingered. James and Larry still needed to make trade-offs among the speed of rollout, its quality, and its expense. Some colleagues argued that the opportunity was so large that speed was of the essence. Others, taken aback by the financial and resource costs of the rollout, argued that those with program experience should teach the first round of store managers, but that the newly taught managers should then teach others. Others argued this might be short-sighted, because someone who had just studied this program for two weeks could not be expected to teach it as well as managers who had been working on it for three months. However, assisted by Denise and her team, James and Larry ultimately made the needed decisions and extended the program across the entire store network.

The Cost of Change

The Capri case illustrates the complexity of driving new solutions in a large organization, but it also traces a proven process through which some of that complexity can be managed. What is required? Commitment of leaders. Harmony with organizational and personal values. Aligned organizations. Appropriate technology. Tailored processes. Superior talent and mindset. We have suggested also that successful implementation programs have several characteristics in common: aggressive goals, the succession of quick wins to build momentum to convert the doubtful, a pragmatic program, and modifications in organization, technology, processes, and talent to sustain the change.

But, one might ask, at what cost? In this case, heavy casualties. At one point Capri suffered a nearly inconceivable 50-percent employee turnover. We could not post vacancies, review resumes, hire and train new employees fast enough to keep the lights on in its stores. We even lost Capri's CEO, a true *garmento*. If the Global GasCo project gave me gray hairs, then this one gave me ulcers from worry. I personally had never seen anything like this turmoil. It nearly brought Capri to its knees.

For most of Capri's original employees, the change in aspirations, focus, and values was simply too great. They liked Capri's products; they did not want to learn to sell services. They had neither the confidence nor the competence to give customers advice on creating new outfits. Loving only the design of new fashion, even the CEO had no interest in leading a service-focused company.

But what was the alternative? Capri's competitive position, market performance, and very future were spiraling downhill. We needed to break that downward trend. It is not clear that we could have foreseen just how much chaos our program would trigger.

In the end, the main outlines of the program stuck, although not in the ways we had expected. After a hard-earned reputation for excellent frontline service and a number of triumphant seasons, Capri is back to its former glory.

Why did I dedicate eighteen exhausting months of my life to this Capri project? Especially after the eighteen months with Global GasCo? Because I have come to believe that an insightful solution to a difficult problem is an accomplishment, but actually making it work is an achievement of a different order. Because it was not enough for me to be an excellent problem analyst. Because I wanted to become a true *problem solver*. My clients and my teams, in both circumstances, set high aspirations, screwed up our courage, and then sustainably improved the performance of two large, complex organizations. That will be our legacy.

Leadership and Problem Solving as an Ongoing Conversation

Father John Jenkins
President, University of Notre Dame

For the past two years, I have been privileged to lead the University of Notre Dame. Throughout my travels, I am struck by how much each generation thinks it loves Notre Dame more than the prior or subsequent generations of alumni. Individuals' passions for the place lead them to fiercely protect the Notre Dame they love and care about.

I have learned much during my tenure as president. I observe, for instance, that a very important part of my job is considering how to create dialogue among various constituencies about Notre Dame's future—whether they be students, parents of students, administrators, professors, alumni, benefactors, ecclesiastical leaders, or supporters. These ongoing conversations are important. They certainly help me to identify the unique perspectives on various matters ranging from curricular content to campus planning to intercollegiate athletics. These discussions also help to develop a common understanding and language regarding Notre Dame's mission and identity. When the inevitable challenges, problems, and disagreements arise, we can, as a result of these conversations, better and more quickly understand and resolve these matters as a community.

During the coming years, for example, our community's common enterprise will be to build an even greater university while maintaining and enhancing its distinctive Catholic character. To accomplish this vision, we need to develop preeminent research programs without sacrificing our commitment to outstanding undergraduate teaching—the long-established strength of Notre Dame. My sense is that conducting the analysis to determine which academic areas to invest in, which scholars to attract to Notre Dame, and where to raise the funds will not represent our most difficult problem-solving challenge.

Rather, because of each constituent's strong personal conception of Notre Dame, one of my most difficult leadership challenges will be to communicate consistently and effectively the vision for how the University needs to grow and, in some instances, change. This message must reach everyone, and I anticipate that many groups will seek to share their hopes and concerns with me. The faculty, for example, will likely respond enthusiastically to the promise of investment in research, although they will anxiously wait to see where the resources are distributed. Alumni and benefactors, in turn, have pulled me aside and expressed their concern that Notre Dame not abandon its distinctive focus on excellent undergraduate teaching—and they will continue to voice their fears. And unlike many of my peers who serve as presidents at other institutions, I must consider our institution's critical relationship with the Catholic Church. Bishops and other Church leaders will encourage us to display fortitude in our commitment to our Catholic character. Even sports fans will weigh in to tell me how important it is to keep up Notre Dame's winning tradition in athletics. They will worry that an increased focus on academic excellence will be accompanied by fewer wins on the field or court.

Given all of these pressures from constituencies that have their own perspectives and priorities, how can we bring people together around a common vision for Notre Dame's future? Some leadership theories suggest that the challenges of leadership can be summarized by three themes: establishing a compelling vision, driving alignment across the organization, and energizing community members toward the vision. At Notre Dame many of our supporters already hold tightly to a vision of what we should be, are completely aligned behind that vision, and are totally energized to help make it happen. My job, as president, is to communicate a well-crafted and compelling vision for what Notre Dame can and should become. This vision must be grounded in our strong Catholic mission and values, and it must explicitly state our aspirations of becoming a truly great university. Yet, to achieve the kind of alignment we need among all of our constituents, it must include the perspectives of various groups, and thus be a comprehensive vision for an even more ambitious future.

How can a leader accomplish this? Communication is critical. University presidents and other leaders must listen carefully, share stories, manage expectations, and make connections among very different groups of constituents. Listening is particularly important during a leader's first days in office, but becomes even more so when the time comes to solve problems and implement change. Once we have carefully listened to the ideas and interests of various members, stories are a powerful way to humanize the mission and identity of Notre Dame, giving personal expression to its core values. Through these stories, we can effectively communicate that our values are served through a multiplicity of aspirations, including excellence in undergraduate education, in graduate education and research, and in athletics. We can also communicate their service in how we pursue and achieve our goals, consistently expressing our Catholic character.

I am confident that Notre Dame will strengthen undergraduate teaching while also investing in scholarship and research. The best professors excite students intellectually and build an even richer Notre Dame experience for them by exposing them to both the creation of new knowledge through research and dissemination of known truths through teaching. And I believe we can and must maintain the distinctive character of a Catholic university. The founder of the university, Father. Edward Sorin C.S.C., predicted that the university would be a great force for good. We must be focused on the good we seek to serve. I hope that Notre Dame will have an even bigger impact on the world at large because of its commitment to excellence in teaching and inquiry and its mission and the values arising from that mission. I firmly believe that the world needs a place that can combine the highest level of intellectual inquiry and teaching with a sense of faith, with a sense of mystery, with a sense of moral purpose.

Conclusion

Great leaders are masters of charting the course to successful solutions. Like captains at sea, they assess the current environmental conditions, set a direction, and then encourage their crews to overcome any challenges they may face. For the captain, the vessel's seaworthiness and the crew's readiness constrain the possible destinations. So, too, leaders must discern underlying problems from symptoms, hazard informed guesses at the solution, and then marshal all possible resources to prove (or disprove) the guesses. Yet leaders must always iterate between execution and elegance, because an answer that the organization cannot implement is essentially worthless.

Drawing this work to a close, we offer both a few reflections on the problem-solving methods and also several alternatives for those situations in which these methods may not seem to apply; finally, we offer our aspirations for you, the reader.

Parting Reflections on Values and Habits of Mind

Integrity regarding one's personal values, and ideally with one's organization's norms, is the necessary starting point for efforts to discover solutions. Our values constrain and enhance both what may be defined as the problem and what may be the truest solution. Priorities, analyses, trade-offs, even the acceptable ways to implement solutions—all rest on the combination of personal values and organizational norms. The essence of the argument is that business is about performance, that performance rests on judgment in decision making, and that judgment is not possible without well-examined, coherent values.

Rigor in the form of thorough inquiry, like what we have described, lies at the heart of successful problem solving, particularly when the problem is ambiguous and truly complex. In times of great uncertainty, leaders can count on only those solutions that are derived from structured inquiry and that are true to values.

The approach we have outlined depends on deductive logic in its early stages, to develop a hypothesis of the solution that becomes essential to organizing further activities. With a hypothesis in hand, the problem solver adopts inductive logic, thereby deriving conclusions from the results of collecting and investigating more data. Deductive logic is how one formulates the hypothesis or Week One Answer; inductive logic is how one tests, proves, disproves, and revises that hypothesis. The problem-solving approach is fundamentally iterative, with the problem solving moving back and forth between these two reasoning methods on the path toward discovering the solution.

This approach is also efficient, effective, and open to plenty of creativity. Although we have presented the framework in a linear manner, make no mistake—the problem solving here requires and enables nonlinear thinking. Still, the best creative solutions are often built on a thorough assessment of available conventional options. These can serve as a tool for unearthing potentially more creative ones.

Aspiration and pragmatism are two more watchwords of successful problem-solving efforts. Nothing compares with successfully getting an organization to embrace a new change, a new solution, in a timely manner. Shying away too much from adopting a potential new course of action is a decision in itself. It represents nontrivial costs—namely, out-of-pocket expense and the cost of lost opportunities elsewhere—while also siphoning off the general manager's analytic attentions. Recognizing when a good enough solution is indeed both *good* and *enough* is a hallmark of good managers everywhere.

Handling the Limits

There are situations for which our approach may not be quite appropriate, although truthfully, in our experience such situations are few and far between. We are more concerned that novice problem solvers may be reluctant to settle on *any* hypothesis for fear of its being wrong. To them we suggest thinking not about whether any early hypothesis is right or wrong, but rather whether it effectively organizes the subsequent problem-solving work. Being wrong, at least temporarily, is critical to the problem-solving process. Indeed, if your experience turns out anything like ours, subsequently gathered data will prove that half of your initial hypotheses are "wrong," but the inquiry can still proceed to a workable solution.

If you do feel reluctant to adopt a hypothesis, we suggest a few options. One is to ask yourself whether the problem is new to the company. If so, then perhaps there are lessons from how a competitor addressed a similar challenge. If the problem is new to the industry, insightful analogies may lie with companies in another industry that have already faced a comparable test. More often than not, the problem is new only to the problem solver, and it pays to discuss other analogies and insights with one's thought partner, who with any luck stands somewhat outside the problem.

Deductive problem solving in business depends on developing logical hypotheses based on understanding, knowledge, and principles of how a particular market works. Inductive reasoning depends on the effective collection of data to test and revise those hypotheses. But what if the workings of a market are obscure, seemingly chaotic, or quickly changing? Without landmarks, in uncharted seas, it becomes nearly impossible for a ship's captain to set sail safely. Similarly, absent such familiar markers—or principles of how a market might evolve—it becomes nearly impossible to generate an informed hypothesis for the potential solution. Under such rare circumstances, we would counsel the problem solver to adopt, temporarily, the following stance.

In such circumstances, intuitive leaps may be necessary to land on solutions. In spite of intuition being difficult to plan for, problem solvers can still take a few other pragmatic steps. They can catalogue everything they already know, to identify which subset of variables—such as consumer adoption rates and technology performance attributes—may materially shape or swing the potential market. The problem solver must then be the ever-vigilant observer, tracking these indicators and looking for trigger events that foreshadow the market's evolution. With time, one can develop a range of hypotheses that collectively account for a probable range of future possibilities. Having settled on a set of hypotheses, however tentatively, the problem solver employs the same iterative problem-solving framework, with its inherent strengths of structure, analytical rigor, and pragmatism.

Let us take two examples of rapidly evolving markets with misleading landmarks, or no landmarks at all. Imagine, first, the chaos facing a consumer products company from Western Europe as it attempted to expand into the Russian market in the early 1990s. With the collapse of the Soviet Union, simultaneous changes in many factors made it nearly impossible to chart an effective course of how to invest, export, and make a profit in Russia. In the future political and legal infrastructure, would property rights and contracts be enforced? Would Russian consumers purchase foreign brands? Roads, railroads, and ports were crumbling, so perhaps the Western imports might never arrive in Russian markets. In foreign exchange markets, the ruble's exchange rate was tremendously volatile. Under such circumstances, a captain would be navigating in unexplored waters, with no familiar sights to help determine the ship's course.

Confronted with a similar challenge, the general manager of the Western European company had no stable landmarks on which to base hypotheses on ways to launch new consumer products into the Russian market. So he dedicated resources to finding and charting those market landmarks. Focusing on the affluent consumer segments in major markets with some access to Western distribution, he devoted a certain amount of budget and time to launching experiments in the market, from which he gathered invaluable information about its evolution. As it turned out, Russian consumers loved Western brands, as long as they were delivered to their local markets.

Or imagine how existing market landmarks might have completely misdirected those in charge of marketing Tang in the United States in the 1960s. Tang was an orange powder that, when mixed with water, created an orange-flavored drink. Judged by previous experience, Tang could have been relegated to use as civilian war rations or for military expeditions, as these had been the main earlier uses for powdered foods. But as things turned out, children were eager to drink the Tang that the astronauts drank in space.

We would stress again, however, that such situations—in which multiple unknown or changing market factors might prevent the effective use of the problem-solving methods outlined here—are rare indeed.

Problems as Opportunities in Disguise

Problems are opportunities in disguise—opportunities to drive extraordinary results when expectations are lowest. Tough problems do demand fortitude, but courage flows from confidence in the systematic process to tackle those problems. That self-assurance starts with asking probing questions about the mess of symptoms you face and then proceeds through diagnosis, analysis, trade-offs among potential options, and execution. Once you have practiced the ideas outlined in this book, we feel sure you will gain the confidence to ask better questions and thereby take on tougher challenges.

We hope that by now you can also recognize the beauty in solving a difficult problem. If one can feel the magic of a well-played symphony or a well-hit baseball, one can understand the beauty of resolving complex business challenges. Great problem solvers tend to seek out difficult problems. You will know you have arrived as a problem solver when you find yourself seeking rather than avoiding the toughest problems in your business.

Our aspirations then for you, the reader, are that you adopt a mindset of seeing problems for their possibilities and their beauty, rather than as threats. Developing great solutions is about recognizing and evaluating that possibility. With the values-based habits of mind and action described in this book, you will gain faith in the solutions you discover and implement. With that rigor comes both the great beauty of solving a difficult problem—and the great rewards of executing it and driving results.

Notes

Chapter One

1. Aristotle, *Politics*, Book 1, Chapters 1–2.
2. Thomas Hobbes, *Leviathan: Or on the Matter, Forme, and Power of a Commonwealth Ecclesiastical and Civil*, Chapters 13 and 17. (New York: Simon & Schuster, 1997)
3. Gerald F. Cavanagh, *American Business Values*, 2nd ed. (Upper Saddle River, NJ: Prentice Hall, 1990); Daniel Bell, *The Cultural Contradictions of Capitalism* (New York: Basic Books, 1996).
4. Milton Friedman, "The Social Responsibility of Business Is to Increase Its Profits," *New York Times Magazine*, September 13, 1970, p. 1.
5. Keith Davis, "The Case For and Against Business Assumption of Social Responsibilities," *Academy of Management Journal*, 16: 2 (1973): 312–322.
6. "Too Much Corporate Power," *Business Week*, September 11, 2000, p. 3.
7. Lynne Sharp Payne, *Value Shift: Why Companies Must Merge Social and Financial Imperatives to Achieve Superior Performance* (New York: McGraw-Hill, 2002).
8. Ralph S. Larsen, "Leadership in a Values-Based Organization," *The Sears Lectureship in Business Ethics* (Waltham, MA: Bentley College, 2002).
9. Daniel Katz and Robert L. Kahn, *The Social Psychology of Organizations*, 2nd ed. (Hoboken, NJ: Wiley, 1978).

10. Brackley, Dean, *The Call to Discernment in Troubled Times: New Perspectives on the Transformative Wisdom of Ignatius of Loyola* (New York: Crossroad Publishing, 2004).

Chapter Four

1. Teresa M. Amabile, *Creativity in Context: Update to the Social Psychology of Creativity* (Boulder, CO: Westview Press, 1996).
2. Teresa M. Amabile, "How to Kill Creativity," *Harvard Business Review*, 76:5 (Sept/Oct 1998).

Chapter Five

1. Michael, E. Porter, *Competitive Strategy: Techniques for Analyzing Industries and Competitors* (New York: The Free Press, 1980).

Chapter Six

1. Barbara Minto, *Pyramid Principle: Logic in Writing and Thinking* (London: Financial Times Press, 1987, 2002), and *The Minto Pyramid Principle: Logic in Writing, Thinking, and Problem-solving* (London: Minto International, 1996); Mary Munter, *Guide to Managerial Communication: Effective Business Writing and Speaking* (Upper Saddle River, NJ: Prentice Hall, 2000); James S. O'Rourke IV, *Management Communication: A Case-Analysis Approach* (Upper Saddle River, NJ: Pearson-Prentice Hall, 2007).

Chapter Eight

1. Abraham Wald, *Statistical Decision Functions* (London: Chelsea Publishing, 1971) and *Sequential Analysis* (London: Doner Publications, 2004). For a good overview text and reference for this area of research, see also Y. S. Chow, H. E. Robbins, and D. Siegmund, *Great Expectations: The Theory of Optimal Stopping* (Boston: Houghton Mifflin, 1971).

About the Authors

Viva Ona Bartkus is an associate professor of management at the University of Notre Dame. Dr. Bartkus graduated *summa cum laude* from Yale University with master's and bachelor's degrees in economics, and then completed her doctorate and master's in international relations at Oxford University while on a Rhodes scholarship. Her book investigating nationalism, self-determination, and why groups attempt secession, *The Dynamic of Secession*, was published by Cambridge University Press (1999). Her current teaching and research interests concentrate on two distinct areas: the leadership approaches most effective in solving complex business problems and the social capital of communities that enables collaboration. Her book, *Social Capital: Reading Out, Reading In*, with James H. Davis and published by Edward Elgan (2008) investigates the networks, norms, and trust that underpin social capital. Prior to joining the faculty at Notre Dame, Dr. Bartkus spent ten years serving health care, industrial, retail, and high-tech clients to overcome their strategic, operational, and organizational challenges while at McKinsey & Company, the last four years as a partner of the firm.

Edward J. Conlon is the Edward Frederick Sorin Society Professor of Management, and associate dean for graduate programs in the Mendoza College of Business of the University of Notre Dame. Professor Conlon earned his undergraduate degree from the Pennsylvania State University and his master's and doctorate degrees from the Graduate School of Industrial

Administration of Carnegie-Mellon University. He has served as the editor of *Academy of Management Review* and on the editorial boards of several other academic journals in the field of management. He has published research on a variety of topics in organizational behavior including the challenges of change and management decision making. Professor Conlon currently teaches courses on organizational change, leadership, and business consulting in the MBA and executive programs of the University of Notre Dame.

Index